Twice to the Gallows

Twice
to the
Gallows

Bennie Swim and the
Benton Ridge Murders

A New Brunswick
Non-Fiction Novel

Dominique Perrin

Chapel Street Editions

Published by
Chapel Street Editions
150 Chapel Street
Woodstock, New Brunswick E7M 1H4
www.chapelstreeteditions.com

ISBN 978-1-988299-24-2

Library and Archives Canada Cataloguing in Publication

Title: Twice to the gallows : Bennie Swim and the Benton Ridge murders /
    Dominique Perrin.
Names: Perrin, Dominique, 1956- author.
Identifiers: Canadiana 20190118164 | ISBN 9781988299242 (softcover)
Subjects: LCSH: Swim, Bennie, 1899-1922. | LCSI I: Murder—New Brunswick. |
    LCSH: Trials (Murder)—New Brunswick.
Classification: LCC HV6535.C32 N42 2019 | DDC 364.152/30971551—dc23

Book design by Brendan Helmuth

Dedication

Dedicated to my two sons, Derek and Steven, who both trudged all over Carleton and York Counties with me to find information about people and places relevant to this story.

Contents

Foreword

When Truman Capote published *In Cold Blood* in 1966, those of us in the literary world and the book industry scratched our heads. What is this? It's not fiction or journalism; it's not history, sociology, or biography. It was a book without a category.

Capote was already a well-known novelist and short story writer, but *In Cold Blood* was something different; it was the telling of a true story based on extensive research, but the book had the characteristics of a novel. The reviewers and critics all agreed it was a strange kind of masterpiece. Capote's book defined a new genre of literature — the non-fiction novel.

Dominique Perrin has written a New Brunswick equivalent — a non-fiction novel based on extensive research into the circumstances of a shocking crime. He has creatively imagined the characters and their circumstances. He has narrated the arc of events with the skills of good storytelling. The author has brought the Bennie Swim story from folklore to literature.

The tragic story of Bennie Swim's crime, and the fact he was hanged twice, has been a legendary tale in Carleton County, New Brunswick ever since it all played out in the early 1920s. The story was even turned into a musical theatre production by Nick Lawson and Amy Anderson and was performed by the Carleton County players in 2009.

Now, thanks to Dominique Perrin's research and carefully applied imagination, we have the complex scope of the story retold in its various facets of character and drama. The author has given us a detailed and highly credible account of what brought Bennie Swim to Benton Ridge with a gun in his pocket. He has given us a gripping account of the crime and its aftermath. He has provided a detailed narrative of the legal proceedings and the infamous hangings. But behind and around all this, the author has also created a portrait of the social and cultural life of the times.

Almost a century has passed since this tragic drama of crime and punishment captured the attention of Carleton County residents and the interest of many others around the province and across Canada. Now, with this first well-researched and highly developed account of the Bennie Swim story we have the opportunity to understand motives, action, and outcome in a more fully rounded way.

This book is distinctly different from a conventional true crime story because it is anchored in the wider reality of time, place and character. Even at the remove of a century, we recognize the people, places, and communities involved in this story. The author's creative imagination brings to life the character of the men and women who lived through this tragedy and had to deal with its aftermath. Due to the author's carefully imagined dialogue and his portrayal of the character's thoughts and feelings, people, who would have otherwise faded from history, now have a continuing place in cultural memory.

The story, of course, swings around Bennie Swim but he is not the only character to stand out in bold relief. Sheriff Foster, in particular, takes centre stage in this drama as well. Even minor characters are captured in dialogue in a way that creates a sense of recognition — for example, the taciturn Mr. Doherty.

The work of writers in the case of the non-fiction novel is not to invent characters and develop drama, but to surround the people and events revealed to them through their research with a plausible narrative that brings out the textures and colours of their lives and circumstances. This is a task of sustained discipline for the creative imagination that is very different than writing straight fiction.

When a writer succeeds in this task, they add something of enduring value to our sense of cultural history and, in this case, to our understanding of the difficulties and disastrous consequences that can unfold from an accumulation of seemingly unavoidable circumstances. This is the definition of tragedy as derived from classic Greek drama.

Such stories bring up a deeper awareness of the human condition than do ordinary crime novels or typical true-crime books. This is the difference between entertainment and literature. With *Twice to the Gallows*, Dominique Perrin has moved this New Brunswick story from the shadows of folklore into a fully developed non-fiction novel.

Keith Helmuth
Chapel Street Editions
Woodstock, New Brunswick

Preface

I have tried to make this book as accurate as possible, but so many records have been lost or misplaced that, in some instances, I have had to create the events using my own experience and knowledge. I tried to familiarize myself with the general mood of the time and with the way people thought and felt during this period. I have taken the liberty to imagine the thoughts and feelings of the characters, and have composed conversations between them. These elements of the story, although realistic, are obviously the work of my imagination.

I have used many second-hand stories given to me by older members of the community and by relatives of the main characters. They provided me with a wealth of information from their knowledge of the people and circumstances involved in the tragic events of this story. I thank them all for their invaluable assistance.

Where possible, I have used official documents to verify what I have written, but I also used old newspaper accounts that I hoped were accurate. Unfortunately, many of them contradict each other, so I used those that seemed the most logical or came from the most reputable sources. All names and dates are accurate according to birth certificates, death certificates, marriage certificates, trial transcripts, Canada Census, New Brunswick Vital Statistics, family trees, military records, grave markers and old maps. Where newspaper reports and official documents are quoted, they appear *verbatim*. Grammar and punctuation have not been corrected. Occasionally in the public record, Bennie's name is spelled "Benny." This appears to be an error. All court records and legal documents use "Bennie." "Bennie" is used throughout this book except where quoted material uses the other spelling.

There are some stories in circulation about Bennie Swim and the circumstances of his life that I have not included in this book because I could not corroborate them in a way that gave me confidence they were true.

I have included the stories of Bennie Swim haunting the Woodstock Jail, although I don't personally believe in ghosts. However, if a spirit someday contacts me, I hope it will be the ghost of Olive Swim. I have a lot of questions to ask her.

Dominique Jean Rene Perrin
Fredericton, New Brunswick

Prologue

The forest is an entity. A person who does not spend time in the woods may never see it for what it really is. It doesn't matter what part of the world it's in; the similarities remain the same. A forest is like a separate being, calling and answering to all who heed its presence. Some see only trees or the occasional animal, but those that cannot stay away feel a definite presence every time they enter the forest. They feel it more at night than in the daytime, for in the darkness there is no control. The forest wins and everything in it becomes more alive. Humans can never fully understand this. They need to feel in control, so they always bring with them something that puts them at ease. It may be a gun, a source of light, or a companion.

The forest does not want them there. It shuts down and becomes silent. It waits and watches. Then, like machinery, it starts up again and grudgingly accepts their presence. But the animals wait. Once you leave the road or the trail, you know that anything could happen. The forest swallows you, and the animals rule. They know you're there, and where you are at all times. They have the advantage of surprise, they know how to hide, and stalk you without being noticed. They are always watching you, but you don't know it. If you do, you should be worried because it means they have lost their fear of you and are ready to strike.

Beginnings

On a day in early October of 1899, Jesse Herbert Foster goes into the forest with some family members. They trudge along the well-worn path to a cabin several miles from any road, up behind the village of Coldstream in Carleton County, New Brunswick. They continue in an easterly direction that brings them along the Becaguimec River to the area known as the Mainstream. Jesse thinks about what he is going to say when he gets there. He doesn't want to be put in this position but the honour of the family is at stake. He must go and confront a man called William Swim who has been living with his sister, Eva. He wants them to get married and is willing to be very persuasive if necessary. He has a shotgun slung on his back.

Eva is near ready to give birth. Her belly is large and bulging, but marriage for her is not a concern. Folks have been living like this for years up here on the Mainstream, deep in the forest. Half the people here are unrecorded, never making it on any government registers or ledgers until well into their sixties when it becomes necessary in order to get the pensions the government so generously provides.

William is 42, but that doesn't much bother her. She is 24, an old maid by most standards. Out here, life turns young people old in short order. Almost everything is done by hand, but she's used to it. Truth to tell, she's just glad she's got a man, a man with two hundred acres of land, passed down from his family. That's important. A man with land is somebody. Many women don't have a man in these parts, and look at the way they end up. Taking care of other people's kids and cleaning someone else's house, or being a burden on a family that can't afford them anymore and resents their presence. She doesn't have it so bad; the cabin may be small but it's dry in the rain and warm enough in the winter so long as the stove is full of wood.

She sits outside the cabin waiting for something to happen. She can feel it in her bones. Something is going to happen and it's not good. William sits inside and works on his figures, counting out the money in the tobacco can several times over, as if it will grow in value if he counts it one more time. It doesn't, and he feels the concern, knowing it will be many more months before he can find any kind of paying work that will add to his savings. It looks like he'll be poaching another deer this winter to add to the food supply; it happens often, it's nothing new to him.

It's not his fault if there isn't enough work or money to make it through the winter.

He hears Eva yelling and quickly goes outside. He sees her brother, Jesse, and the others; they stare at Eva's large belly and then turn their attention to William. William knows he is not going to like the reason they are here. He knows about Eva's family. He's heard lots of stories about them; half of them are insane, the other half can be mean, real mean. He's glad to see the one with the shotgun is Jesse. He's probably the most normal of the bunch. He waits for them to state their business and it doesn't take long. He likes that Jesse doesn't waste words. He lets William know that his choices are few.

"Get married or get buried," Jesse says in a demanding voice.

William believes him and gets his coat; they all head into Hartland to get a marriage license. With the marriage license in hand, William and Eva go to see Reverend H. J. Shaw who agrees to perform the ceremony on October 8th. William doesn't want his new in-laws to know his real age and tells the Reverend to write down 30 on the marriage certificate. He also lists himself as a farmer but he is really just a labourer who does whatever it takes to make a few extra dollars.

The wedding day arrives and they get the ceremony over with quickly. Friends and relatives have brought plates of food and large jars of home-brewed beer. There are pitchers of lemonade for the women and children, and they all proceed to enjoy the bounty. All goes well, and when they have had their fill they begin the dances. The festivities continue well into the night, and then they all depart for home.

Eva is now Mrs. William Swim and her children won't be born bastards. That should make her family happy, and maybe they will leave them in peace now. They go back to the cabin and wait. She knows it won't be long before her first child arrives. She is right. She feels the pains start early on the morning of October 22nd. She yells at her husband to get the doctor, but it's a long ride and instead he brings back a local woman who lives closer to the cabin. Eva again yells at him to get the doctor, and this time he goes to Hartland as fast as he can. When the doctor and William arrive back at the cabin, Eva is groaning in agony as the head crowns. The doctor takes over, and within minutes Bennie Swim enters the world. If he had known how his life would end up, he may not have wanted to come out at all.

*   *   *   *   *

Life on the Mainstream had its advantages for Bennie. It was a wonderful area, rich in game. The Becaguimec and other rivers were abundant with fish.

3

He could while away a whole day with nothing but a fishing pole and a can of worms. Bennie was a moody boy who liked his own company more than that of others. He could lose himself in thought while walking through the forest with no one to bother him. Like most boys of the area, he learned to hunt at a young age and became adept with a rifle, a necessary skill needed to insure an adequate food supply.

Bennie didn't much like going to school. Because of the poverty of his family, his clothes were threadbare and often patched. The kids at school teased him mercilessly. He tried to avoid them but it wasn't always possible and coming home with a black eye or bruised ribs was not uncommon for Bennie. His father just figured it would make him tough and better prepare him for life ahead. He wasn't much for book learning, but it wasn't really necessary because as soon as he was big enough to work, he would be joining his father on the local farms, or in the logging business.

His sister, Cassie Elizabeth, was born on the 2nd of February in 1902. More than year later, on December 22, 1903, a brother, Alexander Cameron, also joined the family. William now had five mouths to feed. Life did not get any easier for the Swim family.

The Mainstream was a poor area when it came to farming. Land was cheap, but trying to grow crops was frustrating. The forest soil, once cleared of trees, was thin and filled with rocks. It broke many a farmer trying to eke out a living. Long days of hard labour brought only small returns. Apple trees grew well, so everyone had a small orchard close to their house. Raspberries also grew easily and patches were allowed to spring up everywhere. Children and adults alike harvested the wild crop and made extra money by selling them in the village of Coldstream and the town of Hartland.

People of the Mainstream mostly kept to themselves and did not enjoy the presence of outsiders. Homes were far apart, with lots of privacy, which is what many of the residents of the area preferred. They were aware of their circumstances and the poverty in which they lived. They did not want to be judged by others who looked down on them and did not understand the way they lived. Bennie's family was of Irish descent and even though it was now more than third generation Canadian, their way of life was not much better than that of the early settlers who had come directly from Ireland. That they were here at all was a tribute to their toughness and strength and their ability to endure stringent conditions and real hardships.

When it came to relationships and marriages, most of the families in the area were interconnected. Swims married Fosters, Fosters married Rosses, Rosses married Derrahs, Derrahs married Swims and so on. Sometimes it was even less complicated, with direct marriages between cousins. It wasn't unusual for married women to not even change names, their maiden names being the same as their married names. For men, it was never a problem to find a wife. There was often a spinster daughter still living with her parents who was eager to have a husband. A girl was often married soon after she turned sixteen. If she didn't find a husband, about the only thing she was able to do was to work as a domestic in a local family that was better off than her family.

That kind of work usually started soon after the age of twelve when the girl was big enough to handle a load of laundry or bring in the firewood and keep the woodstove burning. She often lived with the family, typically given a small room in the attic, working fifteen-hour days taking care of the children, preparing meals, and any other chores the lady of the house could think of. Her wages might be twenty-five cents a day and perhaps some the mistress' cast off clothing as a bonus.

With that kind of life to look forward to, young women were often happy to get married to a man who could provide them with little more than a cabin in the woods and a subsistence homestead. Girls were often still in their teens when they married men in their forties and even older. They looked more for a better life than for love. It wasn't uncommon for a girl to be married within weeks of meeting her prospective groom. Up in the Mainstream many couples didn't even bother with the formality of marriage and just started living together. In the case of Bennie's parents, they probably would have continued doing just that if not for the intervention of Eva's brother, Jesse.

Church going was important to many folks who lived on the Mainstream. One of the most important activities of the area were the regular revival meetings held at the local churches. Without much else to look forward to, these were social events that most local folks would not want to miss. Bennie and his family were Baptists, and not the silent type when it came to worshiping. If the preacher didn't have the congregation convinced of their sins and calling out for forgiveness, he wasn't doing his job properly. For example, Reverends Quigg and Bragdon knew how to work up a congregation. A meeting began with lively songs about the joy of knowing we have such a wonderful and merciful God. The church choir sang loud for all to hear; "Sitting in our church we worship Jesus, raising our hands to make sure he sees us, that's what we do in our little old church back home."

The songs went on for an hour or more. Once the crowd was sharing the joy of the Holy Spirit, the preacher changed his tone. Now it was time to convince the congregation that heaven and God's mercy did not come without a cost. Now was the time for the fire and brimstone message. The preacher reminded them that sin is a very powerful force that must be cast out.

"The Devil is very real," the preacher shouted. "He wants you bad. It wasn't God who invented liquor; it was the Devil. If you think drinking a bit of whiskey now and then is OK, then you are sadly mistaken my friends. God hates whiskey and beer and anything that takes you away from him. The kingdom of heaven is only for the righteous and you will not get there by sinning. So now is the time to confess your sins and get right with Jesus. Don't think he doesn't notice you men in the congregation staring at the women in the church pews with lust in your eyes; God is watching you. And you women, with your dresses showing a bit too much of your bosoms, God is watching you too. Your dress should cover your legs. When you women out there like men's attention and push the limits of modesty, then I say to you the Devil is pleased. He knows what God hates and he wants to bring you down through those fiery gates of hell with him."

At this point, the description of hell that followed was enough to move the most unrepentant sinner. Some would call out to God, begging forgiveness that the preacher would later grant. He worked the crowd for all he was worth, shouting that God is a merciful God and as long as you take Jesus into your heart and accept his love then heaven is waiting for you. Once the preacher was totally spent, having directed all his energy into saving the congregation, he said a final prayer. He asked God to forgive and save his flock. And then, the service was over and a collection was taken. The preacher never expected a show of gratitude except, of course, the donations and tithes which were God's money, not his.

With the congregation saved and once more at peace, the ladies brought out the fried chicken and the homemade bread. The preacher thanked them, and thanked God for His bounty, giving the prettier young women a bit more attention than the others. The men stuck around long enough to show their support and have a good feed, but then, out of sight of the preacher, the flasks came out; whiskey for the better off and moonshine for the rest. The preacher knew about this. He waited for everyone to leave before bringing out his own. Saving sinners was hard work, but worth it. So if a bit of whiskey helped rejuvenate him that was OK. And besides, he was a preacher; the Devil couldn't touch him.

Life in a Cabin

The forest was home for Bennie and his neighbours. Most of them lived in cabins made from a hodgepodge of used building materials and with whatever local materials they could find. Split logs or flat stones brought up from the river were often used for flooring. Cabins were often well hidden within the dense parts of the forest. Many of the folks out there in the backwoods were not always hospitable, and did not welcome intruders. Those who had a still near by were especially secretive.

Whenever a house was deserted or a barn left for good, the men of the area turned out with crowbars and hammers, demolished the deserted buildings, and hauled away anything they could use. Once they had completed their work and packed off everything that could be reused, the sites would be so well cleaned up it was hard to tell there had ever been a building there in the first place. The Mainstream men were ingenious builders and quite skilled at making sturdy dwellings that often lasted longer than the occupants themselves. Appearance was not a consideration; it was practicality that mattered. When possible, the cabins were built near a stream so a water supply was close by until wells were dug.

Most of the cabins had a large room that would be sectioned off by blankets draped over a rope, or with plywood tacked up for walls. Washboards and washtubs hung on nails outside the cabin ready for clothes washing and the weekly scrub-down on Saturday night to make sure the family was nice and clean for church the next morning. Outhouses were built far enough away from the cabin so the odour would not be noticed, but close enough to be reached in a hurry when digestive maladies occurred.

Sleeping two or three to a bed was common, which was an advantage in winter. With closeness of sleeping quarters and light partitions, hearing the sexual noises of their parents was something that kids just took for granted. This was sex education for kids of the Mainstream.

During the summer, the mosquitoes and black flies nearly ate them alive. It was a time when the worse you smelled the better off you were. Even though the odour of an unwashed body repelled insects, this often wasn't enough. After a while, you just didn't notice the mosquito and black fly bites that covered your body. Despite the warm weather, residents of the

Mainstream would often wear long sleeved clothing day and night to prevent insect bites.

Once fall arrived, the bugs disappeared and, for a spell, life was more comfortable until it became cold. By that time, a good stack of firewood had to be built up. A small cabin would commonly go through three or four cords of wood each winter. During the winter evenings there was not much to do living in a cabin. With the kerosene lantern lit, the family might sit around and discuss the day's events or plans for the future. Those who could read might have a book. There was always mending and washing to do. Washtubs were now brought inside and filled from big pots of water heated on the cookstove. Clothing was put in the washtubs and allowed to soak overnight. The next day, they would be scrubbed on the washboard and then hung out on the clothesline to freeze-dry. It wasn't uncommon for children to be hustled off to school with their clothes stiff and creaking because they were still partially frozen.

Chopping, sawing, and splitting firewood was something that was needed. It could take up any spare time available. The stove needed to be kept full since it was used both for cooking and heat. The best stoves were the Franklin and the Kootenay Range, but they were big and expensive. More commonly used were the smaller stoves made by local blacksmiths and foundries. The cabins were often hard to keep comfortable. When the stove was going full blast during the day, they could be too hot. But no matter how much wood was put in the stove the night before, the occupants of these cabins would wake up in the morning with teeth chattering and bodies shivering. Someone would need to get up early to restart the fire, but it would be sometime before the heat could be felt throughout the cabin. When it was warm again, it would be time to get up, light the kerosene lantern, cook up a breakfast of porridge or left-over beans, or maybe some buckwheat pancakes with dried berries thrown in for flavour, and then send the kids off to the one room schoolhouse a couple of miles down the road.

For the men, it was out to look for work. Finding work was not a problem during the rest of the year, but in the winter there wasn't much going on, although keeping the family warm was work enough. Some men might have trap lines but the animals with pelts that brought in good money had been heavily trapped for generations and were scarce. Poaching deer was always an option if you didn't mind risking a few weeks or months in jail for your efforts and having your gun confiscated.

The people of the Mainstream had a good system for dealing with this problem. Jail was not a deterrent for single men because the food in jail was often better than their regular fare. Going to jail was not considered shameful since many families had members who had been locked up for poaching, or had a relative who had spent time behind bars.

As for the confiscation of firearms, the community had a good working system. When a man was caught poaching, his gun would be confiscated and then later sold at a local gun auction to the highest bidder. Since everyone knew whose firearms were being sold, no one would bid except the owners. They were usually able to buy them back for pennies on the dollar. Woe to the person who did not go along with this system and bid higher than the owner. He would find himself severely beaten on his way home from the auction. There was a good chance that some day he would also be caught poaching, so it was for his benefit that he be taught to follow the neighbourly plan.

The people of the Mainstream were fiercely loyal to each other. They shared many of the same difficulties and traditions. Surviving on the Mainstream required being strong, tough, and loyal. Family meant everything and you did whatever it took to protect your relatives, legal or not. People looked out for each other and lived by a certain code. They understood it, and if others didn't, then to hell with them. They didn't belong here anyway.

And Then Came Olive

One day in 1920, when Bennie was walking home from his job peeling pulp at Hex Fosters place out at Mount Pleasant Corner, he met a very pretty girl. She was walking with an older man Bennie recognized as his Uncle John, brother to his father. He carried a suitcase for the girl. When he saw Bennie he waved, and waited for Bennie to catch up. John and Bennie shook hands and then his uncle said, "Olive, this is your cousin, Bennie. Do you remember him?" Olive said "No", but gave Bennie a smile that almost made him blush. He was not used to attention from females near his age. She looked to be about fifteen. Although Olive was six years younger than Bennie, the age difference did not seem to bother her. She was used to attention from men and was comfortable being friendly. Bennie was totally smitten. She told him she would be working as a housekeeper in one of the homes in Hartland, and that she would be staying in the cabin with Bennie, his brother Cameron, and his parents. By this time, Cassie Elizabeth, Bennie's sister, had married Frank Ogden and moved out. Bennie thought this arrangement was wonderful and started thinking of her as his beloved.

Olive was born in Rockland near Mainstream on July 10th 1905. Her mother was Phoebe Ann Wiley, daughter of Rebecca Jane Swim and George Wiley. Olive's parents met when John Swim was staying with Phoebe's family and working on a local farm. She had an older brother, Roy, who was born on the 17th of June in 1899, and a sister, Alice Pearl, who was born in 1906 on April 16th. Although Roy was the same age as Bennie there is no indication they knew each other. As a matter of fact, when Roy was later in court as a witness, he would deny Bennie was even his cousin. Whether he knew that Bennie was his cousin and just didn't want to accept it, is unknown.

John Swim was known as a good, hard-working man and was often sought out for employment by local farmers. He readily found work in different areas of the province as well as in the state of Maine. The family frequently pulled up stakes, living and working with different farm owners. John often worked in Hartin Settlement in York County where Alice Pearl, the youngest daughter, was born. John often went alone to work on farms in Maine. On special occasions, his wife would travel with Alice Pearl to visit him, leaving Olive and Roy with family. As Roy got older and stronger, he also became a farm hand. Eventually, on Benton Ridge in southern Carleton County, John was able to realize his dream of having his own farm.

Olive was taught the skills needed to run a household. When she was old enough, she would be sent away to look for a job as a housekeeper. Life was work for both men and women. But for women, short of marrying rich, it meant especially long hours. For men, it was the physical labour of farm work. For women, it was the cooking, cleaning, washing, sewing, knitting, mending clothes, and garden work. There were always the younger children that needed taking care of as well. Work for girls started as soon as they were big enough to heft a washtub or strong enough to knead bread. When that time came, few would ever return to school; it was considered a waste of time for them. "Girls don't need no education; they just need to know how to take care of youngins and menfolk." This was the prevailing attitude at the time.

There was always so much housework to do. It was the training ground for girls, preparing them for running a household of their own when they married, or a means of gainful employment for those who were single. When Olive was in her early teens, she heard through family connections of a place in Hartland where she could find employment as a domestic. So this is how it happened that her father brought her and her suitcase filled with all of her personal possessions to the cabin on the Mainstream to live with his brother William and his family.

Bennie and Olive developed a special relationship. Bennie could not have been happier. For the weeks before her job started, he and Olive spent all of their free time together. Bennie would soon begin to believe that Olive was as much in love with him as he was with her. He even got a fiddle and learned to play it. He figured Olive would love and admire him all the more if he could play a few tunes for her.

At first, Olive enjoyed being with Bennie and being the centre of his attention, but as time went on her feelings changed. She came to feel smothered by him. At first, she traveled to her job in Hartland in the morning and returned at night, but that took so long she soon went to live with the family where she was employed. She was gone for long periods of time. Bennie became morose and began to think she didn't love him anymore. While Bennie was pining away for Olive, she spent most of her time working. Eventually, Bennie began scheming on how to get Olive to come back to the cabin to stay. One day it came to him, more from frustration than anything else. He went to the house where Olive was working and made a ruckus, telling Olive that he wanted her home with him and he wasn't leaving until she came. Seeing this, Olive's employer fired her because he didn't want the annoyance of some crazy guy like Bennie coming around and making trouble. There were plenty of girls like Olive who were available for employment. Olive was furious but had no choice but to go back to the cabin with Bennie.

Life in the cabin was boring and then became intolerable for Olive. She longed for another job. Bennie did his best to discourage her from thinking about getting another job, even promising marriage and spending what little money he had on special little presents for her. Olive began to feel more and more oppressed. She longed for a job to take her away from Bennie and make her more independent with an income of her own.

After weeks of sitting around and being hounded by Bennie's mother to do more work to earn her keep, Olive took a walk down to Estabrooks General Store in the village of Coldstream. While chatting with the owner's wife, she mentioned her situation. Mrs. Estabrooks pointed her towards a notice posted on the wall for employment as a housekeeper in Houlton, Maine. This seemed like a perfect plan for her. Houlton would be far enough away from Bennie so she would not be bothered by him, and close enough to Benton Ridge that she could visit her parents once in awhile.

That night, she packed her meagre belongings and hid the suitcase under her bed. Once morning broke and Bennie and his family were out of the cabin, Olive grabbed her suitcase and walked to Hartland where she boarded a train for Houlton, Maine. She could imagine what would happen when Bennie came home and read the note she had left on the bed explaining that she had left to find work in Maine. She was glad that she wouldn't be there when he found it.

When Olive arrived at the address given in the ad for employment, she was impressed with the size and stature of the house. She could only dream of being able to live in such a house one day. But for now it would be good enough just to work there. When the owner of the house opened the door and saw how beautiful Olive was, he hired her on the spot. The lady of the house, on the other hand, was not as enamoured of this young woman as her husband, but she saw that Olive was strong, knew how to work and would be able to do the chores well.

Life for Olive at this house went on as expected for a domestic. She was the first one to get up in the morning and start up the fires for the stoves. Once they were going well, she would fill up the large pots with water for cooking and for making coffee or tea. She would then mix the batter for pancakes, which were a regular part of the breakfast meal. Some days breakfast included eggs and bacon, some days porridge, and in large enough quantities to satisfy the whole household.

Life and work in the big house became routine and Olive felt at ease, although the wife always found extra chores for her to do. The work was hard, and except for a bit too much attention from the husband, she began to enjoy herself there. The children were a handful, but she was happy enough, and hoped her life would stay the same for a while. She was also glad that Bennie was far away and, as yet, had not tracked her down. She thought that perhaps he had found someone else and began to think he was now out of her life.

But Bennie had not forgotten about Olive, nor had he found someone else. He was tearing his hair out trying to find her. He tortured himself with thoughts of her in the clutches of another man or worse, being taken advantage of by a new employer. He wrote to her parents for information, but they were unhelpful. Her parents seemed not to know where she was, or if they did, had no intention of telling him. He would have to come up with another way of finding her.

Finally, a chance encounter with Mrs. Estabrooks at the general store revealed some useful information. She recalled the notice about a job in Houlton, Maine that Olive seemed interested in a short time before she left the area. Mrs. Estabrooks could not remember the name of the family that was looking for a housekeeper, but that was not going to stop Bennie. He would find her and bring her back. This time, to make sure she stayed with him, Bennie would build a cabin of their own so they could live together as a couple. That would surely convince her he was serious about marriage.

Before he left to find her, Bennie's father and his brother, Cameron, helped him build a cabin in the woods a short distance from his parents. It was a pathetic little thing, not much bigger than a tool shed, with barely room enough for a bed and table. He installed a small wood stove in one corner that would keep them warm. At first, the roof leaked when the rain came down and Bennie had to work on it several times before he finally made it waterproof. Bennie was happy with the cabin and was convinced that Olive would also be happy to live there.

With the cabin finished, Bennie went to Houlton to find Olive. Locating her was not difficult. After asking several people in town, he was directed to the house where she worked. He waited outside and watched to make sure she was really there. Finally she came out with a big basket of laundry and began to hang it on the clothesline.

The husband of the house also came out and started helping her, making sure he got a eyeful of Olive's bare legs as she reached up to hang the laundry. Olive had gotten used to his lingering gaze and just ignored him. Bennie, on the other hand, did not. With a rage that surprised even him, he went up to the man and started yelling curses at him, threatening him with bodily harm. This sudden verbal assault by a complete stranger scared the man half to death. He ran back into the house and bolted the door. Olive was at first too stunned to react, but that didn't last long. She turned on Bennie with her own litany of profanities and then walked back into the house. Her employer, not wanting to risk another such episode with the crazy man, told her in no uncertain terms that she was no longer needed or wanted and she should get her things and leave.

Bennie was overjoyed when he heard this. So once again, Olive left her employment and followed Bennie back to Mainstream. Bennie apologized all the way home, and by the time they arrived Olive was somewhat pacified. But instead of going down the trail to his parent's cabin, Bennie turned off on another path and led the way to the new cabin.

With a jubilant step he stopped in front of it and exclaimed, "This is our new home, Olive dear." Her reaction was not what he expected. Instead of a joyful shriek of surprise, Olive, who had been used to living in a proper house for months, took one look at the cabin, sat down and burst into tears. This was not what Bennie had expected. He thought she would be happy to finally have a place they could call their own. A cabin that she could dress up any way she wanted. Instead, Olive was totally despondent. Was this the way her life was going to be from now on? Finally she went inside and accepted, at least for a while, that her fate was to live with Bennie in this cabin in the woods.

But Olive's days were filled with despair, She tried to keep herself occupied while Bennie was at his job removing bark from the logs at Foster's sawmill. She kept herself busy with whatever chores she could think of. At night, on the small bed, it was always the same. Bennie would lean in close to her and try to remove her clothing. Olive would burst into tears and scream at Bennie to leave her alone. Her best excuse for not having sex with Bennie was to feign terror at the thought of going to hell because they would then be living in sin. Bennie didn't see it that way because as far as he was concerned they were a married couple and should be starting a family. He figured that Olive would eventually give in and they would then live as a normal husband and wife.

Olive knew that if she were to get pregnant she would be stuck with this kind of life forever. She had other plans; she knew she had to get away from

Bennie once and for all. She had no intention of spending the rest of the winter in the small cabin. She had written her family recently and had found out that her father had finally realized his dream and now owned a farm near the town of Benton, and that the rest of her family was now living there.

Near the end of February 1922, Olive once again wrote a note to Bennie, careful to not mention any references to where she was going, and put it on the bed after he had left for his job at Mount Pleasant Corners. She then walked to the railroad station in Hartland and boarded the train going south. She was headed for Benton Ridge where her father's new farm was located.

When the train pulled into Benton, her father was waiting for her. She was happy to see him and especially happy to get to the farm at Benton Ridge, which was in a pleasant area, just off Lewin Rd. There were apple trees close to the house and large swaths of raspberry bushes near by. This would mean canning enough fruit to last all through the year. There would be no shortage of cakes and pies in this household.

The land was difficult to work as was evident from the many large piles of rocks that dotted the fields. As with most farms in the area, it would take long days of hard labour to make this farm successful, but with what her father knew about farming, he could make it work if anyone could. As they drove up the road to the property, she could see many large sugar maples that surrounded the area. These trees would be great for the sap that was needed to make maple sugar for their coffee and maple syrup to pour generously over buckwheat pancakes. Olive was again happy for the first time in many months. She was a beautiful young woman, seventeen years old, and back with her family on their own farm. She could now relax and see what life would bring.

That night, after a hearty meal of roast beef with mashed potatoes and gravy, several types of vegetables, and with apple pie for dessert, her father lit the kerosene lamps and Olive told her family what her life had been for the past two years. She spared no details as she recounted the good times with her employers and the bad times with her cousin Bennie. When she had finished the family was stunned. Her father vowed that if he ever saw Bennie again, he would give him a thrashing for what he had put his daughter through.

Later in the evening, after much conversation and laughter, there was a knock on the door. A man her father had recently hired to help out on the farm had come to the house. John brought him inside and introduced him to his daughter. "Olive, I want you to meet Mr. Harvey Trenholm; he's been working around here for the last couple of months. He's going to buy the Sharp farm just down the road." Olive took one look at Harvey, sized him up, gave him her warmest smile, and watched as he blushed. This was the man she had been looking for and he would soon own one of the nicest farms in the area. He had Bennie beat by a country mile in every way. He was stronger, taller, better looking, and evidently had money. He would be quite the catch.

And Then Came Harvey

On March 15th 1883, Harvey Dixon Trenholm drew his first breath while his mother was drawing her last. It was not a good time in the Trenholm farmhouse near Baie Verte in Westmorland County, New Brunswick. Mary Emaline had already given birth to five children, four of which were still living, when Harvey's birth cost his mother her life. Her screams were desperate as she fought a losing battle trying to handle the pain that came with such a difficult delivery. The doctor was doing what he could, but sometimes it just does not go well. He contemplated whether it was time to make a decision to either save the baby or the mother. When the decision was left totally up to him, it was always the mother he saved. Mary Emaline saw the look in his eye and knew what it meant. She grabbed his arm and with a feeble voice said, "Not yet, not yet, I can do this for the both of us."

The doctor looked over at her husband, James Herbert Trenholm, but could see no reaction. He was beyond scared and in shock at what was happening. This was not the way it was supposed to happen. All her other births had been fine, so why was this one different? God's will? That's what everyone said when they did not have a better explanation. Well if this was God's will, then God was not in a good mood. The baby was still not coming out, and Mary's screams just got louder. The doctor had already used his scalpel to enlarge the opening of the womb, but it was all he could do. He couldn't make it any larger without serious harm to the mother. Finally just before he was about to end the baby's life to save the mother, Mary gave one more terrifying scream and the baby's head began to crown. Several more attempts by Mary to push were successful. Harvey was definitely on his way out of his mother's womb, and into the harsh light of the world.

Once fully out, Harvey was quickly wrapped in a blanket and passed off to the nurse while the doctor began working on Mary. It did not look good. He was unable to stop the haemorrhaging and, despite all his efforts, Mary died. She was thirty-one years old. James Herbert, her husband, couldn't believe what had happened. His Mary, dead so young, and now he was the single parent of five children. He looked down at his new son and didn't know whether to hate Harvey or just accept what had happened. For most of his life, he could not look at the boy without remembering the sight of his beloved Mary writhing in agony and finally passing away before his very eyes. Life would go on, but for now James was silent; even when others came up to him to offer their condolences, he did not acknowledge them.

Finally, with a sigh he got up and came back to life. There were four children and a baby to take care of and a funeral to plan. He knew that the only way he was going to get through this would be to marry again, and soon. He couldn't run the farm and raise his children alone. Luckily there were many single women close by wanting a husband, even one with five children. In the meanwhile he did have family and friends that would help out. His oldest child was only nine but James Teed was strong and able to do some of the chores. The next in age was Edger at five, then Florence at four, Alfred at two, and now Harvey the baby. The only thing the younger ones would be good for was getting in the way.

With the help of others, James worked hard to keep the family provided for and the farm running. The long tiring days were a blessing for him as they kept him from thinking of his beloved Mary too much. He knew he was going to need another wife so he asked his friends and relatives if they knew of any possible women he might start courting. One name kept being repeated over and over—Annie Lanchester Polley Murray. She was an orphan who had been adopted as a child, and was almost twenty years old. James took to seeing her whenever he could find the time. It wasn't much of a romance but often that's the way things worked out.

Finally he asked and received permission to marry her. They went down to the Methodist church on the nineteenth of August 1884 and became man and wife. There were no thoughts of a honeymoon, and Annie was fine with that. After all, she was an orphan, and as the way of thinking went at the time being an orphan was sort of a curse that God placed on certain children. She considered herself lucky to find a husband at all, even if he already had five children. James settled his new wife into the family routine. He spent long days in the fields while Annie took care of his children in the farmhouse. Annie was young and was determined to have children of her own. It didn't take much convincing for James to make her pregnant several more times before she would have the children she wanted.

First came Oscar, born in 1885, but unfortunately he did not live long and was dead at the age of 4. Next came Marie Gussie in May of 1886. She would live until the age of 24. Roy soon followed in 1887, and then Eva in 1888. If she thought that James was going to stop wanting more children she was mistaken. Since she was not one to deny her husband, the children kept on coming. Luckily for her there was a six-year break. Harriet Jane (Hattie) was born on the 22nd of March 1894, Leona on the 22nd of May

1895, Margaret Marie in 1897, followed by Kenneth Secord in 1904, and last of all came Harry Frederick in March of 1908. So now James had given his new wife nine children plus five from his first wife. By the end of her childrearing, there were more than a dozen children living that she would have to take care of.

Young Harvey was brought up in the middle of this chaotic household. With so many children in the house, he did not get much attention from his father or stepmother. He was a good child but James could not look at his son without being reminded of the pain and sorrow that he had unintentionally caused with his birth. While he loved his new wife, she never completely took the place of Mary.

Harvey worked hard on the farm and learned all of the skills necessary to become a good farmer, but his heart was not in it. When he had time to himself, he would go down to the docks, stroll among the large ships, and talk to sailors who filled the boy with incredible stories of adventures in far away lands. Harvey decided that when he was old enough he would become a sailor. No smelly barns for him, or working long hours in the fields. There were other members of the family to carry on the family farm. When he told his father of his plans, James understood. He took his son down to the docks and introduced him to one of his uncles who was a fisherman.

Harvey was happy to be on the open water. It gave him a sense of freedom he would never have back home on the farm. Most of his time was spent with the local fishermen on the smaller boats but also he was able to work on the large schooners that plied their way from New Brunswick to the Grand Banks of Newfoundland and beyond. He was adept at learning all the skills that were needed to become a good fisherman and sailor.

He learned how to make every knot, the names of every sail, and the uses of every line, sheet, halyard, and rope on board. There wasn't a thing he didn't learn when it came to reading the oceans that would supply an abundance of fish to fill the holds. Hauling in the nets made him strong and healthy and Harvey grew into a man on the water. Coming from a large family gave Harvey a desire to have a family of his own. He looked forward to that, and when he was on shore he would spend time with a local girl, Bessie Gertrude Hayward.

Bessie was a lively, pretty girl. She and Harvey spent hours talking and laughing about almost anything. Bessie was born to father James W. Hayward and mother Jemima Matilda in 1888 in Port Elgin, New Brunswick. She was a happy girl and was quite smitten with Harvey when they first met. Though he was five years older, she just saw him as more mature than the other men she had occasion to meet. It did not take long before she would realize that this was the man she wanted to marry and he felt the same way. After asking her father for permission to marry her, Bessie and Harvey went to the Reverend Henry Brown for a marriage license. He was happy for them and they set a date for the wedding ceremony. On July 4th 1907 they became man and wife. Family and a few friends attended the wedding. When it was over, they moved into a house near Harvey's home place and settled into married life.

Times were good for the couple even though Harvey was away much of the time making a living on the fishing boats. Bessie didn't mind though, as Harvey's family was close by to keep her company when he was away. On September 8th in 1908, their daughter Gladys Gertrude was born. Bessie couldn't have been happier. She now had a child of her own to take care of. She was hoping that it would be the first of many but fate would not be kind to Bessie. She loved the child as most parents do, but the pregnancy and birth had taken a lot out of her. She found herself getting weak for no reason, and couldn't spend as much time doing the simple chores that were needed to run the household. She didn't think much of it and carried on as best she could. When Harvey came home, they enjoyed taking little Gladys on picnics in the fields overlooking the ocean.

Bessie wanted desperately to have another child but as much as they tried it did not happen. It didn't make sense to her or Harvey. The first child had come easily enough. So after years of trying and failing to get pregnant, Bessie went to see a doctor but he could not see any immediate problems. When she told him of her weak spells, he decided she should have some tests done. When he received the results, it was not good news. Not only was she not going to have any more children, she would not be able to live as long a life as she had hoped. She was dying. Slowly, the disease was getting worse. She hoped for a miracle but it did not come.

Bessie continued to live as normally as possible, not even telling her husband about her illness, hoping that if she ignored it, it would not be real. It was real and after a long spell of weakness Bessie died. In the latter part of 1915, Harvey came home after an extended fishing trip on one of the larger schooners and instead of his wife and child to meet him, it was his father-in-law and little Gladys crying uncontrollably. The sad look in their eyes was enough to tell him that his Bessie was gone. He asked how it happened. Bessie's father told him that it was the disease that killed her.

Harvey was devastated. He picked up Gladys and walked back through the countryside to his house. One thing for sure, he would not be going fishing anytime soon. He had to stay close to home to care for his daughter. For now, he would work with his father on the farm. It was not a long-term solution but it would have to do. But he missed his wife so terribly, and his depression made his life so wretched that he couldn't give his young daughter the attention she needed. He also started drinking. At first it was just a glass or two of whiskey at the end of the day but it soon became an all day activity. When his father-in-law saw his condition, he threatened to take Gladys away from him unless Harvey straightened up.

One day when Harvey was walking through town coming home from the tavern, he saw a recruitment poster for the 26th New Brunswick Battalion. The more he thought about it, the more joining the military seemed like a good idea. That could be just the thing that he needed to get his mind off losing Bessie.

During this time, he also began keeping company with a local woman, Dorina Rose Burgess. She was a forty year old widow with a son in his teens, but Harvey wasn't much of a catch anymore either. They were both available and took advantage of each other. Harvey was definitely not in love. Dorina was simply a drinking companion with whom he could pass the long evenings and enjoy sexual activity.

On December 4th 1915, Harvey travelled to Sussex to sign up for the army. When the recruiting officer asked him his date of birth, Harvey gave it as March 15th 1883. The recruiter frowned and said they were looking for men under thirty. He saw Harvey's disappointment and then again asked for his birth date. This time Harvey shaved two years off his age and declared that he had been born in 1885. The recruiter nodded and Harvey was signed up for the army. After a medical exam, he was told to go home and wait for orders.

Harvey spent the next month at home waiting to be notified. Finally, in February, he was given orders to report to the army base in Saint John, New Brunswick. He took young Gladys to his father-in-law's house and reported for duty. Harvey trained for several months with his fellow recruits, learning all the military skills needed for the making of a good soldier. As one of the older lads, Harvey was looked up to by the younger men and fit in well. He was an excellent shot with a rifle and well respected by his superiors. They could see that his athletic ability would serve him well in the trenches. The recruits in training were fearful that the fighting would be finished before they were shipped overseas, but they needn't have worried; there was plenty of fighting left to be done before the war was over.

When Harvey was given leave, he would return home to spend the days with Gladys, and the nights with Dorina. She was pressing for a wedding date but Harvey had no intention of marrying her. He was just using her to pass the time and for the sex that would usually happen after a few glasses of whiskey. Dorina was aware that his feelings for her were not love, but she would settle for just having a husband. She knew Harvey was still very much in love with his deceased wife, Bessie, and that she would never mean that much to him. She could accept this, but what scared her was that she had now missed her period for two months and was probably pregnant. She figured Harvey would have to marry her now.

When Harvey returned to the base he was glad to hear that the Battalion had been given a departure date. They were to sail for England in September of 1916. When Dorina learned of this situation, she knew she had to act fast. She went to Nova Scotia by train, where Harvey was now stationed, and confronted him with the news. He was furious, but more at himself than her. Being a man of honour, he agreed to marry her. Harvey was given a few days leave. They went to Amherst, Nova Scotia and got married. He planned to keep the marriage a secret, even from his own family. On his military records he still claimed to be a widower. Dorina did not want to keep it a secret. She was happy to be married again and wanted everyone to know.

On the train ride back to New Brunswick, she started to get cramps and was feeling miserable by the time she arrived home. She made it in the door, dropped her bags and headed straight to the outhouse. She was about to start the longest and most painful flow she ever had in her life. She was definitely not pregnant. She knew she had to tell Harvey but put it off as long as she could. She was sure he wouldn't believe she really thought she was pregnant. She knew he would think she had just concocted the story to get him to marry her. Once he knew she wasn't pregnant, she figured he'd be furious. She was right. Harvey was so upset when he found out that he wanted a divorce, but with all that was going on in his life he decided to wait until he returned from the war.

The 26th New Brunswick Battalion was deep in the trenches for the rest of the war. Harvey distinguished himself often and showed great bravery through the battles in which he and his fellow soldiers were engaged. He was there at the Somme, Paschendale, Ancre Heights, Vimy Ridge and several other battle sites. One battle almost ended his military career. At one point, he was one of the first out of the trenches. He felt the explosion before he heard it. Suddenly, his legs were not working. When he looked down he saw a mess of blood. His left side was also bloodied and he knew it was bad.

Luckily for Harvey, he was quickly evacuated to a hospital where they removed as much shrapnel as they could find. When he was well enough, he was sent home on the next hospital ship. He arrived in Saint John in late 1917. Harvey was glad to get home, but worried that his injuries would prevent him from having any employment. With good care and strength-building workouts, he was soon on the mend. He missed the army terribly, but for now he would have to get used to being a civilian again.

Harvey went back home and demanded a divorce from Dorina, but she refused. Disgusted with her and not wanting to be anywhere near her, Harvey took off to Fredericton to join the home guard. He was refused. They had many healthier men to choose from and didn't need wounded soldiers. Harvey was devastated, but more determined than ever to get back into shape. He went for long walks and found employment in forest work. He built up his body to the point where he was as strong as before he was wounded.

One day he was in a tavern on Queen Street in Fredericton when he ran into an officer he had served under. They started talking and Harvey mentioned how much he missed the army. The officer said that he would see what could be done. Luckily for Harvey, by that time in the war it was getting harder and harder to recruit new soldiers. The boatloads of casualties that descended from the troop ships left an indelible mark on the local populace. Fewer and fewer men wanted to join up. That worked in Harvey's favour, and when he went back to the recruiting office he was accepted once again. So on the eighteenth of April 1918, Harvey went to Saint John and was re-inducted into the military. Since he was already trained, he was quickly shipped back to Europe.

This time the mood was different. They knew the enemy was weakening. In order to end the war as fast as possible, battles had become bloodier and more intense. Fewer leaves were given and the men spent more time in the trenches than before. The bombardments lasted longer, and the time between them became shorter.

Three days before the end of the war, Harvey was wounded again. Shrapnel entered his leg and he was sent back to a hospital. On November 11, 1918, the war came to an end. This time, Harvey was going home for good. But he was a very changed man. While the war had ended for Canada, it had not ended for Harvey. It would take years before he could find peace. He did not feel like he belonged in his old life. Fishing was not an option. Though he had a daughter, he didn't know her anymore and she didn't know him.

The Harvey that returned from the war was not the man his family and friends remembered. When he arrived back in New Brunswick, he decided that instead of going home, he would do some travelling. His first stop was Edmundston, where he had a cousin, Theo, who owned a bowling alley.

Harvey spent some months helping his cousin at the bowling alley while deciding what to do next. He needed to get back to hard physical labour. That was the only thing that calmed him and prevented the nightmares that continually plagued him. He decided to head south and see what work he could get.

Everywhere Harvey went he developed a reputation as a hard worker. His employers were happy to give him good references and pass him on to others that needed someone to work in the woods. Many of them wanted him to stay and work for them, but Harvey was adamant about moving on after his job was completed. In 1921, Harvey was working as a lumberjack for Judson Hale and stayed with him until after Christmas. While working for Judson, he learned of a farmer at Benton Ridge who needed help and was willing to board a hired man to get started. So Harvey moved in with John Swim and his family. The family consisted of John and his wife, Phoebe Ann, their sixteen year old daughter, Alice Pearl, and twenty-two year old son, Roy Byron and his wife, Rita. The house was quite full, but they could put up Harvey until he went to work for someone else.

One day in late February, Harvey was walking down the Benton Road when a man stopped and asked him if he needed a ride. Harvey said yes, and they began to talk. William Sharp owned a farm about a mile and a half from the Swim farm and he needed someone to help him work it. Harvey agreed and started to live with William as a hired hand. Harvey would take to visiting the Swim farm on occasion and it was on one of these days that he met John's other daughter, Olive. When Olive came to Benton Ridge in late February, life for Harvey took a turn for the better. He fell immediately in love with her and she with him. He took to visiting Olive whenever he had a chance.

Olive's parents watched the two lovebirds and passed knowing glances at each other. They knew it wouldn't be long before Harvey would ask to speak to John outside and ask for Olive's hand in marriage. They were right. John and Phoebe were very happy. They knew Olive would be well provided for and best of all she would be close by. The Sharp and Swim farms were only a short distance apart. Harvey had approached William Sharp with an offer to buy his farm and all it contained, including the buildings, equipment and livestock. He knew he could get a loan from the Soldier Settlement Board for the funds needed to purchase the farm. He had already filled out the paperwork and sent it off.

The Settlement Act of 1919 was set up to help returning soldiers of World War I obtain land and property for farming such as the machinery and livestock. The Board provided up to $5000 in low and no interest loans for those who could convince them they had farming experience. Harvey was well qualified. While he was waiting for the loan to be approved, William Sharp agreed that Harvey could work the farm as if it was already his. It was a good arrangement for both of them, and it gave Harvey a sense of peace he had not felt in many years.

The same week all these arrangements were completed, Harvey went to Woodstock to get a marriage certificate and purchase a wedding ring at Dahling's General Store. Since he needed a bondsman for the marriage certificate he took William Sharp with him. Next, he went to the Meductic Baptist Church, which stood on the shore of the St. John River, and talked to Reverend Worden about performing the wedding ceremony. He wanted the wedding to be as soon as possible. They settled on the date of March 15th. Olive was ecstatic. Finally, her life was going on the right track. She busied herself making sure she would have the nicest dress she could afford. With her mother to help with the sewing, it would be ready in time for the wedding.

However, something was bothering her. She talked to her father and asked him what she should do about Bennie. She had not mentioned this part of her past to Harvey, and she sure didn't want Bennie mucking things up. She told her father how things had ended with Bennie. He told her not to worry. He would take care of Bennie if he dared show his face anywhere near Benton Ridge. That was good enough for her. She sent out invitations to friends and family inviting them to the wedding. When she asked Harvey about his side of the family, he told her he would take care of it. She was surprised that he did not send out any invitations and realized that Harvey was keeping secrets of his own. She never found out what they were. For starters, he was still married to Dorina even though he claimed he was a widower. He never mentioned he had a daughter who was just a few years younger than Olive. He had given his age as thirty-three instead of thirty-nine. Olive put her age down as eighteen instead of seventeen when Reverend Worden completed the marriage certificate. She figured it would make her more appealing to her new husband.

Bennie Goes to Visit Olive

When Bennie got home from work and found the note Olive had left, he was furious — and then sad. What more could he do for his beloved? Hadn't he given her everything he could, a place of her own and all the love he could offer? He couldn't understand what more he could do for her.

He went down to one of the local moonshiners and bought himself a jug. He began drinking in his little cabin and pondered his situation. The more he drank the more furious and despairing he became until he smashed everything in sight and tore down the walls of the cabin. After he was done, he packed up what was left of his belongings and went back to live with his parents. They were surprised to see him since they believed he and Olive were happily living in the cabin they had helped him build.

"She's left me," explained Bennie. "Just up and took off again. I don't have a clue where she went."

"I'll make some inquiries," his mother offered.

She went to visit one of her relatives and sure enough found out that Olive had gone to her parents' farm near Benton. Bennie and his parents discussed the situation concerning Olive and came up with a solution.

"She probably just wants to know you are serious about her," his father suggested. "Look, just give her a few weeks to realize how much she misses you and then go and see her. I'm sure she'll come back with you then."

"And here," said his mother handing him her wedding ring. "Give her this when you see her. It will guarantee she will want you back. A girl can't say no to a guy with a ring in his hand. She'll melt into your arms and you two can get married for sure."

This sounded like a great plan to Bennie. At the time, of course, he had no clue Olive had become seriously interested in someone else. He did just what his parents suggested. He waited a few weeks and then went to see Olive on Monday the 13th of March. As he sat on the train watching the scenery go by, he couldn't help smiling to himself at the thought of seeing Olive again and how happy she would be to see him. Just when she would ask to come and live with him again he would take out the ring, fall to his knees and propose. He was dressed in his best suit and tie and thought himself quite dashing.

When he got off the train in Benton, he went to William Porter's store and asked the way to the Swim farm. William told him how to get there and

Bennie started walking. It took about an hour to reach the farm on Benton Ridge. When Olive saw him coming up the lane, she yelled for her father to come.

"Damn it all, Bennie must have found out where I am living. No way in hell I'm going to see him," she told her father.

"Don't worry," he said. "You go out to the woods and keep walking towards your grandmother's house. I'll say you're visiting her. Wait there, and I'll get rid of Bennie. I'll come get you when he's gone."

So before Bennie saw Olive, she slipped out the back door and walked rapidly into the woods. But even from a distance, she could hear the loud cursing with which her father greeted Bennie, and the threats of bodily harm if Bennie ever came back.

"But I love her," Bennie wailed, close to tears with frustration. "I want to marry her."

"Well that ain't never going to happen," John roared. "There's a train leaving for Woodstock soon and you'd best be on it. Now clear out of here and don't you ever come back—got it?"

Bennie left, heartbroken and frustrated. Then he got mad; he knew if he could only speak to Olive personally and tell her how much he loved her, she would surely want him back. He would try again later, maybe in a week or two. By then her father would have calmed down, and Olive would want him more than ever. She wouldn't care what her father said. She would want to come back to the Mainstream with him and get married. That's the thought that Bennie hung on to while he trudged back to the station and waited for the next train to Woodstock.

When John came to the woods to let Olive know Bennie was gone, she asked him what she was going to do when he came back. She knew Bennie well enough to realize he wouldn't give up so easily. She also asked if he had told Bennie about her getting married to Harvey. John said he hadn't. He said the best thing to do was for Olive to write Bennie a letter telling him about Harvey and getting married.

"And make sure you write it after you're married and then send it to him," John advised. "That way there's no chance he will ever bother you again."

Olive agreed that was a good plan and this is exactly what she did.

When Bennie got home he told his parents what happened at Benton Ridge. His father couldn't believe the way his own brother had treated his nephew. At first he thought there must be a misunderstanding, but soon realized there must be something more going on. After all, hadn't Bennie and Olive already lived as man and wife? They were together in the cabin for months. Didn't that mean anything? He discussed it with Bennie and once again, suggested that time would make things right. Olive must not have known that Bennie visited her that day; if she had, she would have returned with him.

Bennie, in the meantime, went back to his sad, lonely life of peeling logs for Fosters and drowning his sorrows in moonshine. But he wouldn't give up on Olive. He would try again as soon as he had the chance. The next time he would make sure to speak to Olive personally. He would wait until he knew her father would be away from the farm when he went to see her. His mother, on the other hand, was not so sure about Bennie's determination. She tried to convince him to forget about Olive and find another girl. Bennie dismissed this idea immediately because the only girls that would give him any attention at all were usually fat and ugly with crooked teeth. Not one of them could come close to Olive in looks or figure. No, it would be Olive or no one.

Olive and Harvey Get Married

On the morning of the 15th of March 1922, Olive woke up with the joy and anticipation that all brides feel when they are going to be married to the man of their dreams, and Harvey was that man. Her beautiful dress, long, white, and flowing, was hanging on the wall beside her bed. She couldn't wait to put it on. This was her day and she was going to make the most of it.

The rest of the family slowly got moving and were sitting down to breakfast when Olive came in. The wedding ceremony wasn't until the afternoon, but Olive was much too restless for breakfast. She counted the hours until she and her family would hitch the team to the wagon and head down the Ridge to the Meductic Baptist Church by the St. John River. She did up her long hair and set it with the special combs she had recently purchased at a local dress shop. They had cost more than she wanted to spend, but for this occasion it was well worth it. After all, a girl only gets married once and she wanted to do it right. In the kitchen there were large trays of food they had been cooking for the last couple of days and were now ready to be loaded on the wagon. The food was for the reception that would be held after the wedding ceremony. For the men folk, there was a keg of beer and a few jars of whiskey that would be hidden somewhere convenient and taken out during the day. For the women and children there would be large pitchers of lemonade and raspberry juice.

Olive had written a letter to Bennie the day before telling him about her marriage to Harvey, but she was waiting to post it until after the ceremony. She wanted to make sure it would get to Bennie after it was too late for him to do anything about it. She could only imagine his reaction when he read it. Well, that was his problem. She had a right to her life and her choice in who she married. She was older now and wiser, and knew what life with Bennie would be like. She shuddered at the thought. But now, everything would be all right. Harvey would take good care of her and she would take good care of him. After all, she had already spent many years as a housekeeper and knew just what to do. They would have lots of children and Harvey would be so proud of her in the way she ran their household.

Olive was shaken by Bennie's visit. She didn't expect him to show up so soon, but she knew now that she had made the right choice in not seeing him. He was a problem she did not want to deal with and was happy to let her father take care of it. She watched as her mother and sister bustled around the kitchen doing the last of the morning chores. She pitched in to make the time go faster. She was sure the old clock on the mantle was mocking her with its slowness. She could almost hear her heart beat three times for every tick of the clock. No matter how much she did, the hands on its face hardly moved. Finally, she stopped looking at it and just did whatever she could around the house to keep herself occupied.

Her brother Roy and his wife Rita were also in the house putting on their Sunday clothes. This would be quite the special occasion for them all. Not since Roy's wedding back in 1918 had there been this much excitement in the Swim household. The invitations had been sent and all was ready. They expected family members and local friends to show up. Finally, Olive saw her father and brother go to the barn to get the team. It was now time to put on the dress she and her mother had spent so much time making and were so proud of. Wouldn't Harvey just melt when he saw her in it? She hummed happily to herself with the thought of the upcoming ceremony. Her father and brother finished hitching the team to the wagon. John called out to the family to get a move on. They loaded up the wagon and proceeded along the Benton Ridge Road and down the long hill to the Meductic Baptist Church by the St. John River.

Harvey woke up that morning like nothing special was going on but in an odd state of mind. It was his birthday as well as his wedding day but he was conflicted. He loved Olive dearly, but he wasn't sure if he loved her for being Olive, or because she reminded him of his first wife Bessie. They were both about the same age when he married them, but he was thirty-nine today. That was more than twice the age of Olive. He hadn't told her his real age. She thought he was thirty-three. It shouldn't matter, really. What were a few extra years? If she found out once they married, it wouldn't be a problem. He would shower her with love and take good care of her—that's what mattered.

When he was fully dressed in a suit borrowed from his employer, William Sharp, he felt better about the situation. He thought about his daughter and wondered how she was getting along. He had thought about inviting her to the wedding, but that would make it very uncomfortable with all of the questions it would raise. He had not contacted her for fear that Dorina, still technically his wife, would find out about his new life and mess it up. It would be a serious problem if Dorina were to show up at the wedding. It would ruin everything and he didn't want that to happen. He had avoided contact with her since returning from the war but legally she was still his wife. Even so, he was getting married to Olive today and didn't want anything to spoil that.

To calm his now troubled nerves, he reached for his flask of whiskey and took a long swallow. No matter what, he would act like the happy bridegroom and all would go well. When it was time to leave, he put on his coat and hat and went out to the barn to saddle his horse. William Sharp had already saddled his and was waiting for him in front of the house.

"You were takin' so long, I was startin' to think maybe you'd changed your mind about marrying Olive," he said with a chuckle. "She's quite the catch and if you don't marry her there are plenty of guys around here who would."

Harvey knew that was true, but he just nodded to William and they started off down the road. The church was about an hour's ride and, with snow still on parts of the road, it was slow going. As they rode, Harvey told William how thankful he was for all he had done in helping him fill out the forms for the Soldier Settlement Board so he could buy the farm. William shrugged it off, saying he was happy to do it. He was thinking that once Olive moved in they would to have a real housekeeper to make excellent meals they would all enjoy.

When they arrived at the church, Harvey saw the yard filled with the wagons that had brought the guests. He was surprised to see so many people and happy for Olive. He knew this large attendance would help make the day even more special for her. He took one last swig of whisky and then with William walked to the front of the church. The Reverend Worden was already there in his robes looking out over the congregation. He liked the attention these ceremonies brought him and felt quite powerful looking down at the nervous groom and the smiling bride. It was nice to see so many people for a change. Normally, a much smaller crowd was on hand to hear his sermons due to the larger churches in nearby Benton.

When Reverend Worden saw Olive standing at the back of the church, he motioned to the piano player to start the wedding march. Gladys Marston had been practicing this piece for days but still had not managed to perfect it. She missed several of the notes, but the guests didn't pay much attention. They were all looking at Olive. She looked radiant as she walked up the isle on her father's arm. The older women were looking at the dress, trying to see imperfections. The young women were wondering when their wedding days might come and they would be the centre of attention. The men were looking at Olive and wishing they were the ones that would be getting to do to her what lucky Harvey would be doing tonight.

Reverend Worden waited for Olive to take her place beside Harvey. As she stood by her husband-to-be, she noticed the faint smell of whisky that wafted from him. But she was too enamoured to worry about it; it was just what men did. She could tolerate it to a point and hoped his drinking would not get out of hand. She would put a stop to it if she had to. For now, she would just glow in the adoration he showed her as they looked into each other's eyes.

The Minister opened his well-worn Bible to the place he had marked for this occasion. He had performed many weddings and he was feeling calm as he gazed over the guests. It was now his time for attention.

"Dearly beloved," he began. "We are here to join this man and woman in holy matrimony."

When he got to the part about whether anyone present knew of any reason why this man and this woman should not be married they should "speak now or forever hold their peace," Olive almost feared she might hear Bennie's voice come shouting out from the back of the church. Harvey almost expected the same from Dorina, but silence prevailed and no one contested the marriage.

Reverend Worden waited for a few seconds to make sure before he carried on. "By the power invested in me, I now pronounce you man and wife. You may kiss the bride."

And Harvey did just that. The guests applauded and the happy couple turned to face the crowd. They walked arm in arm to the back of the church followed by the guests. The celebration could now begin. While the men clapped Harvey on the back and offered the couple their congratulations, John, Roy, and Alice Pearl went to the wagon, and, with the help of several others, unloaded the food and beverages on the tables that had been set up at the back of the church. As everyone ate and drank, they enjoyed the opportunity for lively conversation and catching up on local doings. When most of the food had been consumed, and after again congratulating Olive and Harvey and wishing them well, the guests began to leave. After everyone had departed, William Sharp, Harvey and Olive, and Olive's family loaded up the wagon and set off for the Sharp farm. When they arrived at the house, they put out food and drink for the evening that had been kept back. William brought out a jug of whiskey he had been saving for this occasion and the party continued well into the night.

Finally, John announced it was time to leave. They had planned for William to spend the night at the Swim house so the newlyweds could be left alone. Olive's family and William departed. He would give them this one night alone before coming back in the morning. After that, they would live together. Olive would be the housekeeper while William and Harvey worked the farm. When the Settlement Board approved the financing, William would officially turn over the farm to Harvey and Olive.

When the family left, Olive looked at Harvey expectantly. He gave her a big smile and she blushed. She went to the bedroom, carefully took off her wedding dress and hung it in the armoire. She put on her nightgown and crawled under the covers. The blast of cold shocked her, but she knew she would soon be warm when Harvey crawled into bed beside her. It didn't take long before that happened. Harvey had a last sip of whiskey and joined his new wife in the creaky old bed.

Olive's last thought that night was that she was glad she had kept herself pure for her husband. The next morning Olive awoke before Harvey. When she got out of bed, she was sore but not unreasonably so. She had expected some pain, mixed with the pleasure, so she wasn't surprised with what happened. Her mother had assured her it would only hurt the first time but not much after that. Olive started up a fire in the woodstove. She put on water for tea and got out the large cast iron frying pan and set it on top of the woodstove. She got out eggs and bacon and waited for the stove to get hot. Before long, the eggs and bacon were cooking and the scent wafted through the house.

Harvey woke up and smelled breakfast. He was hungry and ready to eat. He came into the kitchen with a big smile on his face and sat down at the table. Olive was smiling as well, knowing this would be her routine for many days to come, and, hopefully soon, with children bustling around the kitchen with their noisy laughter. She heard a knock at the door, but before she could open it William came in. She welcomed him and bade him sit at the table with Harvey while she served the eggs and bacon, giving each man a generous portion. For herself, she ate little. Olive was quite aware of her slim, attractive figure and wanted to keep it as long as possible. Once the children came she could put on a little weight and not feel guilty about it.

The men discussed the day's activities while they ate. There would be no honeymoon for the newlyweds. It was business as usual on the farm. There was the livestock to feed, eggs to be collected and wood to be cut. The maple sap would soon be running and they needed to make more spiles for tapping the trees. Olive told Harvey she needed to go to her father's place to get the rest of her clothing.

"Fine," he replied. "If you need help let me know."

Olive said she could handle it on her own. The real reason she wanted to go alone was because she didn't want Harvey to see the letter she was posting to Bennie. She had never told Harvey about Bennie, not that it would have mattered, but it was best to keep some things secret.

Olive ran up the road to her father's farm and found them all sitting in the kitchen. Her brother Roy grinned at her and she gave him a dirty look. She went to get the letter where she had left it in her room. Her father knew about the letter and said he could take her to the post office in Porten Settlement. They departed immediately to mail the letter.

When they arrived, the postmaster, who had been a guest at the wedding ceremony, said in a loud voice, "Good morning Mrs. Trenholm. What can I do for you today?"

Olive gave him the letter. He weighed it and said the postage would be three cents. When he turned it over, he saw it lacked a return address.

"Better put on your return address," the postmaster advised and handed the letter back to Olive.

She thought for a moment and then wrote on the back of the envelope; "Mrs. Olive Trenholm, Sharp Farm, Benton Rd. Benton Ridge, New Brunswick "

She counted out the three cents and asked how long it would take to reach Mainstream.

"I'll make sure it goes out on the afternoon train to Hartland so it should arrive there by Saturday," the postmaster replied.

That was fine with Olive. As she and her father rode back to his farm, he asked her what she thought about being married. She laughed and said that it felt good. It made her feel complete. They stopped at the Swim farmhouse, picked up the rest of her clothing and other small belongings and returned to the Sharp Farm. Now that she had mailed the letter to Bennie, she would never have to think about him again. That part of her life was over and done with, and good riddance. Now she had a husband to take care of and her own household to run. Life was good.

Bennie Gets a Letter

On Saturday the 18th of March, Bennie stopped at Estabrooks General Store in Coldstream on his way home from peeling logs at Pleasant Corners. He was thinking about going to see Olive and bringing her back to the Mainstream. He smiled at the thought. He knew that by now she would be desperate to see him, and no matter what her father said she would defy him and come back to the Mainstream with him. They would live as man and wife once again; of this he was dead certain and it gave him a feeling of happiness.

As he finished making his purchases, the mail carrier came in, motioned him over and said, "Got a letter for ya Bennie. It came down from Benton Ridge today."

Bennie was overjoyed. He knew it had to be from Olive, writing to say how much she missed him, begging his forgiveness, and that she wanted to come back to the Mainstream and live with him. He turned the letter over and noticed the return address. When he saw the words "Mrs. Olive Trenholm," he was dumbfounded and then exclaimed, "What the hell?"

He ripped open the envelope, pulled out the letter, and read the message.

Dear Bennie.

I have married Mr. Harvey Trenholm on March 15th at the Baptist Church in Meductic. I hope you find a nice girl yourself to be with but it will never be me. Please do not come around here anymore. Good luck with the rest your life.

Mrs. Olive Trenholm

Bennie couldn't believe it. He read the letter over and over until with a rage he couldn't contain began cursing the heavens, hell, damnation and everything else he could think of. It must be a mistake. She would never do this to him. Maybe it was just a ploy of her father to make sure he didn't come around. But when he examined the letter closely he recognized Olive's handwriting. It was her handwriting for sure. No, it had to be real. He then trudged back to his parents' cabin feeling morose and defeated but still with flashes of rage.

When he arrived, his father took one look at him and knew something was dreadfully wrong. Bennie showed him the letter. William read it a few times and passed it to his wife, Eva. She also read it several times before giving it back to Bennie. His parents knew life for their son would never be the same. They didn't know just how bad things would get, but they would find out soon enough.

At first, they tried to console him. They told him that there were plenty of other fish in the sea. Lots of girls in the area that would be happy for what Bennie had to offer. That didn't get much of a response. He knew exactly what kind of woman he would have to settle for and that thought kept him from considering it. No, it would be Olive or no one. Then his parents tried to denigrate Olive. They came up with plenty of bad things to say about her. But that didn't placate Bennie either. He sat and thought, drank and thought, cursed and thought, and inbetween was lost to utter melancholy.

When his parents tried to get him to go to church with them Sunday morning, Bennie declared that he had no interest in ever going to church again.

"Why pray to a God that would do this to me?" He asked.

He watched his parents depart and then went out to buy another jug of moonshine from one of the locals, who would also not be doing any worshiping that day. When his parents returned from church, Bennie was still sitting in the same position except more drunk than usual. The next day they tried to convince him to go to his job, but Bennie had no interest in going back to work. On the third day, Bennie came up with a plan. Actually it was several plans, depending on what the outcome of each part would be. As he thought about it all, he became happier but more apprehensive at the same time.

The first plan was that since he and Olive had actually lived together she was his common-law wife and if she married someone else she would be committing bigamy. He could now get the Sheriff to arrest her and her new husband. That idea seemed like it might work and it would help counter the jests he would have to put up with from others when they heard about Olive's wedding and tried to make him look foolish. He talked the idea over with his parents, but they didn't think much of it. After all, Bennie and Olive were not legally married so there was nothing preventing Olive from marrying someone else. Besides, the Sheriff would probably laugh in his face if he tried it.

The second part of his plan would be to murder Harvey Trenholm and maybe Olive as well. Even though he stilled loved her, he also felt she deserved it for what she had done to him. On the other hand, if she agreed to get back together with him murdering her wouldn't be necessary.

"No, that won't work, she'll never come back. I'll have to murder them both," he thought with despair.

But he realized that if he murdered Olive, it would hit him so hard he would probably want to kill himself as well. Why would he want to live? He kept going over and over the idea hoping to decide on the best course of action. But in his despair and frustration, he couldn't come up with an exact plan. He would just see how it all worked out and decide what to do as things happened. For now, he decided he would get everything he needed to carry out the plan. He made a list.

First, he would need a gun. He had a good deer rifle, but it would be too obvious. He needed something he could easily hide; he needed a handgun. Next he needed some cash to take the train down to Benton. That shouldn't be much of a problem. He looked around the sparse cabin and took inventory. At barely twenty-two he had not much in value to show for his life. He had been working since he was a teenager, and all that he had that might get him a few dollars was the rifle and maybe his winter coat and a sturdy pair of work boots. He also had the violin.

On the 22nd of March, he bundled these items and headed down to Estabrooks General Store. As he was walking, he realized what all of this meant. Once the deed was done, he would not be coming back. It didn't matter if he sold everything because he wouldn't need any of it anymore. What he didn't sell, his parents could use. There would be no escape route and no plans for anything after the shootings. Well, it wasn't done yet; maybe something would happen to change his mind, but for now he would do what was needed to carry out his plan.

When he entered the store, Edmund Estabrooks greeted him from behind the counter. "What can I do for you today, Bennie?"

Edmund had known Bennie since he was a child and was also familiar with the rest of the family. Bennie proceeded to tell him what he needed. He showed him the coat, rifle, boots and violin, and although curious why Bennie would want to trade these items, he didn't say anything. Business was business and it was not his place to inquire. Edmund inspected the items carefully turning them over and checking for wear. Finally he looked up and came to a decision.

"Here's what we can do Bennie. I'll give you this revolver I picked up from your cousin Raybon Swim. He got it from a jeweller in Hartland. It has a broken trigger spring but works good most of the time. I'll add ten rounds of 38-long rifle ammunition. They're the right calibre but they're a bit too long. You'll have to shave them down and they'll work fine. I'll also give you a cap, raincoat, shoes, rubbers for the shoes, and seven dollars. I don't need your rifle or the boots; I got too many of them already. I'll just take the violin. What do you think?"

Bennie didn't have much choice, but he tried without success to get more cash from Edmund. When he got back to the cabin, he took out the gun and made sure it would fit into a side pocket of the raincoat without showing. He carefully took the bullets out of each cartridge and filed them down so they would fit properly in the chambers of the revolver's cylinder. As he was working, one of the cartridges fell to the floor spilling the powder. He gathered up as much of the powder as he could and put it back in the cartridge before reinserting the bullet. He went outside and test-fired the gun twice. It worked fine each time. He noticed the trigger felt loose because of the broken spring, but it didn't affect the firing.

The revolver had a five shot cylinder. That was all he would need to carry out his plan. He put the revolver under his bed and smiled for the first time since hearing the news of Olive's wedding to Harvey. He would show them that Bennie Swim was not a man to mess with. He kept his plans secret. He didn't want his parents to know any of it for fear that they would interfere. They would surely try to dissuade him from carrying out his plan. No, he would act like nothing was happening and they would be none the wiser. His parents were glad Bennie was now in a better mood and thought he had gotten over the fact that Olive would never be his wife.

Bennie sat around for a few days thinking about when it would be best to carry out his plan. He bought more moonshine with some of the money he had gotten from Edmund. He sat and drank and wiled away the days until it was gone. His parents figured he would soon go back to work so they left him alone with his thoughts. They had no idea what Bennie was thinking. The night before he left the cabin for the last time, he spent hours in his parents' bedroom talking to his mother. She noticed something odd was going on with her son, but that was just Bennie, so she thought nothing more about it.

The Murders at Benton Ridge

The next morning, Bennie got up early. He told his parents he was going to visit some family and then go down to Woodstock to pay a note on the violin. His mother had no clue what that meant, so she just said goodbye and expected to see him back that evening. Without another word, Bennie got up and headed out the door. His parents wondered if he was getting ready to go back to work or find a different job.

March 27th was a fair day. The sky was cloud free and the temperature was mild for late March. Bennie walked to the train station in Hartland. He purchased a ticket on the C.P.R. line to Woodstock and boarded the train. With the five dollars he had left he could have gone all the way to Benton, but he didn't want to get there too early. He would enjoy the walk and think things over again while travelling. He would need to ask directions to find the Sharp Farm, but he had plenty of time for that. By coincidence, Sheriff Foster was also travelling on the train from Hartland to Woodstock. His destination was unknown to Bennie, but he didn't like seeing him. It was a bad omen. When Bennie arrived at the Woodstock station around noon, he started walking down the River Road toward Meductic.

Alfred Ball had just picked up a load of supplies from the feed store and was heading home when he saw a young man walking along the River Road. He pulled his team over to the side of the road and asked Bennie if he would like a ride.

"I'm only going as far as Lower Woodstock but your welcome to hop on if you want. Save you some shoe-leather," he offered.

Bennie was happy for the lift and jumped on the wagon.

"So where might you be going this fine day?" asked Alfred.

Bennie was not thinking it was a fine day at all, but did say, "My wife Olive left me and married another man. I'm going to the Sharp Farm to look into the matter."

Alfred was surprised. This was a story he was definitely not expecting to hear. He looked more closely at the young man and tried to place him but could not. He was sure he had never met him before.

Alfred nodded gravely and replied, "That's a very unfortunate situation."

He was surprised to see the situation didn't seem to cause the man any grief or anger. He would have expected a much more emotional expression from his passenger. He seemed quite calm about it all. No undue excitement, nothing. Quite a strange young man indeed, thought Alfred. When Bennie left his company, Alfred continued on to his farm.

Bennie kept walking until he reached John Marston's house. He knocked on the door and was invited inside. Mrs. Marston was sitting at the table drinking coffee with Enoch Gilbert. John Marston, a constable, was in Woodstock for the day. Bennie asked for directions to the Sharp Farm. He also asked where the nearest telephone was. That was an odd thing to say and Enoch pressed him for more details. He asked Bennie why he was going to the Sharp place.

"I'm going to have my wife and another man arrested," Bennie replied.

Enoch did not like the sound of this but said he was going in the same direction and would show Bennie how to get to the Sharp farm. Enoch was curious and just to be sure he knew who Bennie was talking about, asked Bennie who his wife was.

"Olive Swim," Bennie replied

It was who Enoch thought it might be so he said, "Look, they're married now; don't meddle with them."

"You needn't tell me that," Bennie replied. "I got a letter from her on Saturday that told me all about it, but I don't care".

"Well why do you want to meddle with them?" Enoch asked. "Why don't you let the law do it?"

To which Bennie replied, "They can't but kill me anyways."

Enoch was stunned. "So who might you be?" he asked.

"I'm Bennie Swim," was the reply.

It was what Enoch expected to hear but wished he had not. He had heard stories about Olive's ex-boyfriend and now, with what he knew, it all made sense.

"Well, they're married now and that's the end of it," he calmly offered one more time.

He wished Bennie would go back home but knew he had not come all this way just to forget about whatever he planned to do. He had tried to see if Bennie had any weapons but there was nothing obvious. When they got close to Wellie Rogers place, Enoch pointed out the road to the Sharp farm and left Bennie off. He watched him going down the Springfield Road and wondered what he should do. He decided to go to John Swim's farm and let them know what was going on.

Before he got to the Swim Farm he saw Roy Swim, Olive's brother, at the Sewell's place. He had been cutting wood and was taking a break. Enoch called him over and told him his cousin Bennie was headed for the Sharp farm to see Olive. Roy thanked him for the information, quickly leapt on his horse and took off down the road. He had a bad feeling about this.

As Bennie approached the Sharp house, he saw Olive standing at a window. If she knew what was about to happen, she wouldn't be so relaxed he thought. Actually, Bennie himself didn't know for sure what was going to happen. He had rehearsed in his mind what he was going to do but it did not seem real. Even as he walked up to the Sharp house, he still could not believe what was about to happen. He had a moment of doubt. He could change his mind and go back home. No, he came to do what he had to do and would not back down now.

Bennie looked around one more time, took a deep breath and walked up to the Sharp house. If only Olive had come back to him none of this would now be happening. Well, she didn't so she was going to get what she deserved. He pulled out the gun just to make sure it was still fully loaded. He spun the cylinder and heard the click for each of the five bullets. Well this was it, time to set things right.

Olive was feeling especially happy as she made the preparations for dinner. She looked over at Harvey. Here she was, a farmers wife, taking care of two men. Soon the farm would be officially theirs. Harvey was making cedar spiles for the maple sap run. She thought about how they would work together. There were large maple trees on the farm that would give plenty of sap. They were so big they could be tapped in more than one place insuring a large amount of sap could be collected each day. They would boil down the sap outdoors in a large iron pot and then finish the process on the kitchen stove until they had maple syrup. They would continue boiling some of the sap further until all of the water was evaporated and they would have maple sugar for their coffee and tea. Maple sugar was a special delicacy and a point of pride for the household when served to guests.

Olive hummed to herself, secure in the knowledge that life was good and her handsome husband was going to take care of her for many years to come. She imagined the children that would soon be running around the kitchen or playing in the yard. She had even begun to think of names for her brood. Good biblical names would be the best. That way they were sure to lead righteous Christian lives and end up in heaven.

As she thought of all this, she stirred the Irish stew cooking on the stove. The delicious odour wafted throughout the house. It was an old family recipe she knew Harvey and William would especially enjoy. She often found herself smiling at Harvey for no apparent reason. He knew why and smiled back. He was more in love with his young bride with each passing day.

For Harvey, the war was finally over and he could appreciate the simple things that life had to offer. He no longer suffered the nightmares that had plagued him for years after the war, and he was content to live the rest of his life with Olive and any children that they might have. He was still waiting for the Soldier Settlement Board to make their decision to help him to buy the farm, but he was confident it was only a matter of time before he was approved. Then, all of the machinery, livestock, buildings and land would be his and Olive's. He was proud of what he had accomplished and was looking forward to living here for the rest of his life.

He looked over at his beautiful wife and thanked God for what he had been given. Olive was just what he needed; she was kind and gentle but could also get fired up when the situation called for it. At "eighteen" she was wonderful at being a wife. In many ways she seemed much older than her age and he sometimes wondered what it was that had made her that way. He hadn't pressed her about her past life. They probably both had things to be kept secret—he certainly did.

As he continued whittling the sap spiles, he thought about when William would get back from Benton with the supplies they were laying in for spring planting. The days were getting longer and soon much work would be required to produce all that the farm was capable of providing. Harvey was awakened from his reverie by a knock on the front door. He and Olive looked at each other. They were not expecting anyone, but it was not unusual for neighbours to drop by unannounced. He shrugged and got up to answer the door.

Bennie stood waiting for several seconds on the front doorstep after he had knocked on the door. He heard footsteps coming in his direction. He was going to ask to speak to Olive, but when he saw Harvey looming in front of him with a curious and steady gaze, blind anger took over. He pulled out the revolver, aimed it at Harvey's head and fired. The noise stunned him for a second but as he saw Harvey fall in front of him on the doorstep, he regained his composure and looked up.

Olive, who had been in the kitchen preparing dinner, heard the shot and ran to the front door. She looked at Bennie, still holding the gun in his hand and then at Harvey and screamed. She couldn't believe what she was seeing. She then bent down to help Harvey. Bennie, furious that she would try to help her husband, grabbed her by the dress, pushed the gun into her chest and fired. It threw her back but she did not fall. She stumbled backwards a few steps then turned and ran. Bennie took aim and fired at her back. She stumbled and dropped to the floor.

Bennie entered the house and stood for a moment looking down at Olive. A heavy flow of blood was pooling beside her. He was momentarily surprised by the damage the bullets had made, but then was suddenly overwhelmed with shock and grief. It hadn't occurred to him that filing down the bullets to fit the revolver would cause them to shatter on impact, causing much worse damage than if they had not been altered. That, plus the fact they were rifle bullets with a heavy charge of powder, had caused the massive damage to Olive and Harvey that he now witnessed.

Bennie began to feel remorse for his actions and then a sense of utter despair. Not for what he had done to Harvey, that barely gave him pause, but what he had done to Olive, his true love. He sank onto a kitchen chair and then noticed a writing pad and pencil on a table. He picked it up and wrote, "Good Bye Olive Swim and Sleep."

With one last look at Olive, he turned and stumbled out the door towards the sheep pen. The gun still had two bullets left in the cylinder. He thought about what he had to do. There was no escape from his grief. The sight of Olive dying in front of him would never leave his mind. He knew when he left home this morning he would kill himself right after he had killed Olive if it came to that, and it had. He didn't deserve to live. He took a deep breath, closed his eyes and put the gun to his head. He pulled the trigger. He felt an explosion go off in his head and his ears rang to the point of deafness.

Bennie fell to the ground, but instead of a sweet black cloud of unconsciousness that would mean he was dying, he just felt an extreme headache in his right temple. He felt blood dripping from his head. For a few seconds, what had happened didn't register. Then it came to him; he was not dead. He saw the blood falling in slow steady drops onto his coat. What the hell had happened? Why wasn't he dead?

It didn't occur to him the bullet he had just fired was from the cartridge that had fallen on the floor back in the cabin. He had gathered up as much of the spilled powder as he could, but that cartridge ended up with much less powder in it than the others and had much less firing power. The bullet had gone in at an angle, travelled only a short distance under the scalp, and lodged above his right eye.

Bennie didn't know what to do. He had a bullet in his head but he was not dead. The pain was incredible. Should he try again or should he forget about killing himself and think about escaping? He figured it must be a sign from God that he didn't die. If God wanted him to live, then so did he.

With the pain throbbing in his head, he started to walk. There were still several hours of daylight left so he had to be vigilant. He didn't know if anyone had heard the shots and even if they did, so what. It was a common sound in the country. As he was coming out from between the barn and the house, he noticed a carriage driving down the road in front of the Sharp house. Better not to take any chances. He quickly darted into the woods so as not to be seen by anyone travelling by. When he thought it was clear, he went out to the road. Blood was still dripping from his wound so he took out his handkerchief and wrapped it around his head, covering the wound as best he could.

Mrs. Jesse Kirk, housekeeper for William Woodman, lived about a quarter mile from the Sharp farm. When she looked out the window that day in the late afternoon, she saw a young man wearing a light raincoat and cap walking towards Benton. It looked like he had come from the Sharp house. She had never seen the young man before. As he disappeared from sight, she thought no more about it and went back to her cleaning.

Leslie Bell was out in the woods north of the Sharp house with his team and sled. He was cutting and loading wood with the help of Mr. Hempel who was deaf. Winter had been especially cold this year. Bell had gone through his wood supply sooner than expected and needed to replenish it. He had been working all afternoon and was taking a break about 4:30 when he heard what he thought were several rifle shots. He didn't pay much attention and went back to cutting wood. As he did so he looked towards the road and saw his father, Robert Bell, travelling by. He waved and his father slowed his carriage to a stop. They talked for a few minutes and then Robert went on towards his home.

He had been travelling down the Benton Road coming from Elmwood. When he passed the Sharp farm, he noticed a man wearing a cap and light raincoat coming out from between the barn and the house. He didn't recognize him and paid him no heed. He noticed the man pulled his cap over his eyes and turned away. It looked like he was trying hard not to be noticed. The man then turned quickly and headed in a westerly direction. Robert was thinking of his friend and comrade in arms Harvey Trenholm. They had met overseas, when both had been soldiers of the 26th New Brunswick Battalion. Robert was a sergeant, and somewhat older than Harvey. He had been meaning to go over and visit Harvey for some time. He wanted to meet Harvey's wife and felt a visit was long overdue. But he continued on home, looking forward to supper.

Bennie felt his head and realized he was still bleeding from his right temple. He tried to stem the flow of blood but was not very successful. Drops of blood fell on the snow every few feet. Although the pain had subsided somewhat, he was still in a state of shock. He couldn't believe he had actually killed two people. That was a hanging offence for sure. He fully realized the gravity of what he had done. He also understood he had to get away, fast. But first, he had to get rid of the gun.

About two hundred yards from the Sharp house, he stopped at a large tree and stashed the gun and remaining cartridges under debris at the base of the trunk. He then continued walking through the forest towards the west. He tried to think about his options. If he could make it to the Maine border he might have a chance. First he needed to get as far away from Benton Ridge as possible without being seen. The forest was still filled with deep snow and the going was painfully slow. He came out of the woods and walked across several fields. If he stayed in the open, even with the sun starting to go down, he could easily be seen if anyone were looking for him. If he stayed in the woods, it would be long after dark before he would reach the border.

Bennie wasn't sure how far it was to the border and he was rapidly tiring. He was feeling increasingly weak and knew he couldn't go much further before he passed out. Risking the road seemed to be the only option. He was also hungry. If he could get something to eat it might give him enough strength to keep going through the night. He settled for walking along Caldwell Road. Although he didn't know anyone around here, he decided to take a chance and ask for something to eat at one of the nearby farmhouses. He didn't think news of the murders would be spreading in the neighbourhood for several more hours or maybe even a day or two.

He saw a house far off the road that looked inviting. He walked up the lane and saw a man sitting on the veranda. Henry Carr had seen Bennie walking across his field. As Bennie approached the house, Henry could see he was covered in blood. He looked like he had been in an accident. He was bleeding from the forehead and appeared very weak. Bennie asked if he could have something to eat. It seemed an odd request but since Henry and his wife had recently had supper, and they had plenty left over, he went to the kitchen and filled a plate with food. Bennie sat down on the veranda and began to eat. He was ravenous. He hadn't eaten since breakfast. He ate like it was his last meal.

"What's the matter with your face?" Henry Carr finally asked.

"I'm tired," Bennie replied. "I got into trouble with a man and woman at Benton and they shot me."

Mr. Carr was surprised and then asked, "Who were they?"

"Donahue or Donavon," Bennie replied.

"What place was it?" Henry Carr asked.

Bennie ignored the question and asked, "Do you know Alexander Rogers, where he lives?"

Mr. Carr said, "Yes."

"How far would Roger's place be from the Sharp place?" Bennie continued.

"Over a mile cross-country," Mr. Carr replied.

"What road does Rogers live on?" Bennie asked.

"He's on the Springfield Road," Carr told him.

Bennie hesitated and then asked, "Is that a different road than where the Sharps live?"

Mr. Carr said, "Yes it is."

He now thought there was something seriously wrong with this young man. Maybe it's his wound. He seems calm but scary as well.

He finally asked Bennie, "Who are you?"

"I'm Swim," Bennie replied. "I'm awfully tired; my head hurts something awful. Where's the nearest *doctor*?"

Bennie emphasized the word doctor. He was worried Mr. Carr would send him to the nearest hospital.

"The nearest doctor is in Debec, about four miles." Mr. Carr replied.

Bennie asked, "When does the next train leave from Debec for Woodstock?"

"About nine tonight," Mr. Carr told him. "You'd have time to get your face dressed before the train leaves."

"Good," Bennie said in a voice that was growing weaker.

Mr. Carr then asked Bennie the name of the woman he had been in trouble with.

"Swim," he replied.

OK, thought Mr. Carr, maybe it's just a coincidence that this is the same name as the young man in front of him, though he doubted it. He tried one last time to get the whole story from Bennie.

Bennie closed his eyes and told Henry Carr the following story. "I went to the door and this fellow opens it and he says, 'What are you doing down here?' So I say, 'I'm down here on a little business.' The man hits me three times, and I tell him 'Careful, I have hands too.' Then he takes out a gun and fires at me; I grab the gun and throw it away. And that's it."

This was the story Bennie came up with to satisfy Mr. Carr. He didn't bother to tell the part about killing the man and Olive.

"Listen, I need a place to spend the night. Would you be able to put me up?" he asked.

No way in hell, thought Mr. Carr. This is too strange a person to risk my safety and that of my wife. So, he said to Bennie, "I can't, but there's a man down the road about a mile, James Doherty, that may give you a bed for the night. You can't miss his place; it's the next farm towards Oak Mountain on the same road as this."

Bennie thanked him for the food and left. He walked as quickly as he could down the Caldwell Road. He was feeling better since he ate, but he was afraid it wouldn't last. His head was still throbbing. He kept moving northwest up the road toward Oak Mountain and the border. He cut back into the woods to stay out of sight but it was slow going and it was getting dark. He didn't know what to do. In despair, he sat down by a tree to rest. He then tried to stand but a wave of weakness forced him to sit down again.

He waited for some time beside the tree and then, back on the road, continued slowly for over an hour until he came to Jim Doherty's house near Oak Mountain. He was totally exhausted. He knocked as loudly as he could with what was left of his strength and then practically fell through the door when it opened. Mr. Doherty took one look at the frail young man, and though he was covered in blood and offered no explanation for it, agreed to put him up for the night when asked. Doherty had to practically carry Bennie up the stairs and into one of the bedrooms. Bennie was grateful but didn't want to talk. He lay on the bed and pretended to fall asleep. Mr. Doherty left him in peace for the rest of the night.

* * * * *

Roy Swim was flying towards the Sharp house as fast as his horse would go. There were still some large snowdrifts on the road so he had to be careful and give the horse its lead. The news that Bennie was cruising for Olive made him prepare for the worst. He had seen the row that his father and Bennie had got into back on the 13th of March. They all hoped that the marriage of his sister would finally put an end to Bennie's desire for Olive. Obviously, it hadn't. After what Bennie had said to Enoch, it was apparent that Bennie had something bad in mind; what it was he didn't know. He knew Harvey Trenholm would have no trouble thrashing Bennie if it came to that, but who knew what his crazy cousin was capable of.

As he approached the Sharp House, he had a sense of foreboding. Everything seemed far too quiet; no one seemed to be around. He was just about to jump off the horse, when he saw Harvey lying face down at the front doorway with his hands folded underneath him. He stared dumbfounded at the body for several seconds making sure what he thought he was seeing was what he was really seeing. It was definitely Harvey, lying dead on the doorstep. He cried out for Olive, but got no reply. She must be dead as well or she would be out here trying to help Harvey, or screaming uncontrollably somewhere close by. Maybe she had gotten away.

Roy looked around to see if anyone had him in their gun sights. He decided to go for help. He went to Archie McElroy's house, which was close by, and told him what he had seen. Archie came back to the Sharp house with Roy and saw for himself what had happened. Roy stayed at the house while Archie went to John Woodlands' house where there was a telephone. He called the Sheriff. He explained about Harvey Trenholm being dead just outside the doorway of William Sharp's house and that Roy Swim was still there. The Sheriff told him to go back to the house and stand guard with Roy until he arrived, and to make sure no one went inside the house. When Archie got back to the Sharp house, he walked up close to Trenholm and saw the wound in Harvey's head. He then walked around the house and looked in a window. He saw Olive, lying dead on the floor in a large pool of blood.

*　*　*　*　*

Albion Rudolph Foster was the High Sheriff of Carleton County, but was also a farmer. That made him a very busy man. The idea that each county should have its own Sheriff and Deputy Sheriff was started in 1833 and had continued. The workload was enormous and for the amount of hours spent doing official duties, it did not pay very well. Sheriff Foster was paid about $1000 a year plus the expenses of his office. He began his official duties as Sheriff in 1917, replacing John Tompkins. Prior to that he had been Deputy Sheriff.

In 1922, he was fifty years of age but still in good health. He liked his job, or at least most of it. He had seen two hangings and was hoping not to see anymore. His duties involved serving writs, evicting tenants, transporting prisoners, arresting people, setting up juries and providing all services required by the judges. This is a short list of what he actually did. He was responsible to the Attorney General of the Province to whom he answered if anything went wrong. It was a big responsibility that he was good at fulfilling.

Being the High Sheriff had one big downside—you might be killed in the performance of your duties. He had to deal with some of the worst miscreants that society had to offer: rapists, murderers, arsonists, moonshiners, thieves, rustlers and every other type of criminal behaviour around. If he were killed, his widow would receive a pension.

Albion Foster had seen it all in his term as Sheriff. He was a large, powerfully built man who, with his gentle manner and intelligence, exuded confidence. But when needed, he could be very intimidating. On the evening of March 27, 1922, he had just finished supper when he got the call from Archie McElroy—a man murdered and he needed to come immediately. He didn't need to be told to come immediately, but he understood how excited people got when reporting a crime, especially murder.

He knew Benton Ridge but was unfamiliar with the Sharp farmhouse. He gave the order to Archie to not go in the house and to make sure the body or bodies not be moved. He next called his partner, Deputy Sheriff Mooers, and told him of the situation. Mooers then called the livery stable and had them prepare a team of horses and a sleigh. He contacted a Mr. John Bragdon to be the driver of the team. He figured a car would not be able to make it through the large snowdrifts that would still be blocking the way once they got closer to the farming community of Benton.

Sheriff Foster called the County Coroner and told him to prepare for an autopsy. Coroner Hays then called Dr. Griffin, and told him they needed to go to the Sharp farm at Benton Ridge where there had been a murder. The Sheriff also called and then picked up Mr. Robert Simms, the County Clerk of the Peace, and they all proceeded to Benton Ridge. When they arrived at about 8 p.m. they found Roy Swim and Archie McElroy still guarding the house as they had been told. They had also contacted William Sharp and told him what had happened. William was in Benton when he received a phone call from Mr. Gibson and immediately left for home where he arrived at about 7 p.m..

Sheriff Foster asked Roy to tell him all he knew about what had happened. When told of Bennie's visit and what he had said to Enoch Gilbert, it was pretty clear that Bennie had committed the crime. Enoch had also arrived at the Sharp house by this time and confirmed what Bennie had said to him. Sheriff Foster then went to the Woodlands' farm and called the border guards at Houlton, Maine and several local police stations. He told them to be on the lookout for Bennie Swim and arrest him if they saw him. He also called undertaker Henry DeWitt in Woodstock and asked him to come and pick up the bodies. He then set about systematically examining the crime scene. Mr. McKinley, a photographer from Woodstock, had come to take pictures of everything of importance.

By this time, people from the nearby homes had congregated outside the house. Inside the house, he took note of the woman who had also been murdered. She had on a drab coloured dress. She was lying about six feet away from a large pool of blood. A smaller pool of blood was about three feet away. William Porter was also helping search the house. He found a fully intact bullet at the entrance to the front room. He handed it to Mr. Simms. Mr. Simms then passed it back to William, who then passed it to Sheriff Foster. It was verified as a 38-calibre and gave the Sheriff an indication of the type of weapon that had been used.

Dr. Griffin had given the bodies a quick examination and spoke with the Sheriff about it. His findings were that Harvey had been killed with a single bullet to the temple. Olive had first been shot from the front through the rib cage. The bullet had exited her body. Then, she had been shot a second time in the back. The second bullet was still in her body. When the undertaker finally picked up the bodies, the Sheriff let others into the house to help search for any more clues.

Sheriff Foster then went outside and checked all of the buildings. He found footprints between the barn and the house. They indicated someone had recently left the property walking in a westerly direction. He got a lantern and examined the footprints more closely. He noticed drops of blood in the snow beside the footprints and surmised that Bennie was injured in some way. Someone mentioned to the Sheriff that there was a considerable amount blood just outside the sheep pen. When that was examined, it confirmed that Bennie was injured. Footprints from the sheep pen led to the place where the Sheriff had first found footprints. It was clear that Bennie had crossed the road into a field and was headed for the Caldwell Road.

Bennie is Captured and Taken to the Woodstock Jail

Sheriff Foster and Deputy Sheriff Mooers went back to where the footprints started and with the aid of a lantern began to follow them. The going was difficult when they came to places where the snow was still deep. When they came to where Bennie had entered the woods, they couldn't see well enough by lantern light to continue. They stopped for the night and planned to continue in the morning. They went to Mr. Woodland's house and spent the night there.

Early the next morning they went back and picked up Bennie's trail. They continued to follow the drops of blood and the footprints. When they came out of the woods to the edge of a field, they looked in the direction the trail was leading and could see it was heading for Henry Carr's place. They went directly to the Carr house and talked to Henry. They were right; Bennie had stopped there the evening before. Henry told them he had given him supper and told him to try the Doherty's for a place to stay the night.

After a quick cup of coffee, they continued following the trail and in about a mile they came up to Jim Doherty's place. That was where the footsteps stopped. Sheriff Foster was conflicted. He knew that Bennie's mother was a Foster, so Bennie must be some relation to him. He didn't know exactly what, maybe a second cousin or something, since the Fosters that lived in the Hartland area were pretty well all related. He would do what he could for Bennie but a job was a job and right now it was his duty to apprehend the murderer. Before he even knocked, the door swung open and Jim Doherty came out. The Sheriff asked him if a stranger had come by.

"A young fella came in last night," Jim replied. "He was injured. He needed to rest. He's still sleepin' upstairs."

The Sheriff went to the foot of the stairs and called in a loud voice, "Is that you Bennie? What happened?"

The Sheriff waited and then came a weak reply, "Yes, this is awful; I think I'll hang for it."

The Sheriff was a bit worried that Bennie might take a shot at him because he thought he still had the gun, but even so he spoke out firmly, "Bennie, I have to arrest you for shooting Olive Swim and Harvey Trenholm down at the Sharp place. Did you know both of these people were dead?

You are not bound to make any statement. You are arrested under a serious charge and whatever you say may be used against you at your trial."

Bennie came down the stairs fully dressed and ready to go.

"This is a bad scrape, Sheriff, a bad scrape, "he said offering no resistance as he was handcuffed and led out to the waiting sleigh. The Sheriff searched him for the gun. Bennie told him he had buried it beside a tree close to Sharp's house.

"I'll get it for you if I can," he offered.

Sheriff Foster and the Deputy Sheriff Mooers put Bennie in the back of the sleigh and proceeded to the Sharp farm. When they arrived, there was a large crowd of people hanging around. They were all surprised to see the Sheriff with Bennie. They figured Bennie would have been taken directly to the Woodstock jail.

Sheriff Foster addressed the crowd; "Now listen up; I need your help to find a revolver used in the crime. It's buried at the base of big tree somewhere nearby."

Turning to Bennie, he asked, "Where is it Bennie?"

"It's beyond the well-house," Bennie replied pointing in that direction.

With Bennie's guidance, the gun and the extra cartridges were soon found at the base of a big maple tree about two hundred yards from the house. This was no doubt one of the trees Olive had been looking forward to gathering sap from for making maple syrup.

The gun and cartridges were brought to the Sheriff. He carefully examined them. The gun was a five shot double action revolver, with a weak trigger spring. There were four spent cartridges and one live cartridge in the cylinder. The bullets in the remaining cartridges had all been shaved down to fit the gun. Without unloading it, Sheriff Foster placed the gun and cartridges in a wooden box and put it in the sleigh. Their work here was done. The Sheriff, Deputy Mooers, and Bennie began the long ride back to Woodstock.

On the way back, Bennie started talking. "It's a terrible thing I've done and I'll probably hang for it," he said. "I loved that girl with all my heart."

The Sheriff told him once again that everything he said was going to be retold at the trial. Bennie became silent and didn't say much more for the rest of the ride back to Woodstock. The full gravity of what he had done and the consequences that would follow weighed heavily on him and he became pensive. He now realized he had better start thinking of saving his own skin anyway he could. He thought about his parents and brother and sister and what they would have to live with. Having a murderer in the family would be very difficult for them. For his own sake and for that of his family, he needed to come up with a believable story of the murders that put him in as good a light a possible. He would claim he had shot Trenholm in self-defence. He would say Trenholm had threatened to beat him up and then pulled out the revolver and tried to shoot him. He over-powered Trenholm, took the gun away from him and shot him with it. That was good for one murder, but it wouldn't explain the murder of Olive.

Eventually, there would be several versions of the murders, but no one except Bennie would ever know what really happened. The end result was what mattered. Bennie had killed two people and now the wheels of justice would start to turn.

*　*　*　*　*

When Roy Swim didn't come home for supper on Monday night, Rita and Phoebe wondered what was going on. As Rita shooed away her three-year old son, Ellery, and continued cleaning up, the door burst open and Roy came in. She looked at his contorted face, and before she could say a word, Roy blurted out, "Bennie killed Olive and Harvey."

"What?" Rita screamed. "What do you mean?"

Phoebe collapsed against the kitchen wall, speechless in horror. Alice Pearl, who had heard Roy from the front room, came running in, the colour drained from her face

Without bothering to sit, Roy grabbed a plate of food and wolfed it down.

"I've got to get back there," he said. "Me and Archie are guardin' the bodies 'till the Sheriff comes."

After Roy left, Rita was at first too stunned to react. Phoebe was sobbing uncontrollably at the kitchen table. Alice Pearl was completely distraught. Little Ellery stood silently looking in fright at the adults. Rita scooped him up and took him off to bed.

Rita then went out on the porch and looked towards the Sharp farm. She could see lanterns glowing in the dark. She was overcome with a sense of foreboding. What had happened made no sense. Murders didn't happen here, but now they had. Her whole world felt unhinged.

By this time, most of the neighbours had heard that something bad had happened at the Sharp house and had come over to find out what was going on. John Swim was in Woodstock on business and wouldn't find out about the murders until the next day. When Roy came home later that night, he was completely exhausted. He told his wife, mother, and sister what had happened that afternoon starting from the time Enoch Gilbert came to warn him that Bennie was going to see Olive, up to the time of the Sheriff's arrival.

"That bastard killed her," he told his family. "Killed her and Harvey. Shot them in cold blood."

Phoebe just couldn't believe it; their precious Olive, gone, her little girl, only seventeen. It couldn't be. As the reality of Olive's murder sank in, her anger at Bennie exploded. She cursed him with profanities she didn't know she knew.

"They better hang him fast," she thought. "Because if they don't, John will."

Actually he would have probably killed Bennie in a much more painful way if he had had a chance. To hell with hanging, that was too good for him. The women fell silent in their grief but then asked Roy for more details. So Roy started again and told them everything he had seen and what he heard from the Sheriff.

It was all so terrible. Olive was so happy to be married. Alice Pearl had been visiting Olive whenever she had a chance. They would sit at the kitchen table laughing and talking about anything and everything. She would miss her sister terribly. Her death was an incomprehensible loss, especially because of the way it had happened.

*   *   *   *   *

After the bodies had been loaded on a wagon and taken to Woodstock, William Sharp and his neighbours stood around talking for several hours. They discussed all aspects of the crime, and then slowly drifted back to their homes. It was unreal that the day had started out so normally and now he had to deal with this, thought William. He had gone to Benton for the afternoon for supplies and had enjoyed himself with a few beers and some lively talk with his fellow farmers. When he was called to return home, he had no idea what to expect. He had been told to come as fast as he could. The scene that had greeted him when he arrived was unreal. Several of his neighbours were already there standing in the front yard talking about what had happened. They were waiting for the Sheriff to arrive.

William wanted to go in the house but Enoch Gilbert and Roy Swim would not let him do so. They told him they were obeying the Sheriff's orders. William understood, but it still vexed him. It was his house after all, but the sight of Harvey Trenholm lying on the doorstep was a stark reminder of the seriousness of the situation. He went to a side window and looked inside. He saw Olive lying on the floor with her blood pooled nearby. What a shame, he thought to himself. She was so young and full of life. He was overcome with sadness for her and Harvey. After all those years of fighting in the trenches of the war and surviving, it had come to this for Harvey — taken down by Olive's cousin, Bennie.

He wondered if he could have done something to prevent the murders if he had been here or if he would have been shot as well. That's something he'd never know. One thing for sure, he wouldn't be selling the farm anytime soon, not with the reputation it had now. Some people would think it was cursed. The stories would travel far and wide and people would gawk at his house now every time they passed. The story of the murders at the Sharp farm was sure to be told and retold over and over.

Robert Bell was the last person to leave that night. He'd seen a lot of blood and gore on the battlefields during the war, but this was different. It wasn't supposed to happen so close to home. He said a silent farewell to Harvey as one soldier to another, and then left the property. William watched Robert leave and waited until he was out of sight before he went back into the house. He went into the kitchen and sat down at the table. He looked over at the two empty chairs where Olive and Harvey usually sat. He remembered last seeing them when he left for Benton. Olive was working at the stove, stirring a pot of stew; Harvey was making sap spiles at the kitchen table.

William walked over to the cupboard and pulled out a bottle of whisky and a small glass. He filled it almost to the brim and downed it in one gulp. The whiskey burned but within seconds its numbing effect made him feel better. It was what he needed to take the edge off. He couldn't imagine going to bed just yet. It would be pointless. He knew that sleep would not come, besides farm chores still had to be done. He poured himself another drink. He sat and thought. He was still there, slumped over the table when the sun came pouring into the room the next morning. The whiskey bottle was almost empty, and a headache was forming in his temples. He got up, lit the stove and put on the coffee. He then noticed a crowd was forming outside. His neighbours had returned along with people who hadn't been here the night before.

*   *   *   *   *

As Bennie, Sheriff Foster, and Deputy Mooers bounced along the road, they didn't talk much. At one point, Bennie spoke up and gave his second version of the shooting. The Sheriff thought it sounded false. He was tired and wished the ride back to Woodstock would go faster. Bennie was just kind of numb. He looked at the countryside wondering what would happen next and if he would ever see it again. He tried to memorize each farm, orchard, woodlot, and stretch of forest, believing correctly this would be the last time he was going to be in the open countryside. He was cold, but he wouldn't say a word to the Sheriff about it because he didn't feel he deserved compassion. He would remain stoic and take what was coming to him.

After several hours they reached Woodstock. People on the street gawked at Bennie like he was a prize heifer going to the fair. Some of those staring at him knew about the crime but others didn't; they just liked the distraction of seeing the Sheriff taking a prisoner to jail. It didn't happen often and it was a sight to see. Some folks noticed the handcuffs on this prisoner and figured he must be a dangerous felon. They would find out soon enough just who he was and the nature of his crime. They reached the jail and Bennie saw for the first time what his temporary home looked like.

The two story brick and sandstone building with a square Romanesque tower, is located on Maple Street adjacent to the Courthouse. It was designed by Saint John architect H. H. Mott and built in 1901. Prior to Bennie's arrival, two people had been hanged in its courtyard. George Gee, in 1904 and Thomas Cammock in 1905. The jail had the capacity to hold up to fifty inmates but was rarely used to house convicts for such a serious crime as murder. The history of the place didn't much concern him. He just looked at the imposing structure and wondered how secure it really was.

When they arrived at the Woodstock Jail, the Sheriff placed Bennie in a cell at the far end of the corridor. Bennie watched him leave then sat on the small thin bed that was pushed up against the wall. He had never been in jail before, so it was a new experience for him. He knew he would not be left alone for long. The Sheriff told him a doctor would soon be in to tend his wound. While waiting, he began trying to convince himself everything would turn out all right. God would protect him from the hangman's noose. He continued to think through different versions of the murders that might give him a chance of staying alive; the right story might get him a sentence of life in prison. That would be better than hanging, wouldn't it? At least it would be better for his family.

Time dragged on as he sat there pondering his fate. He was given his supper on a plate passed through the meal slot, but he wasn't hungry and just picked at it. It didn't look particularly bad. He was thankful for that. He had no clue how long he would spend in this cell, but he figured he might as well get used to it; nothing was likely to change for a while. Later that night, as he was lying on his bed, he heard footsteps coming down the hall. Sheriff Foster and Deputy Sheriff Mooers had returned. They opened the cell door and ordered him outside. He was cuffed again and taken to Dr. Griffin's office.

Dr. Thomas Griffin, the jail house physician, had been practicing medicine for twenty-five years. He had done his medical training at the Jefferson Medical College at the University of Pennsylvania in Philadelphia. He had done his autopsies of Harvey and Olive earlier in the day and was now ready to take care of the prisoner. He told Bennie to sit in a chair while he examined the wound on his head. He probed the wound and found a bullet lodged over his right eye; it had not penetrated his skull. He removed the bullet and patched Bennie up using several stitches and a dressing around his head. Bennie would suffer no ill effects from the wound and would recover completely. After the procedure was finished, he was taken back to the jail. This would be the only time Bennie left the jail for the rest of his life except when taken to the nearby Court House.

Sheriff Foster was not happy. He was tired and emotionally drained but still had much to do. He asked Dr. Griffin for a full account of the autopsies. From a legal standpoint it wouldn't matter much because he knew the victims had both been shot to death, but it would give him a better understanding about what had actually happened. He didn't trust Bennie's account because it wasn't consistent with what he had seen at the house. Doctor Griffin went over the autopsy reports with the Sheriff.

When he first looked at the bodies, he tried to envision the body of the young woman he had known at several stages of her life. When Olive was young, Dr. Griffin had performed a few minor operations on the girl. He remembered her as a smiling, happy child with a mischievous look in her eye. He remembered as she had grown into a beautiful young woman, full of life and vigour. And now, here she was, dead at seventeen; far too young and killed in such a brutal way. He was saddened to be doing his job today, but he was a professional, and would do it right. He didn't know the man; he had never seen him before today, but could see that he was relatively young and had been in good shape up until his death. He sighed, cut away the clothes sticking to the bodies and began the post mortem examination. Dr. N.P. Grant acted as his assistant. They began with Harvey.

> *Subject: male, white, well developed, about 35 years of age. No scars on body, no deformities, numerous powder marks on face, two puncture marks on head, one an inch over the left eye, the other, one and a half inches above the left ear. The nostrils are filled with blood. Numerous abrasions of the skin over the forehead. Examination of the skull shows a large irregular perforation of the left temple. The wound is about an inch and a half wide, the brain*

badly lacerated. A portion of the bullet was found in the brain tissue. Numerous spicules of bone embedded in the brain tissue together with a portion of the bullet. There was only one shot, the bullet divided and a part went out and a part remained within.

Next, they turned to Olive.

Subject female, Mrs. Trenholm was between the ages of 18 and 20, a well developed girl, light complexion, light hair, no deformities. Operation scar in the middle line, operation scars in the appendix region, two puncture wounds in the front part of the chest, one small about the size of a five cent piece in the left breast over the region of the heart, another somewhat larger, one inch to the right of the sternum between the first and second ribs, two puncture wounds in the back of the chest, one to the lower edge of the left scapula with blood oozing freely through it, Another puncture wound at the lower part of the left lung, two inches from the spine between the seventh and eighth ribs. Bullet found in tissue of the left breast. On opening thorax, both plural cavities filled with blood and clots. The top of the left lung was perforated and also the heart. The bullet perforated left ventricle. Examination of the abdominal and pelvis organs negative. The bullet, a 38-calibre was found in the tissues of the left breast, both cavities filled with blood, left and right lungs both perforated, one bullet came from the front and one came from the back. Deceased could not walk after second shot. Death was caused by second shot. She was shot in room where found or body carried there. The first wound, although she might have been able to walk, would also have caused death.

Sheriff Foster read the report several times and then handed it to Deputy Mooers. It was mostly what the Sheriff expected. The woman had been shot twice and the man once. It was clear that Bennie wanted to be sure they were both dead before he left the house. The woman must have scared him when she didn't go down right away like the man. She must have had some fight left in her when she took the first bullet, then turned and tried to make it out the back door. Bennie had to fire a second time to kill her. That made Bennie one cold hearted killer for sure. Kin or not, there would be no sympathy for him now. With the autopsies completed, Sheriff Foster asked the doctor for the bodies to be bundled up and sent to their next of kin for burial. For Olive, this was easy; they knew a lot about her, who to contact and who her parents wanted to do the burial service, but for Harvey it was a problem.

Bennie was feeling better when he was taken back to his jail cell from the doctor's office. The doctor had given him pain medication, and his wound was now just a dull ache. As he sat there on that Tuesday night, he sorted out his thoughts on his story. He had already made up a complete fabrication of what had happened at the Sharp farm on Monday and maybe he could make them believe it. He had told the Sheriff that Harvey attacked him first and he had shot him in self-defence with Harvey's own gun. He didn't stop to think there was evidence that would refute that. Either way, he wanted his family to believe he was not a cold-blooded murderer and others to believe he had overcome Harvey in a struggle. That would make him look better, but it wouldn't explain why he had shot Olive. Shooting a man in self-defence was one thing, but shooting an unarmed woman was something else. He didn't sleep much that night.

When morning came, he was given a light meal. Later, Deputy Sheriff Mooers told him that in the afternoon he would be brought into the courtroom for the Coroner's Jury. He explained that a Coroner's Jury officially established the cause of death of the victims. Coroner Hays would handle the proceedings. Next, would come the Preliminary Examination. That would be like a mini-trial to establish for the official record what had happened at the Sharp farm on Monday.

After his noon meal, Bennie was taken to the courthouse, which stood close to the jail facing Woodstock's Main Street. Coroner Hays asked him if he wished to be present for the inquest. Bennie said, "No," and was taken back to his cell. The Coroner ruled that Olive Trenholm and Harvey Trenholm had been murdered and died from gunshot wounds. The date for the Preliminary Examination to determine if and when the case would go to trial was set for the 3rd of April.

The Burials of Olive and Harvey

Sheriff Foster called on John and Phoebe Swim to offer his condolences. He didn't talk about the autopsy findings and they didn't ask. They would learn more when they attended the trial, so it wasn't necessary to burden them with details now. John and Phoebe were still extremely distraught, but their little girl had to be buried and they had made the arrangements. John phoned Reverend H. V. Bragdon and asked him to accompany the body from Woodstock and perform the funeral service. Reverend Bragdon went to the DeWitt Funeral Home and helped load Olive on the train for Benton. He had known Olive at many stages of her life; from just a toddler, when she came to his Sunday services at the Baptist Church in Rockland with her parents and siblings, Roy and Alice, to other times over the years when he would be invited to dinner at John and Phoebe's place.

He remembered how, as Olive grew older, she happily gained attention from all the boys and jealousy from most of the girls. Her plain gingham dresses had complimented her slim figure and she had worn them like a queen. It was one thing to be burying someone who had had a long full life but when they were so young it was different. She definitely didn't deserve this, but the "Lord giveth and the Lord taketh away." He couldn't argue with God's will, but it still made him sad as he watched the body being loaded onto the train.

When this task was completed, he boarded the train, sat in a window seat and watched as the scenery passed by on his way to Benton. He had done many funeral services in the past so he was familiar with the procedure, but for this one he wanted to make it something special. He knew the family well and wanted to do what he could for them. Funerals are for the living, he reminded himself, and the living deserve to have the best possible attention to their loved one and their feelings of grief. He, of course knew that Olive had gone to heaven and that's what he wanted to make sure her family would believe as well.

When he arrived in Benton, John Swim was already there with a wagon and team. They loaded the coffin onto the wagon. John thanked the Reverend Bragdon for doing the service on short notice, but the Reverend assured him this was part of his duty as a minister, and he was happy to do what he could for the family. He was not happy for the circumstances that brought him here but he wanted them to know he was honoured to do the burial service. It didn't take long to arrive at the cemetery. The Benton train station was less than three hundred meters from the Benton United Cemetery where a grave had been dug for Olive. Friends and neighbours of the Swim family had gathered in the church for the service. It was a solemn and emotional affair with much weeping. A photograph of Olive was displayed on the coffin. Reverend Bragdon looked at it with great sadness, as did the family and guests. He reminded the congregation that they were not so much saying goodbye to Olive as they were going through the sadness of being parted from her for a while. They would be with her again in heaven, and for now, Olive was just fine. She was in the good hands of their Lord Jesus and was at peace, a lasting peace that all of us would hopefully enjoy one day. He mentioned she had been taken early in life because God wanted her in heaven and that was his will.

The Swim family was seated in the front row. John was extremely angry and mostly ignored the sermon. He wanted revenge for the death of his daughter but couldn't show it here. Roy also felt the blinding anger that accompanies the death of a sibling brought on by such horrendous circumstances, but he too kept his emotions to himself. The rest of the family was overcome by grief and sadness — Alice Pearl for her sister and Phoebe Ann for her daughter. Ellery, the young son of Roy and Rita was restless. He knew by seeing the adults like this that something terrible had happened but he was too young to understand.

After a couple of hymns had been sung, the coffin was carried out by the pallbearers, John, Roy and William Sharp on one side and three other friends of the family on the other. The Reverend led the way to the grave. As the coffin of Olive was being lowered into the ground, several of the mourners threw small handfuls of dirt on it. Some flowers were dropped on it as well by Olive's mother. John had spent most of the previous night fashioning a grave marker out of wood, and though it was well made, he felt now that she deserved more. He cursed himself for not having spent the money for a proper gravestone. This one would have to do for now. He intended to later change it for something that would last longer but he never had the chance. (Unfortunately time and the elements would do their work and Olive's grave marker eventually disappeared over the coming years.) Finally, Reverend Bragdon said the words "ashes to ashes, dust to dust," and the service was over. He shook hands with the family and they all left. The men who had dug the grave would come later to fill it in. The Swim family and the mourners took one last look at the grave marker before they departed for home.

*Rest in Peace, Olive M. Swim Trenholm, Born July 10th 1904
Died March 27th 1922.*

*   *   *   *   *

When Sheriff Foster tried to find out more about Harvey Trenholm, he had some trouble. No one knew much about him because he didn't much talk about his past life. Harvey had talked to William Sharp the most, but all he could tell the Sheriff was that Harvey had been in the military during the war and that he had a cousin somewhere in Edmundston that owned a bowling alley. Well, that was a start.

Sheriff Foster looked up the marriage certificate for Olive and Harvey and found out that his father was J. H. Trenholm. He located the cousin in Edmundston and was told that Harvey had been born in Bayfield, but his father now lived in Baie Verte. The Sheriff asked the cousin if he would be willing to accompany the body of Harvey back to Baie Verte. Cousin Theo agreed. The Sheriff didn't want the body to show up unexpectedly so he contacted Harvey's father. When James Herbert Trenholm learned about what had happened to Harvey he was dumbfounded. He hadn't heard from his son in over two years. The news that his son had recently re-married and had now been murdered by the ex-lover of his new wife was a complete shock. He didn't know anything about Olive or what his son had been up to in the last few years of his life, but he would give Harvey a proper burial and make sure he was placed in the family plot.

James Trehholm had already endured a heavy burden of family loss and now he had to bury another son. First it was Earnest Alvah, barely five months old in 1878; then it was his wife, Mary Emaline in 1883; then Oscar died at the age of four in 1889; then it was Edgar at 23 in 1901; Marie Gussie followed in 1910 at the age of 24 and now Harvey at 39. Death seemed to follow him too closely and he was tired of it. He didn't know it then, but it would be the last of his family he would bury. His own turn would come in July of 1923.

As he waited for the train to arrive with the body of his son, he couldn't help but think back to Harvey's birth and the loss of his wife on that sad day in March of 1883. Cousin Theo had let James know the train would arrive sometime in the late afternoon of March 30th. He was grateful to Sheriff Foster for arranging the delivery of his son's body and made note to thank him by letter sometime in the future. The family plot was located in Bayfield Cemetery in Westmorland County. He had contacted all of the family and friends that he could so there would be a good crowd of mourners for the funeral the next day. He had considered contacting Dorina Rose, Harvey's other wife, but that would make things very awkward if she showed up. No, thought James, best if she didn't know about Harvey's death or that he had married again without divorcing her. In any event, she was now living in Saint John so he had no easy way of contacting her.

The Hayward's were all there. Harvey had first married Bessie Hayward and though she had died in 1915, the family still felt a kinship to Harvey. They had been looking after his daughter Gladys Gertrude since Harvey had gone off to war. They had not seen much of him since then, but in a way, they were grateful he had relied on them to raise Gladys. She was the only part of her mother Bessie they had left. Gladys, for her part, had not known much about her father. She remembered him as a young man when she was just a child and her mother was still living. During this time, she enjoyed a close relationship with her father. They were a happy family. Gladys remembered the fun they had on picnics and church outings. They would go for long walks in the country, and in the summer would go down to the beach to spend the day. But all that had ended when her mother died. Her father had become sad and even she could not make him happy.

Gladys was now a beautiful young woman of thirteen who wondered why her father had not remained in contact with her. She had a good life with her grandparents. They took very good care of her and were very loving, but she couldn't help wondering how it would have all turned out if her mother had not died. Life can be cruel, she thought, but you have to go on living and that's what she would do. She looked at the coffin with her father's body in it and tried to imagine what he looked like. She would never know because the coffin remained closed. The injuries caused by gunshot to the head made Harvey unrecognizable. Viewing of the body would not have been appropriate.

James Trenholm looked out over the crowd and saw many of his friends and relatives. He was thankful they had all come out. He had hoped there would be more soldiers there, men who had known Harvey in battle, but they didn't have much time to send out notices so perhaps that was the reason there were so few. Harvey would have been pleased to have his old comrades in arms there to say a last farewell. The thought crossed his mind that if heaven is a real place then he would meet up with some of his fellow soldiers there, as well as his first wife Bessie. That would be a situation, eventually having two wives up there in heaven. But if that's what happens, it's a situation he'll have to deal with himself someday.

He knew his son was not religious, so it probably didn't much matter. Even so, James Trenholm would have a nice service conducted by a Methodist minister and the mourners would be pleased. After the service, Harvey's coffin was taken to the Bayfield cemetery and lowered into the ground. Each mourner said a final farewell, and departed for home. James Trenholm and Harvey's daughter, Gladys, were the last to leave. A wooden grave marker memorialized his final resting place.

Rest in Peace, Harvey Dixon Trenholm Born March 15th 1883
Died March 27th 1922

Unfortunately, it would also be destroyed by the elements over the years and his grave would be difficult to find in the future.

The Preliminary Examination

Several newspapers covered all parts of the legal proceedings in the Bennie Swim case—arrest, inquest, coroner's jury, preliminary inquiry, trial, sentencing and execution—the stories are all so different the reader is left to wonder if the reporters had been covering the same case. There are many inaccuracies, some so glaring it's almost humorous. It seems like some reporters couldn't or didn't bother to find out the truth, and just made things up. The discrepancies in reporting may have also been related to the nervousness of the witnesses. After having given testimony several times and after hearing the testimony of others, some witnesses may have become confused about what they had actually seen, or just couldn't remember exactly what happened, so they may have improvised and changed their stories. Some of the reporters couldn't even get the correct spellings of the names of witnesses and other participants, making it difficult to follow the case accurately. The Woodstock Press published the following report on April 4, 1922.

Coroner W. Hay held his court on Wednesday afternoon, March 29th 1922, in the courthouse to inquire into the circumstances surrounding the murder of Harvey Trenholm and his wife Olive Swim at Benton Ridge at 4:30 March 27th 1922. R.L Simms Clerk of the Peace represented the Attorney General and Miss Sprague was Stenographer. The courthouse was crowded with witnesses, jurymen and spectators, showing the great interest taken by the public.

The jurymen were Delbert Franklin, Foreman, Melvin McElroy, Gorman Steeves, Eugene Smith, Frank Porter, Roy Franklin, Bert Grant, David Grant, William Lewin, Hugh Porter, Murray McPherson, and Chas McMillan. The jury, through its foreman, Delbert Franklin, brought in a verdict that Harvey Trenholm and Olive Swim, came to their deaths from shots from a revolver fired by Bennie Swim.

The Prisoner was not present for the inquiry or all of the Preliminary Examination.

The Preliminary Examination commenced on Monday morning the 3rd of April 1922 at 10 a.m. before Magistrate Comben, and the evidence being adduced is the same as came out at the inquest, which follows.

First up to the stand was William Sharp.

William Sharp sworn said that he resided at Benton Ridge, Parish of Woodstock, County of Carleton, said he was a farmer, saw Harvey Trenholm three or four weeks ago, had hired him to work for him about March 1st, his farm was 10 miles from Woodstock and one and a half miles from the Saint John River. He lived a mile or mile and a quarter from John Swim who lived on the back roads but both roads led to the river. He hired Trenholm to work for a few days at so much a day. Later Trenholm was to buy the farm through the Soldiers Settlement Board. He was a widower. "Two weeks ago I drove with him to the Baptist Minister, Rev. Worden who married him and Olive. He met Olive Swim about five or six days before she was married. He (Sharp) lived at Benton Ridge 10 or 12 years. John Swim moved there about 18 months ago. After their marriage she came to live with me, she was housekeeper. On Monday I left home about 3 o'clock in the afternoon for Benton and got back about 7 o'clock, I was there some hours before the Sheriff arrived. When I left for Benton, Trenholm was there with his wife, when I got back, he was lying there dead. There was three rooms in the hall, and the stove is in the dining room. I was not in the house until the Sheriff came. Before the Sheriff came I saw Mrs. Trenholm through the window, when the Sheriff came we entered and found Olive's body in the kitchen. Archie McElroy and Roy Swim were on guard on instructions from the Sheriff by telephone. Before the Sheriff arrived, no one was allowed to enter. These bodies were the bodies of Mrs. and Mr. Trenholm. These bodies were removed by Henry DeWitt on the advice of the Coroner. Trenholm's body was on the outer doorstep, which was a large flat stone. I had no revolver in the house, neither did Trenholm. There was no evidence of a struggle, I never saw Bennie Swim. Trenholm was an active industrious young man, no viciousness ever and an average gentleman. Trenholm had no firearms in the house. I had several guns that I had for years and one new one that I kept up in the storeroom."

Next up was Roy Swim, son of John Swim and brother of Olive. He was sworn and commenced to say he lived at Benton Ridge about a year. "Olive Swim, my sister, lived in Hartland where she was working out. I saw Trenholm three times before he married my sister. He was at my house before he hired at Sharp's. Last Monday I was home. I was told by Enoch Gilbert that Bennie Swim was on the cruise for Olive Swim. I went over and saw the body of Trenholm and never got off the horse's back, but turned and went to see Archie McElroy who went and examined the body, and said Trenholm was dead. Bennie Swim is no relation of mine as far as I know, I was born in Hartland and our family removed to Hartin Settlement. I saw Bennie Swim once and that was a year ago. Olive and Bennie were not married. I did not see him down at Benton Ridge this spring but I heard he was down on Monday, and Olive and Harvey were married on Wednesday, a fortnight ago today. My father probably knows if Bennie was down on the Monday referred to."

Roy was glad to get off the stand. He knew that he had blundered on several accounts but he didn't care. He tried to ignore all the people in the courtroom staring at him and hanging on his every word, but it was difficult and he became flustered. He deliberately lied about Bennie not being his cousin but he didn't care. He didn't want anyone connecting the two, even though it was made common knowledge soon enough. The report continues.

Next on the stand was Dr. Griffin; he was sworn and said, "I knew Olive Swim, met her at her father's house in Hartin Settlement. I was called by the Sheriff to go to Benton Ridge and found the bodies as Mr. Sharp testified. After the bodies were removed to Woodstock, I held a Post Mortem Examination. I found that Trenholm was about 35 years of age, no scars on body, no deformities, numerous powder marks on face, two puncture marks on head, one, an inch over the left eye, the other, one and a half inches above the ear. The nostrils were filled with blood. There was an irregular perforation in the left temple. The wounds an inch and a half wide, the brain badly lacerated, a portion of the bullet was found in the brain tissue. There was only one shot, the bullet divided and a part went out, and a part remained within.

"Mrs. Trenholm was between the ages of 18 and 20, light complexion, light hair, no deformities, two puncture wounds in the front part of the chest, two puncture wounds in the back of the chest, the bullet, a 38-calibre was found in the tissues of the left breast, both cavities filled with blood, left and right lungs both perforated, one bullet came from the front and one from the back. Deceased could not walk after the second shot; death was caused by second shot. She was shot in the room where found or body carried there. The first wound, although she might have been able to walk, would also have caused death. Bennie Swim was examined on Tuesday night. I found a perforating wound at the base of the right ear, the bullet was found an inch above the right eye, it was a 38-calibre, and I extracted it."

Bennie listened carefully to the doctor's report. He couldn't understand how there could be two puncture wounds in the front part of her chest if one of the bullets had remained in her body. What Dr. Griffin had not explained is that the second bullet had shattered, probably from hitting a rib bone, with a large piece lodging and a smaller fragment exiting the body.

Bennie didn't much understand the medical jargon but he did get that he didn't need to shoot Olive a second time. She would have died from the first bullet. He remembered that she tried to run away, so he fired another time to be sure. Well, what was done was done. He didn't like all the stares he was getting, so he tried to ignore them. He could read some of the faces, and if looks could kill, he would be dead from them. After awhile he just ignored the stares, and acted like it was just another day for him. The Woodstock Press report goes on.

Next sworn was William Porter. He said, "I saw Olive Swim before marriage. I arrived at the house of William Sharp before sundown on Monday, March 27. I saw Trenholm lying dead at the step. After the Sheriff came, went in the house and saw Olive in the front room, we followed the stream of blood through the dining room, in the company of Mr. Simms, and picked up a bullet which is a 38-calibre."

Albion R. Foster, the County Sheriff, was the next to be sworn in. He said,

"On Monday I got a telephone call from Mr. McElroy. I took the deputy and Mr. Simms and left for Benton Ridge. I found the bodies sworn to. I telephoned Dr. Griffin and Coroner Hay. I knew the girl, her parents and Bennie Swim; they live in Rockland,

parish of Brighton. After the arrival at Benton Ridge I arranged for the undertaker, Henry DeWitt, to come from Woodstock. I went to the Woodland house and telephoned to Houlton, and other places to look out for and arrest Bennie Swim. A lady in the Woodland house told us that Bennie had passed there. The Deputy Sheriff and myself, at daylight on Tuesday traced the blood from Swim's wound through the field and on the highway road and we concluded that he had gone to Carr's on Oak Mountain. I found out that he had gotten supper at Carr's. We continued on until we got to James Doherty's. I asked Doherty if a stranger had been there, and Doherty said, 'There is a man upstairs.' When I got to the head of the stairs I asked, 'Is that you Bennie?' he said, 'Yes, this is awful.' I said I would have to arrest him on a serious charge of murder, and warned him that anything he said, might be used against him at the trial. This was at 7:30 in the morning. He put his coat on and came along with us. We went back to Woodland's house and then Sharp's house. I asked him what he done with the revolver, and he said he threw it away. At first he did not give us the right place but finally we found the revolver thirty yards from the well house under a tree; it was put there before Bennie went on the highway road. On the way to Woodstock, or shortly after we arrived in Woodstock, Bennie first told me that he had a row with Trenholm on the front doorstep, that Trenholm shot him first, that he took the revolver away from Trenholm, and then shot the man, then the woman. Later he told me that he bought the revolver at Rockland. It was a five-cylinder revolver and four shots had been fired. He also told me that he was engaged to Olive, but not married. I think that Olive is a relation to Bennie. She had visited Bennie's father's home where they had been acquainted. I did not know Trenholm, did not know of a family by that name in the county. I made inquiries and located Trenholm's father in Baie Verte, Westmorland County, where the body was sent for burial on Thursday morning."

The Sheriff was glad that it was over. He didn't much like speaking in public but knew it was his duty and a part of the job. He had hoped that he got all the facts right. Even though he had rehearsed it all, when the time came to speak, he felt that he had forgotten something important. Oh well, he thought, there would still be the trial later on. The report continues.

Earl McKinney was sworn next. He said, "I live in Benton Ridge, I did not know Trenholm, I found a cartridge near the place on Monday night."

Leslie Bell was sworn. He said, "I was cutting wood a 100 yards away from Sharp's and at 4:30 in the afternoon I heard several shots fired at the Sharp place."

Next, it was Enoch Gilbert's turn. After he was sworn in he said, "I live in Benton Ridge, a quarter mile from Sharp's. I knew Trenholm before and after he was married. I was at Marston's home about four P. M. on Monday when a man calling himself Bennie Swim stopped at Marston's and I accompanied Swim part of the way. He said he wanted to see Olive Swim. 'That's my wife, I'm looking up my wife,' he said. Then he said to Mrs. Marston, 'I'm going to get the Sheriff after her.' He was about 25 years of age. Later, I was accompanied to the Jail by the Sheriff where I was asked to identify the prisoner. He was wearing a light coloured raincoat, light cap and dark brown suit. I said yes that's the man.

Robert Bell was sworn and said, "I and Trenholm served together as members of the 26th Battalion, New Brunswick Regiment overseas. I saw Bennie Swim come from between the Sharp house and the barn at twenty-five minutes to five on Monday afternoon."

John Marston next was sworn into the witness box. He stated that Roy Swim told him that a man was dead at Sharp's. He examined into the matter and telephoned the Sheriff.

John McGann of Benton told of the happenings as outlined by the other witnesses. He visited the Sharp place and was one of the guards appointed to look after the house and bodies.

H. V. Mooers, Deputy Sheriff, gave similar evidence to that of Sheriff Foster. The jury adjourned and came back an hour later. They returned with the verdict that Harvey Dixon Trenholm and Olive M. Swim Trenholm came to their deaths from shots from a revolver fired by Bennie Swim. The Preliminary Examination had determined there was enough evidence to bring the case to trial.

The Aftermath

The decision of the Preliminary Examination was no surprise to Bennie. He fully expected the evidence would be enough to send him to trial. No date had been given, but he expected it would not be long in coming. Even so, it was a shock when the trial date of April 24th was delivered to him. That meant his fate would be decided in less than a month.

Time, for Bennie, now seemed to slow down. His parents came to visit him and he was allowed to see a spiritual advisor as often as desired. He wanted to get information from Reverend Bragdon about Olive's funeral. He had killed the girl he loved, and that was what hurt the most. His parents, while supportive, were not having an easy time of it either. Having a son who was a murderer was not taken well by their neighbours and friends, especially because he had killed a family relative.

Everyone knew that Olive was Bennie's cousin and felt sorry for John Swim and the rest of Olive's family. John's anger and resentment was intense and on going. He would never speak to his brother William again. The family was now divided and would remain so as long as Bennie and his father were alive. Luckily for William, the Mainstream was a long way from Benton Ridge. The distance spared him the possibility of running into his brother at the general store or some other local place. He couldn't blame John for hating him, but still it wasn't his fault for what his son had done. Bennie had never told him anything. He had no idea what Bennie was planning to do until the day after the murders, when a neighbour told him about it while he was purchasing supplies at Estabrook's store at Coldstream.

He was horrified to hear what his son had done. He made a phone call that confirmed the news - his son had killed two people. Then, with a sinking feeling, William began to make sense of what his son had done. Bennie had been extremely depressed during the days after he received Olive's letter telling of her marriage. But William didn't know Bennie had gone to Edmund Estabrook at his store and traded his violin and some other possessions for a gun. If he had known Bennie had gotten a revolver, he would have done something about it. He would have known there was a very bad reason why Bennie would want this kind of gun, and he would have tried to stop him from carrying out his plan. But hindsight is useless. It is what it is, and his son will probably hang.

Edward Swim didn't know what to think. He was also dumbfounded when he heard the news of his nephew's murderous actions. He always knew Bennie was different; but murder? He couldn't imagine it. It just wasn't the Bennie he knew. Edward was close to his brother William and offered what support he could, but that wasn't much. After all, what do you say to a father when in all likelihood his son would soon swing from a rope? As for as his brother John, well he was always off somewhere else working. They had not stayed close over the years.

Edward felt especially sorry for Bennie's brother and sister, Alexander Cameron and Cassie Elizabeth. What must they be going through? Would other people look at them differently now? Maybe give them dirty looks, or worse, avoid them all together. With luck, Cassie would be all right since she was now an Ogden and no longer a Swim. People might not make the connection. Cameron would probably have the hardest time of all. People might look at him like he was just as bad as his brother and steer clear of him wherever he went. He might have to go away somewhere, until all this passed.

Edward also felt sorry for his other nieces and nephew, the children of John and Phoebe, but he hardly knew them. Roy he had known as a toddler, but then the family moved away to Hartin Settlement and they lost touch. As for Alice Pearl, he only knew that she existed but he wouldn't have recognized her if he passed her on the street. He'd seen Olive locally a few times at church or on the road but didn't really know her either. He remembered her as being very pretty and thought she would marry well. Apparently she did, but her marriage had lasted only twelve days. He hoped she was happy for those twelve days. What a shame, just seventeen. She deserved so much better.

Cassie Elizabeth, however, was not having an easy time of it. She learned about her brother's horrible deed when she went to the local General Store at Tracy Mills. As she walked in the store and started to look at some of the merchandise, she noticed that some of the men there were eyeing her intently. She didn't think it was because of her beauty, because though she was still young, she had never been the type to attract much attention from men. She was now twenty, and had been married for two years to Frank Ogden. They had one child and another one on the way. She was large in her belly, so she knew the men were not paying her attention because of the way she looked. It had to be something else. Being the bold woman that she was, she went right up to the men and asked them why they were staring at her that way. They all looked at the floor for a moment and then one of the men handed her a Carleton Sentinel newspaper.

There was her brother's name in large print on the front page. She almost fainted when she saw the article. "Good God," she thought. "It has to be a mistake. Not her brother Bennie!" But the more she read the more she became convinced it was one and the same. Not a murder in self-defence, but a double murder in cold blood; and her cousin, Olive, of all people, one of the victims. She didn't know Olive's new husband, Harvey Trenholm, but the whole thing was just terrible. Now, they had a murderer in the family. How shameful is that? And worse, with the newspaper story everyone now knows that Bennie Swim is her brother.

Cassie stood motionless while she swiftly read the article a second time and then handed the paper back to the man who had given it to her. All the customers in the store were watching her reaction. She left the store without saying a word. She could feel their cold stares following her but it didn't matter now. She hurried home and told her husband Frank about what she had learned. They discussed it over dinner, but Cassie could hardly eat anything.

They tried to remember what had been happening with Bennie over the last couple of years. Cassie knew her brother had taken up with Olive. Considering how hard a time he had growing up, she was happy for him to have found someone who cared for him. She didn't know Olive very well, but from what she had heard it seemed she was a very nice girl. But what a shame; Olive must not have loved Bennie as much he had loved her. Well, life had to go on.

She wondered what she could do to support her brother and decided she would write to him. She didn't know what to say so she just stuck to writing about what was happening on the farm and other ordinary subjects. She knew he would have enough people judging him, so she would not be one more. She never mentioned the murders in her letters. Often, late at night, she would try to imagine her brother locked in his cell waiting for another day to pass, knowing that he would at best be in prison for the rest of his life, or at worst, hanged. She shuddered at the thought and tried to ignore the reality of it all. She remembered them as children laughing and playing down by the stream, or in the churchyard having fun and feeling life was good. Well, it wasn't so good now.

Bennie was not in a good mood either. He now had to face the prospect that his life, both past and present, would be minutely examined by reporters, and everyone else that had been impacted by what he had done. In some ways it was nice to have all the attention, but when he started reading some of the stories about him printed in the newspapers he became angry. Some of the stories were fairly accurate but others made him look like a country bumpkin, too stupid to know what he was doing. It was all right that they maligned him, he deserved it, but when they wrote about his family and friends and life on the Mainstream, and fabricated stories just to sell newspapers, it was more than he could take.

One such story called him Barry Swim, with Olive as his legal wife and Harvey Trenholm her employer. The headline was about a woman and her employer being slain at Benton. Well, they could be forgiven for the Benton part, after all Benton and Benton Ridge weren't much different, but it went on to say that he and Sheriff Foster had been on the same train to Benton. It was true, they were on the same train, but it was on the way to Woodstock, not Benton. Couldn't these reporters get the facts straight before they started writing? It also gave Olive's age as twenty-five. Bennie wondered where they came up with that number. They also had his age as twenty-one when he was really twenty-two. Well, in a year it wouldn't make any difference. If things went as expected, it would be the last year of his life anyway.

He liked that in some articles they referred to Olive as Mrs. Bennie Swim and that she was his soul mate. Well, that second part was definitely false. If they had been soul mates she would never had gone off and married Harvey Trenholm, and he would not be sitting in a jail cell accused of murdering her and Harvey. God, he wondered, how had it come to this? He continued reading other articles about his case and found out he had written a note and left it at the murder scene. The note was reported to have said, "Good-bye Olive Swim and Sleep." The memory of the note now came back to him. He had written that note. He wondered why the Sheriff hadn't brought it up at the Preliminary Examination? That was a good piece of evidence; they shouldn't have left it out. Maybe it was overlooked, or they had enough evidence and it wasn't needed.

He also learned, according to one newspaper article, that the Mainstream was a "free-love" area, whatever the hell that was supposed to mean. He supposed it meant the locals there were so stupid they just slept with whoever they wanted, whenever they wanted. Sure, it may have been a tough place to live, but the people there were good people. They were mostly Baptist and God fearing people who had a good sense of right and wrong. They didn't deserve to be tarnished like this just because of his sins. He felt bad about that, but what was worse is that he was listed as having committed the worst crime in the history of Carleton County. That was quite a feat. One thing for sure, the name "Bennie Swim" would not be forgotten anytime soon.

Preparing for the Trial

While waiting for the trial, Bennie was introduced to his Attorney, Frederick Charles Squires. Frederick Squires was born on November 13th 1881 and was now forty-one. He and his wife, Hattie, had a nine-year-old daughter, Frances Louise. He had been a teacher before he began practicing law. When he took on Bennie's case, he had been practicing for seven years. Mr. Squires started out being quite formal with Bennie. He addressed him as "Benjamin," which Bennie quickly corrected. He had never been called Benjamin; he had always been called Bennie and told Mr. Squires to use his real name.

Mr. Squires was irked. His client was charged with the most serious crime imaginable and he had been given so little time to prepare the case. It was almost as if scheduling the trial so soon after the Preliminary Examination had been done on purpose to lessen his chances of effectively defending his client. He took stock of the young man before him to determine if he should take the stand in his own defense. His first impression was no, it would not be a good idea. He would, however, continue to consider it as the trial proceeded.

Attorney Squires studied everything he could about the evidence. He talked with his client often and at length, but the case did not look promising. First of all, his client had been far too cooperative. He had admitted his guilt from the very beginning. If that wasn't bad enough, he had talked too freely to reporters from just about every newspaper in the province. Bennie seemed to have no idea that the crown prosecutors would also be reading these papers. His talking gave away the story. Even the witnesses were too well prepared. Finding a jury that had not already convicted his client would be impossible. He would give Bennie the best defense he could, but with what he had to work with, it looked bleak. Execution by hanging seemed a matter of certainty.

Mr. Squires pondered the case. There had to be a way of giving his client a chance of being spared the death penalty, but how. He then started to do something he would never normally do. He set out to interview the local people where Bennie had grown up, and they had plenty to tell him.

"The family is all insane," he heard from one woman in Coldstream. "Just all outright crazy."

When pressed for details, she elaborated, "Well, Bennie's grandfather had been subjected to fits"

"What kind of fits" asked the lawyer?

"Well" she said, not wanting to be too descriptive but liking the attention she was getting. "I heard he would sometimes go out and howl at the moon when it was full and then flop around on the ground like a fish out of water. It would scare the neighbours something awful."

"Well, that was a scary thought," Mr. Squires said to himself. What was even scarier would be to have this woman on the witness stand in Bennie's defense. He could just imagine what the prosecution would do to her on cross-examination. He politely thanked her and continued his search for others to talk to. Another woman told him that Bennie's mother had once tried to chew his face off when he was only four years old. She swore it really happened, so the lawyer decided he would ask Bennie about this. If true, it might help to establish that there was insanity in the family. He would need more evidence, however, so he asked others for more details. One local man stated that Bennie's brother, Alexander Cameron, had stoned his own horse to death. That would have been strange, and, if true, made the family extremely weird. But he would need something to establish that Bennie himself was insane.

He had heard that Bennie was prone to fits, but that they were not caused by any medical problem, just mostly severe depression that took him to the point of despair. To use an insanity defense, he would need to prove that Bennie was not mentally or morally capable of understanding the results of his actions. A really crazy person would not have been able to carry out the planning and the acquisition of the gun needed to commit the murders, not to mention that he tried to escape. To complicate matters, Bennie now seemed quite depressed that he had committed the murders, at least of Olive, and even admitted that he expected to hang for the crime. It appeared to Mr. Squires that an insanity defense at the trial would not work. It might be helpful, however, at the sentencing or in a later appeal.

For now, all the lawyer could do was to look at each bit of evidence and go over the witnesses' statements at the preliminary examination. He read and reread every one, but it seemed hopeless for his client. Except for a few minor discrepancies, they all looked very credible. He also knew that the parents of both Olive and Bennie would be called to testify at the trial. That would present more problems for the defense. The statements of John and Phoebe Swim would create a lot of sympathy for Olive. A picture of her presented in the courtroom as a smiling young girl would harden the hearts of almost any juror against Bennie, ensuring a guilty verdict with hanging as the outcome.

Mr. Squires did not like this case at all. While it gave him experience for future cases, it was also going to make him well known in Carleton County and probably all over the province. This would not be good for future business. No defendant would want to have a lawyer that failed to prevent his client from being hanged, that's for sure. No matter how well a case was researched and prepared, sometimes you just lost, or at least your client lost. In this case, Bennie was likely to lose his life. As a lawyer, he could go on to the next case, but this lost case would become part of his reputation.

Mr. Squires mapped out his case. He needed to establish certain beliefs to give his client a chance of not being put to death. First, he needed to give some credence to the idea that Bennie should be considered Olive's husband. Second, he needed evidence that Bennie was, if not insane, at least mentally troubled and unstable. He decided to pay another visit to the Mainstream. He wanted to talk directly to members of Bennie's family. He would never tell them to lie on the stand, but he did need to impress the gravity of the situation on them. He told them what he needed to prove. He wanted them to recall all of Bennie's interactions with Olive, no matter how trivial, such as how much time they spent together and anything else that could prove that Olive considered herself to be Bennie's wife.

Next he wanted them to recall all their relatives that had fits, or did strange things, or seemed emotionally unstable. William and Eva knew a lot that would be helpful in this way and would be ready to embellish the truth if need be. Jesse, however, was a better one to talk to. He knew more than they did about some of the problems that their immediate relatives had. He would gladly take the stand in Bennie's defense. He had been close to Bennie for most of his life. He had hired Bennie at certain times to work for him. He could verify some of the fits that Bennie had been prone to as well. So that was it. Any stories about Bennie and his acting strangely would help. Mr. Squires had his work cut out for him.

Bennie spent his time in jail talking with his fellow prisoners when he had the chance. His day fell into a common routine. When he got up in the morning, the first thing he had to do was make his bed. It would then be inspected by one of the prison guards. His fellow inmates were not there for anything like the sentence Bennie was likely to get. Most of them were repeat offenders and were familiar with the life of a convict. Their convictions were generally for fighting, drunk and disorderly conduct, or stealing. Most would come and go during Bennie's stay, but no matter how bad these men seemed to the outside world, they treated Bennie warmly and wished him luck with his up coming trial.

The Crown Versus Bennie Swim

The trial of Bennie Swim began early on the morning of Tuesday, April 25, 1922. A report in the Woodstock Press described the scene.

> *The courthouse was crowded here this morning when the case of the King Versus Bennie Swim, charged with the murder of Harvey Trenholm and Olive Trenholm, his wife, was called. The prisoner was very neatly attired, and seemed unconcerned about his fate. He acted totally unperturbed by the courtroom attendees, as they stared at him. Chief Justice McKeown presided. The Grand Jury, after hearing several witnesses, brought in a true bill. After dinner, the prisoner was brought into court and the charges were read over to him. Bennie pleaded not guilty. The judge asked him if he had counsel to defend him. He answered that he did not which puzzled the judge. It was then verified that his counsel was Frederick Charles Squires. The prosecution was taken by P. J. Hughes. Mr. Hughes, Lawyer for the prosecution was only a year older than Mr. Squires but had been practicing law for several years longer. He was a family man with five daughters, and an ardent Roman Catholic. He had been practicing Law mostly in Fredericton but had been asked to come to Woodstock for this trial. The case was then adjourned until Wednesday morning.*

The prosecution began the next day. The newspaper reported as follows.

> *This morning Mr. Squires stood aside a large number of jurors, including Hazen Scott, Stanley Barter, Milton Bull, James Banks, Archie Pearson, Murray McCloud, Alex Wallace, Wilmot Caldwell, Walter Estabrooks, Tison Nicholson, Thomas Travis, G. F. Neal, Chas B Caldwell, Edwin Melville, George L. Colwell,*

> *The jurors selected were, Charles Wilkinson, Edwin Lipsett, George Keefe, Wilmot Anderson, Frank Plummer, Clayton Flemming, Frank Foster, Paul Raymond, Harold Smith, Arthur McIntosh, George F. Burpee and Robert Bell.*

J. Jones, the Clerk of the Court, read the indictment, and P.J. Hughes outlined the case for the Crown. The Prosecutor began with the following statement.

"Bennie Swim is charged with the murder of Olive and Harvey Trenholm at Benton Ridge on the afternoon of March 27, 1922. The murder took place at William Sharp's farmhouse. Mr. Sharp was not there at the time of the murder, he was in Benton until 7 p.m.. We will show that suspicion was placed on Bennie Swim early on, because of statements from several different witnesses that had interaction with Mr. Swim on that fateful day. We will propose to lay before you such evidence that will convince you that Bennie Swim committed the crime. Included will be statements from the accused, made to certain individuals that will leave you with no doubt, that Bennie Swim, and only Bennie Swim, was involved in the murders. We will show you the murder weapon, and how it came to be in the possession of Bennie Swim. We will show you the exact route that he took from his home on the Mainstream to the murder house, and his actions afterwards. You will be shown the effects, on the bodies of the victims, by the bullets fired from Bennie Swim's revolver. When we are done I believe that you will all be convinced, without a doubt that the accused is guilty of this horrific crime."

William Sharp was the first witness. After being questioned by Mr. Hughes he gave the following testimony.

"I reside at Benton Ridge, I know Bennie Swim, I saw him the 28th of March. I knew Harvey Trenholm only a short time. I hired him to work for me about the first of March. I live about one and a quarter miles from John Swim. After a short time I made arrangements for Trenholm to buy my place and he was waiting to hear from the Soldier's Settlement Board. If the deal went through, he was to have all that was there. When he came to my place he said he was a widower. I first saw Olive Swim a few days before she and Trenholm were married. I did not know her before that time. I knew her father who came here about 18 months ago. I left home at 3 o'clock on the 27th of March for Benton. Trenholm and his wife were at my home when I left. I know Trenholm was married on March 15th to Olive Swim at

Meductic by Reverend H. C. Worden. After their marriage they took charge of my house and Mrs. Trenholm was the housekeeper. When I left the house, Trenholm was busy making cedar sap spiles and his wife was sitting beside him. When I returned about 7 in the evening, the body of Trenholm was found dead on the doorstep nearest the kitchen. His head was lying in the gravel. Archie McElroy and Roy Swim were near the body, when I arrived. I saw a bullet mark on the left temple of Trenholm. I looked in the front window and saw Mrs. Trenholm lying on the floor. No one was in the house before the Sheriff arrived. Sheriff Foster arrived from Woodstock about 9 o'clock that evening."

He then explained the layout of the rooms in his house. His statement continued.

"I got the lights on and went into the house with the Sheriff. We entered the house from the door where Trenholm was, and passed into the room where Olive was dead. At the door near the front room, in the dining room, Mr. Porter had picked a 38-calibre bullet. I saw traces of blood through the house and early the next morning I found blood by the sheep pen and traced it out to the main road. I saw Swim for the first time the next morning when the Sheriff arrested him. I had no revolvers in the house but had three rifles and a double barrelled shotgun in the store room upstairs."

Looking at Mr. Squires he continued, "Trenholm was an athlete, and I have heard that he was a scrapper. I found him to be a very industrious and able man above the average and a gentleman. The pool of blood was six feet away from the body of Olive; a smaller pool of blood was nearer the body, about three feet away. There was no blood in the outer kitchen. Olive was lying on her right side, with her right arm extended. I never saw Trenholm with a revolver. There was no evidence of a struggle in the house. I saw the bodies removed by Mr. DeWitt, undertaker, assisted by others."

Mr. Hughes questioned Mr. Sharp further, which brought out the following additional details. The revolver was found close to the Sharp house, about 50 yards from the well house. Harvey's arms were folded under him. His feet were at the rear door. His house was about 55 yards from the road. There were three doors on the outside of the house; one on the east side, one on the south side, and one on the west side. Harvey's body was found on the east side in the rear of the house. There were two kitchens in the house; the winter kitchen, or outer kitchen, which ran along the east side and was used for mostly cooking animal feed, and the inner kitchen, which was used by the occupants. He saw Mrs. Trenholm from the outside window. He later saw a pool of blood at the sheep pen door, when he was looking for some haywire around 2 a.m.. He last saw Harvey and Olive in the winter kitchen.

Mr. Squires also posed several questions. It was determined that Mr. Sharp was not sure if Harvey had a revolver or not. He had never seen one, but it was possible that he kept it hidden under his clothing. Harvey was a strong man as seen from his ability to lift very heavy things. It was possible that there was a struggle outside of the house. So ended the testimony of William Sharp.

The next witness was Mr. McKinley, a photographer for the Harvey Studio in Woodstock, who took pictures of the scene where the crime was committed. He described what the pictures showed, and where he had taken them. The following photographs were entered into the record: a picture of the Sharp house taken from the Benton road, a picture of where the gun was found, a picture taken of Harvey lying dead on the doorstep, a picture of Olive lying dead inside the house, and a picture of the prisoner as seen the next morning. The court was adjourned until 2 o'clock.

Bennie was taken back to his cell where he was given a meal. Throughout the proceedings he had remained calm except when the pictures of the crime scene were shown. It was so different than he remembered. At the time he committed the crime he was in a state of shock so he couldn't remember many of the details. Now with the pictures staring him in the face, he couldn't ignore the gruesomeness of his actions. He tried to look away but when he did, he ended up looking out over the courtroom where he saw the faces of those attending the trial. They were anything but friendly, so instead he looked down at the floor.

When the trial resumed at 2 o'clock, Sheriff Albion Foster took the stand. When questioned by Mr. Hughes, he related the story of his summons to Benton Ridge.

"I got a phone call from Mr. McElroy at 5:30 p.m., and it was about the murder, and then I called Deputy Sheriff Mooers and Mr. Simms and explained the situation, and then we departed for Benton Ridge about 8 p.m.. I thought originally that there was only one body. We arrived at the Sharp home about 9 in the evening. We found the two bodies and I called Dr. Griffin and Coroner Hay. The Coroner's jury was empanelled that night. I had known Olive, her parents and Bennie Swim. I then called the Undertaker Mr. Henry DeWitt to come from Woodstock. I was handed a bullet by Mr. Porter, it was a 38-calibre. I also telephoned to Houlton and other places to be on the look out for and arrest Bennie Swim if they were to see him. I had done this from the Woodlands' house. A lady (Mrs. Kirkpatrick) in the Woodlands' house had told me that Bennie Swim had passed by the house later in the day. We started the search the same day, someone pointed out some blood by the sheep pen to me. So I started from there. The snow was very deep in places, up to three feet. It showed that a man had been through there on his hands and knees, and the footprints had taken a westerly course from the barn. I could not say if a man was running or not. I followed the tracks with a lantern. We gave up the search for the night, and stayed at M. Woodlands until morning.

"The Deputy Sheriff and myself waited until daylight on Tuesday and traced the blood from Swim's wound through the fields and on the highway road and concluded that he had gone to Carr's house on Oak Mountain. Mr. Carr informed me that Swim had gotten supper there and continued on. We then followed the tracks to James Doherty's house also on Oak Mountain. I asked Mr. Doherty if a stranger had been there, and Mr. Doherty said, 'There is a man upstairs.' When I got to the head of the stairs I asked, 'Is that you Bennie?' He said, 'Yes, this is awful.' I said, 'Come along you'll be alright.'

Mr. Squires then objected to any testimony along these lines and the judge ruled out any further statements made by the prisoner. The Sheriff continued.

"Bennie Swim, with me alongside of him, went out and he found the revolver himself after I asked him what he had done with it. We then went back to Woodstock with a few stops along the way."

Mr. Hughes was not happy with the Sheriff's testimony. He wanted more details. In further testimony the following information was added. The Sheriff brought Bennie back to Sharp's the next morning after his arrest at Doherty's. Bennie was the one to point out where the revolver was found along with several 38- calibre cartridges with clipped ends. It was at the base of a tree about two hundred yards from the house, and fifty yards from the well house. The Sheriff found the body of Olive Trenholm lying on the floor, beside the north window. She was wearing a drab dress. The Sheriff had seen Bennie Swim earlier on the day of the murders when they were both travelling on the same train. When asked about the revolver, Bennie said "I'll get it for you if I can." The prisoner had about five dollars on his person when arrested. The Sheriff wanted to talk about finding a tablet in the Sharp house with writing on it, presumably written by Bennie. Mr. Squires objected because it could not be proven who had written on it.

Mr. Squires also had some points he wanted to clear up. He asked the Sheriff what his exact words were when he arrived at Jim Doherty's house and confronted Bennie. The Sheriff had trouble recalling his exact words but gave them as best as he could remember.

> *Is that you Bennie? What happened? I have to arrest you for shooting Olive Swim, and Trenholm down at the Sharp place. Did you know both of these people were dead? You are not bound to make any statement. You are arrested under a serious charge and what you say may be used against you at your trial. This is a bad scrape.*

The next question Mr. Squires asked was about the revolver. He wanted a description of the gun and its contents.

Sheriff Foster said, "It's a five shot double action revolver with a weak trigger spring, a 38-calibre with four spent cartridges in the cylinders and one live round."

When Judge McKeown heard that, he wanted clarification. "Are you saying that it's still loaded with one live bullet? Why would you do that?"

The Sheriff answered, "I wanted to bring it to court in exactly the same way that it was found, your Honour."

The Judge shook his head. There was never an account of when or if it was unloaded. That ended the testimony of Sheriff Foster.

Roy Swim was next on the stand. After being questioned by Mr. Hughes, Roy Swim gave the following statement.

I live at Benton Ridge and am the son of John Swim and the brother of Olive Swim Trenholm. My father has lived at Benton Ridge about a year. My sister has been living out at Hartland. I knew Trenholm for a short time. He never saw my sister until four weeks ago when he met her at my home. He was at my home a week working for us, when Olive left [upon correction agreed that he meant to say "arrived"] She said they were going to be married. I saw them the next night at Mr. Sharp's. I was at home Monday afternoon and was told that Bennie Swim was looking for Olive. I went up to Mr. Sharp's and saw Harvey Trenholm lying on his face. I did not get off the horse's back, and went at once for Archie McElroy. Bennie Swim was not any relation of mine. I only saw him once. I never knew that Bennie Swim and my sister were keeping company. They were not married to my knowledge. He was at Benton Ridge on the Monday previous to the Wednesday, the day of Olive's marriage.

When further questioned by Mr. Squires, Roy gave several extra facts relating to the case: He had been chopping wood all afternoon on the day of the crime. He met Enoch Gilbert at Mr. Sewell's place at about 4:30 in the afternoon of March 27. When told about Bennie looking for Olive, he went immediately to Sharp's house. It was about 4:50 to 5 p.m. when he arrived. He saw Harvey Trenholm lying on the ground, with his arms underneath him. He called out to Olive several times but she did not answer. Without getting off the horse, he rode over to Archie McElroy's house, which is about three hundred and fifty yards from Sharps, and told him what had happened. They both went back to the Sharp house. Archie then went to John Woodlands' house and called the Sheriff. They were told to go back to the Sharp house and guard the bodies until the Sheriff arrived. They did that, and around 7 p.m. he went home for a short time. He told his family the news and he returned to Sharp's house. When asked if he had ever seen Olive wearing a wedding ring [the question was in reference to Bennie being married to Olive before she met Harvey Trenholm]. Roy replied that he had never seen her wear a wedding ring. So ended the testimony of Roy Swim.

Reverend Worden gave evidence that he had married Olive Swim and Harvey Trenholm at Meductic on March 15th of this year.

William Porter was sworn in and gave the following testimony.

I am a merchant in Benton. I was at the Sharp house at 7 o'clock and saw the body of Trenholm. I went into the house after the Sheriff arrived and examined the body of Olive Swim [Trenholm]. *While in the room I followed the blood marks and found a bullet in the side kitchen and showed it to Mr. Simms, who gave it back to me, and afterwards I gave it to the Sheriff. I saw Swim* [Bennie] *about three weeks before at my store in Benton.*

Constable John Marston was sworn in and gave the following testimony.

I live on the River road near the mouth of Benton Road. I was not at home when Bennie Swim came to my house. I was in Woodstock. I was at the Sharp place about 7 o'clock. I saw Trenholm lying on the doorstep, and also later saw Olive's body. I was in charge of the bodies until they arrived at the undertaking rooms in Woodstock.

Edmund Estabrooks was up next. After being questioned by Mr. Hughes, the following statement was presented as evidence.

I keep a store in Coldstream. I have known Bennie Swim since childhood. I gave him a revolver on March 22nd. [He was shown a revolver in possession of the court.] *I had no special marks on the revolver; this looks like the one I sold him. It has a defective spring. I got the revolver from Raybon Swim, who said he got it from a jeweller in Hartland. I took a violin as trade from Bennie Swim, and gave him a coat, cap, shoes, rubbers for the shoes, the gun, and seven dollars, all for the violin. I also gave him ten cartridges, 38 long, rifle ammunition. They did not fit very well but I informed him that the cartridges could be used by whittling off the ends.* [Cartridges were shown to the witness.] *Looks like the end was cut off. The gun was made to take 38 short, not the long ones.*

R. L. Simms was sworn in and gave the following.

I signed the information as Clerk of the Peace. I went to the scene of the tragedy with the officers, Sheriff Foster and Deputy Sheriff Mooers. I concur with the description and condition of the bodies as given by previous witnesses. I noticed a distinct trail of blood to the dining room, we arranged for an inquest and I went home.

Earle McKinney was sworn in and provided the following information. He was a farmer at Benton Ridge. He lived about a mile from Sharp's farm. He was at the Sharp house at 7 p.m. the night of the murders. He saw the body of Trenholm on the doorstep. He did not go in the house before the Sheriff arrived, but he did go in the house after that. He saw Olive on the floor and the pools of blood beside her. He also took part in the search for the revolver the next morning. He saw the revolver and verified that it was a 38-calibre. He was still at the Sharp house after the Sheriff left with Bennie Swim and found another 38 live cartridge with the end shortened near the tree where the revolver was found.

Mrs. Jesse Kirkpatrick is sworn and stated as follows.

> *I am the housekeeper for William Woodman. I lived about a quarter of a mile from Sharp's. I live on the same road as Sharp's. I was at home March 27th and I saw Bennie Swim on the highway between four and five in the afternoon. He wore a light raincoat and light cap. I saw him the next morning with Sheriff Foster.*

Enoch Gilbert was sworn in and gave the following testimony.

> *I live at Benton Ridge and met Bennie Swim at Jas* [he used his nickname instead of John] *Marston's on the river road where it strikes off to Benton. It was Monday afternoon between four and five the day of the shooting. Swim came to the door and asked which of the roads led to Benton Ridge. He wanted to know where the nearest telephone was located and said it was to have them both arrested.* [He was talking about Olive and Harvey.] *I said, 'They are married and don't meddle with them. Why don't you get the law?' He said, 'They cannot but kill me anyways.' I said, 'What might your name be, and he replied, Bennie Swim.' We walked out together and I left him at the Springfield road by Wellie Roger's place. It was over a mile to William Sharp's. I continued on until I came to Sewell's place. There I saw Roy Swim, and I told him about the visit from Bennie and what he said at Marston's place. The last I saw, Roy was heading to Sharp's.*

On further questioning from Mr. Squires, it was determined that Mrs. Marston was also at home at the time so she was called next to give her testimony. Her version of what Bennie said to them at the house was slightly different than Enoch Gilbert's.

After being sworn in, she said "Bennie told us, 'I am looking for my wife. I want to telephone to Mr. Foster, the Sheriff. I'm going to have them both arrested. I want to go [to the Sharp place] to speak to Olive Swim.' I said to Bennie, 'That girl was married the other day.' Bennie said, 'I know it, you needn't tell me that, I got a letter Saturday.' "I also told him that both roads lead to the Sharp place when he asked about directions."

There was some confusion about who exactly said what between Mrs. Marston and Enoch Gilbert, but the testimony seemed complete enough, so neither Mr. Squires, nor Mr. Hughes questioned further.

Thomas Thistle was next up. He stated he was a jeweller in Hartland and he was the one who tried to repair the defective revolver as best he could. He said he then sold it to Raybon Swim. He identified the revolver by some marks he had put on it while trying to repair it. He then added that he had traded it off to Roy Swim. [He meant Raybon Swim and then confirmed it was traded and not sold to him.]

Leslie Bell was next on the stand. He stated the following.

> *I was cutting wood near the Sharp place on March 27th. I was working in the woods with old deaf Mr. Hempel. We had a team and sled about 100 yards north from the Sharp house when I heard two shots about four thirty. I was going towards my home, which is on the Benton Road, when I heard the second shot. I saw my father travelling on the Benton Road towards home. He had passed the Sharp place. I returned that night to the Sharp House and saw the bodies of the dead man and woman. I also went back to Sharp's house two weeks later and helped some neighbours clean up the bloodstains.*

Mr. Squires then asked the witness how he knew what time he heard the shots. Leslie Bell replied, "I was wearing a watch, and my watch is correct." Mr. Squires then asked, "Are you saying that the bloodstains stayed in the house a total of two weeks before they were cleaned up?" Leslie Bell said, "Yes sir." [In fact, most of the bloodstains were cleaned up earlier and only a residue remained to be cleaned up two weeks later.]

Robert Bell was sworn in. He was a sergeant during World War One. He was overseas with Harvey Trenholm. They both served in the 26th New Brunswick Battalion. Robert Bell gave the following statement.

I live at Benton Ridge. I remember the events of March 27th as follows: I was returning that day from Elmwood and drove past the Sharp house at four thirty. I was in a light carriage. I saw my son Leslie on the road also. I arrived home before my son. I knew Trenholm but not his wife. I saw a man leaving Sharp's as I went by. He had on a light coat and light cap and brown pants. When he saw me he lowered his head and turned around. He continued walking with his head down, then he looked up at me and he turned again and walked in a westerly direction. I saw him the next morning and it was Bennie Swim. I went back to Sharp's house on the night of the murder at 7 o'clock and saw Harvey Trenholm lying there dead. His head was on the ground. I went in the house with the Sheriff and saw Olive Trenholm lying dead on the floor. Next morning I saw a man that the Sheriff had arrested for the crime, and recognized him as the prisoner here in court. [He Pointed to Bennie Swim.] *I also helped find the revolver, with directions. A crowd was also there looking for it.*

Henry Carr was next up. His statement went as follows.

Bennie Swim had come to my house on the evening of March 27th. He looked weak and ill and was bleeding from his wound on the right side of his head. He asked for some dinner, which was given to him. He didn't stay long, and left as soon as he had finished his dinner. He looked like he was headed west.

Mr. Hughes wanted more so he had Mr. Carr tell everything he could remember from the minute he first saw Bennie to the last and what exactly both of them said. Mr. Carr obliged.

I saw a man coming towards my house from the fields along Caldwell road. He had on a light raincoat, light cap, and shoes with rubbers on them. He had a white handkerchief wrapped around his head with blood dripping from it. His face had blood on it, and it was dripping down onto his clothes. I was sitting on the veranda. It was between 6 p.m. and 7 p.m. The man walked right up onto to my veranda and sat down. He asked me for something to eat. I said, "It's just after supper, but I'll go in and see." Then I said, "What's the matter with your face?" He said, "I'm pretty tired and hungry. I got into trouble with a man and woman out in Benton and they shot me." I said, "Who were they?"

He said, "Donahue or Donavon." I asked him, "What place was it?"
He said, "Do you know Alexander Rogers, where he lives?" I told
him, "Yes." He said, "How far would Roger's place be from the
Sharp place?" I said, "Over a mile cross-country." He said, "What
road does Rogers live on?" I said, "It's on the Springfield road."
He said, "Is that a different road from the Will Sharp place?"
I said, "Yes; so who are you?" He said, "I'm Swim; I'm awfully
tired." I brought out some food at that time, and he ate it on
the veranda. He said, "My head's pretty sore. Where's the nearest
doctor?" He said he was afraid I was going to send him to the
nearest hospital. I said, "The nearest doctor is in Debec, about
four miles." He said, "When does the train leave for Woodstock?"
I said, "About 9 p.m. from the Debec station. You'll have time to
get your face dressed before the train leaves." He then paid me for
supper and thanked me. I told him about James Doherty when
he mentioned needing a place to stay. I asked him if he knew the
woman's name. He said, "Swim." Then he tells me what happened
at Sharp's. He said, "I went to the door and this fellow opens the
door and he says what are you doing down here? I said I'm kind of
down here on a little business. The man hits me three times, and I
said be careful I have hands too. Then the man takes out a gun and
fires at me. He said he was going to shoot again, so I grabbed the
revolver and threw it away." That's what he told me. I noticed he
was calm and not excited. After the story, he asked about directions
to Doherty's. I told him it was about a mile from here on the same
road and same side. Then he left. I thought he was going to get
his face dressed. He was walking at a fast gait, pretty smart like.

So ended the testimony of Henry Carr.

Mr. Hughes figured he now had a better understanding of what had happened at Carr's. It seemed like Bennie was having trouble speaking coherently or logically. He figured this was because of his wound, blood loss and fatigue. It was also the first of several explanations Bennie gave of his presence at the scene of the murders.

The next witness was James Doherty. If Henry Carr had lots to say about his visit from Bennie Swim, Mr. Doherty was the opposite. He had almost nothing to say. When asked by the prosecution, what all had happened from the time he first saw the prisoner to the last he offered only the following account.

89

A man came to my house on the evening of March 27th about 8. I was outside when he came. It was kind of dark. He looked very weak and was bleeding some. I asked him what he wanted. He said he needed a place to stay for the night. I gave him one of the upstairs rooms and he went and slept there. The next morning Sheriff Foster and Deputy Sheriff Mooers arrived about 7:30 and arrested the man I had let into my house. I later found out the man was Bennie Swim.

Mr. Hughes tried to get more out of Doherty.

Hughes: "You must have asked him what happened?"
Doherty: "No sir I didn't."
Hughes: "Are you saying that a man comes to your house covered in blood and you just bring him right upstairs to one of your bedrooms and let him go to sleep?"
Doherty: "That's right sir. I didn't ask him no questions."
Hughes: "Well, weren't you curious about why he was bleeding and where he came from?"
Doherty: "No sir, not enough to ask him no questions."
Hughes: "You didn't even ask him his name?"
Doherty: "No sir. I didn't learn his name till the next morning."
Hughes: "How far is your house from the Maine border?"
Doherty: "Six miles."

So ended the testimony of James Doherty.

Dr. Thomas Griffin was sworn in. He started with some background information.

I have been practicing medicine for twenty-five years now. I began my training at the Jefferson Medical College of the University of Pennsylvania. I now reside in Woodstock. I remember the night of March 27th. I was at Sharp's place that night in the company of Coroner Hay. We arrived at about 8 o'clock and found the bodies of Harvey Trenholm and Olive Trenholm. I knew the latter before she was married. I examined both bodies at the scene and saw that Mr. Trenholm had one bullet wound to the head. Mrs. Trenholm had two bullet wounds. After the bodies were removed and taken to the undertaking rooms, I made a more complete examination.

Dr. Griffin then gave the same testimony about the autopsies of Harvey and Olive that he had given at the Preliminary Examination.

So ended the testimony of Dr. Thomas Griffin.

Constable John Marston also gave his evidence. He was in Woodstock on the afternoon of March 27th and did not see Bennie Swim until the next morning at Sharp's. His house is about one and a quarter miles from Sharp's place, at the mouth of Benton Road where it meets the river road. He was also a guard for the bodies until the Sheriff arrived. He saw the blood that was near a sheep pen at about 2 a.m.. He was present the next morning when the gun was found at the base of a tree, about fifty yards from the well house. Several 38-long cartridges, all with clipped ends, were also found there.

John Swim, Olive's father, was next on the witness stand. He stated:

> *Olive was seventeen on July 10th of last year. I know Bennie Swim; he's my nephew. He came to my house on March 13th of this year and asked where Olive was. I went over to my mother's house and told Olive that Bennie wanted to see her. Olive said she didn't want to see him and wouldn't come home until Bennie went away. Bennie was not happy about that. He stayed for the time that it took to have the conversation. He asked about what times the night train left, and did he have time to catch it. I said I thought he could. Olive had been working at Rockland for over a year. It was where I used to live 23 years ago, before Olive was born. She came home the last week in February and remained there until her marriage. I was in Woodstock when the murder took place and did not see the body until I saw it at the undertaker's room in Woodstock.*

Mr. Squires wanted to stop for the day; it was 6:15 p.m.. Judge McKeown was not happy about this request. He wanted to continue and finish the testimony of John Swim, but he agreed to adjourn for the day. The trial continued on the April 27th at 9:30 a.m. with John Swim back on the witness stand.

Mr. Hughes asked several questions and more details were verified. They included that John Swim was a farmer presently living at Benton Ridge. His mother's house, where Olive was when Bennie came to see her on Monday, the 13th of March, was about a mile and a half, from his house. He was in Woodstock on business on the 27th of March and didn't return to Benton Ridge until the next morning. He returned because of a telephone call that informed him about the murders. John had first met Bennie Swim at the home of his uncle, Edward, John's brother, in Rockland in 1921. Bennie had come down to Benton Ridge for a two week visit in the spring of 1921. Olive was married on Wednesday, the 15th of March 1922. She did not live at home after that. His wife Phoebe Ann was presently in Houlton, Maine and had taken their daughter Alice Pearl with her. He was not able to read or write.

So ended the testimony of John Swim.

Deputy Sheriff Mooers was not able to testify due to illness.

The Defence of Bennie Swim

Mr. Squires first put Jesse Foster, Bennie's uncle on his mother's side, on the stand for the defence. After being sworn in, Jesse described bouts of insanity in the Foster family. Mr. Squires winced when he heard the testimony. He had been up late many nights leading up to the trial trying to arrive at an effective strategy but couldn't come up with a plausible defence. He finally decided to go with whatever he had.

Mr. Squires listened carefully as Jesse recounted incidents of strange behaviour in the Foster family. These were some of the same stories he had heard as rumours when he had previously made his inquiries. This was good; it made more sense. Jesse's testimony confirmed as fact the rumours about the family. Bennie's grandfather did have fits, and so did Bennie. It was Bennie's uncle, Judson, who had stoned his horse to death, and not Bennie's brother, Alexander Cameron. It was the same uncle who had tried to chew the face off of Bennie when he was a child but was stopped by Bennie's mother.

The prosecution listened carefully but did not object. Mr. Squires was waiting for the objections to roll in and was disturbed when they didn't. All the prosecution would have needed to do was to ask Jesse's occupation. When it was established that he was a farmer, and not in a position to decide if Bennie was insane or not, it would have made him look ridiculous. Jesse was trying to do all he could to help save his nephew from the gallows. When his testimony ended, Mr. Squires wanted to clear up certain matters so he began a series of questions, which resulted in many more important details coming to light.

First, was the matter of Bennie's relationship to Jesse. It was verified that Jesse Foster was Bennie's uncle, a brother of Bennie's mother. Bennie had been living with his father and mother at their home in the Mainstream, which was about four miles from Jesse's home. Jesse Foster's brother Judson had stoned his horse to death because the horse had gotten out of its enclosure several times and he was tired of chasing it down. This was in 1921. Jesse elaborated on what happened. He and Judson and another brother, Hex, had corralled their horses in the morning, but they got out again in the afternoon. They tried to keep them from getting in the grain and wanted to take them home. One of the horses ran in the grain. Judson got rocks and went out of his mind. He stoned the horse. Judson Foster had been having fits since he was fourteen. He was now thirty-one. Judson still often acts in an outrageous way. If you cross him in any way, you can't stay in the same place. You have to get away fast. He'll get into a tear and a rage.

Jesse Foster had a "double uncle" [he probably meant his uncle's uncle] that had been confined to a mental institution four different times. Jesse's sister Marie Foster had also been having fits. She would rave and go crazy trying to tear and clutch at things. Her fits usually lasted about twenty minutes, and she had to be held down until they passed. She usually had about three fits a week. Sometimes she would hit people during these fits. Afterwards, she would be weak and need to lie down.

Jesse then told about his father, Alexander Foster who was Bennie's maternal grandfather. He lived with his son Jesse. He was also prone to fits. His fits included spells of outrageous behaviour when he was coming out of them. He would go stiff as a log and fall right down. This lasted five or ten minutes. Then he would begin to tear and rage. He wouldn't stay down. He just rammed around until they got a hold on him. He would try to undress himself and to tear himself to pieces. He would try to tear other people to pieces if he got hold of them. It would take half an hour for the fits to stop. Afterwards, he weakened right down. He would be all right for a day or two and then take the fit again. He has lived with Jesse for the last twenty years. The fits have been going on the whole time. Hiram Hargrove, an uncle of Jesse's was another case. He was out of his mind for three years.

As for Bennie, Jesse hired him to work for him over the last three years. At first, he was a good worker but that later changed. He would no longer work steadily. He would only work for two or three hours and then leave to go back home. He had been hired for a month to help yard pulp. Sometimes he would just linger close to the farmhouse, about four hundred yards away from the yarding site, then leave and go back home.

According to Jesse, Bennie also had fits. He would become extremely angry when he was coming out of a fit. Once, he struck at Jesse with a wooden club as he was coming out of a fit. As a child, he was sent to see Doctor Curtain about the fits. Bennie also had a problem sitting still. He was very restless and always had to keep moving.

Jesse knew Olive Swim Trenholm before she married Harvey Trenholm. When she was living in the Mainstream, she and Bennie would sometimes visit Jesse. Jesse said they passed for man and wife. That was the reputation they had in the neighbourhood. Olive told Jesse that she and Bennie were married. He had never seen her wearing a wedding ring, but she insisted they were man and wife. That was the testimony given by Jesse Foster.

Bennie's mother, Eva May (Foster) Swim was next to take the stand. After she was sworn in she began with this statement.

> *I understood that Bennie was married to Olive. She would have been eighteen years of age this summer. When she came to my home the first time she was about sixteen years of age. She lived with Bennie as man and wife for some months until her father came after her and took her to his home in Benton Ridge. On Monday March 27th, he* [Bennie] *was dressed in a brown suit with a raincoat. He also wore a light cap when he left home. Bennie is now twenty-three years of age.*

She seemed confused about much of her information, some of which was clearly incorrect but neither the defence nor prosecution intervened.

Mr. Squires winced at Eva Swim's testimony. She needed a lot of help. She couldn't even remember the most basic details, and would need guidance for her testimony to be credible. Although she was not a good witness, he believed that most of the jury would feel sorry for her and understand her confusion. Not many mothers had had to deal with a son that had become a murderer and who would probably be hanged. Even so, Squires had a job to do. He began questioning her in a way that helped her give the jury a more sensible description of what was going on with her son and the life he had led in the past.

In the next part of her testimony she also told about her father, Alexander Foster, having fits and falling down. Sometimes he tried to tear his clothes off. Sometimes he would try to grab and bite others. He would go mad. Her father had been all right until he was sixty years old and then the fits started. He is now eighty. With reference to Judson Foster, her brother, she confirmed that he also had fits. He would go crazy and be out of his mind; you couldn't talk to him, nothing would sink in. He would go wild for between one and five hours. One time, when he was about sixteen in 1904, Judson had chewed Bennie's face. She had to tear him away from Bennie. She said her sister, Marie Foster, also had fits. She would get ugly and tear herself to pieces. It took two people to hold her down. It would take about half an hour before she would calm down and she could be let go. Her uncle Hiram Hargrove had fits as well. He was considered insane for three years. James Foster, her second cousin had to be sent to an insane asylum three times.

She also told about Bennie having fits. Sometimes he would be on the floor on his hands and knees trying to pull and twist things. These fits would last about thirty minutes and then he would act strange and stupid. He could not think clearly, or speak properly. She said he had lots of these spells, even during the time Olive lived with them. The fits didn't seem to bother Olive at all. She didn't think less of Bennie because of them, according to Eva.

When questioned about Bennie and Olive, she gave following account. Olive arrived in Rockland about December of 1920. She first stayed with her brother-in-law, Edward Swim for about a week and then came to live with them at their home in the Mainstream. At first, Bennie was shy around Olive. Bennie was a shy person with others as well. When they had company Bennie would often stay in his room. He had few friends. When some of his school chums, trying to be friendly, came over, he would not always want to talk with them. Olive and Bennie became very close soon after she moved in. Two or three weeks after that, they started sleeping in the same room and shared a bed together. Olive said they were married. They seemed very happy. Olive went home to Benton Ridge for six weeks in March of 1921. Bennie became unhinged when she left. He had no appetite, had trouble sleeping, or wouldn't sleep at all. He would sit and talk with her all night. Bennie had a one-room cabin close to his parents place, but he didn't want to sleep in it. He also had his own room at our house. While Olive was gone, Bennie would just walk around in the woods.

It was now the prosecution's turn to question Eva Swim. This didn't go well for the defence. It began with Mr. Hughes questioning Eva about Olive and Bennie's relationship. She said that at first Bennie didn't pay much attention to Olive. It took a few times of seeing her before a relationship started. They started to sleep in the same room and the same bed. Eva said Olive asked her for her ring so she and Bennie could get married. She gave it to them. She said it was common knowledge in the area of Rockland and the Mainstream that Olive and Bennie were married. She said Olive wore the ring everywhere she went and told them they were married in Babytown by a preacher named Foster in April of 1921. When Mr. Hughes asked her where Babytown was located, Eva had no idea. [Babytown cannot be found on any map of Carleton County.] When asked about the preacher named Foster, she said she knew of a preacher by that name but wasn't sure if it was the same preacher that married them. She continued to insist that Olive told her that she and Bennie were married, and that they slept in the same bed together.

Mr. Hughes now wanted to know about the day of the murder; what was Bennie's routine and anything else she could remember about that day. She started off by saying that the night before the murder Bennie spent the whole night in her room talking to her. He said he couldn't live without

Olive. She meant everything to him. The next morning he didn't eat any breakfast. He told his parents he was going to Uncle Tom's. [Tom was Eva's brother-in-law.] Bennie went there and came back and then told them he was going to see Uncle Earn and stay the night and the next morning. [It was never explained who Uncle Earn was.] Eva also said Bennie mentioned he was going to Woodstock to pay a note on the violin.

Mr. Hughes went back to Bennie and his fits. This time Eva denied that Bennie ever had fits. He did run around the woods a lot, and sometimes he would not speak for days, but he didn't have fits. Mr. Hughes let it go. Maybe now she was telling the truth. He also asked her again about Olive and Bennie's relationship. How did Eva know that they were man and wife? This time, Eva said that they were not married to her knowledge. Mr. Hughes also let this go. He wondered, as did the jury, why she changed her story, but it wasn't his problem. Eva Swim was clearly showing the strain and perhaps her memory was fading because of it. That was the end of her testimony.

William Swim, once sworn in, spent most of his testimony saying almost the same thing as his wife, but with a few differences. He stated that he was the father of Bennie Swim. He said that when Olive lived at his home, she and Bennie lived together as man and wife and that he had heard they were married. They slept in the same bed. On two occasions that he could remember, Bennie had fits and on many occasions acted very queer and would leave the house on the run. Sometimes he had no appetite and wouldn't eat. He said he first saw Olive the year before last when she came up with her father. She left before Christmas for Benton Ridge and returned in a few days and lived with Bennie as man and wife. William said Bennie had fits but that he didn't think much about them. Bennie had fits until a few days before he left for Woodstock. He said Bennie began to wander off more and more, but it was probably because there wasn't any work on the farms in the area. He went away on March 27th at 8 o'clock in the morning. He said he was going to Woodstock. William said he had heard that Bennie traded his violin with Edmund Estabrooks for a pair of boots. That was all William had to say.

This wasn't enough for Mr. Hughes. With several more questions asked, these details emerged. William Swim had never asked if Bennie and Olive were married, he just assumed it. Bennie's fits were bad on occasion, and he would then act dumb afterwards. When asked if he knew the meaning of the word "dumb," William admitted he didn't. He also didn't know anything about Babytown or the Reverend Foster, who supposedly had married Olive

97

and his son. As for the day of the murder, he said that Bennie left about 8 a.m. but gave no details about where he was going.

So ended the testimony of the witnesses for the defence. Mr. Squires was tired and emotionally drained. He looked at the jury and they seemed to be as confused as he was. All the testimony coming from the prosecution's witnesses seemed to be accurate, detailed and, worst of all, consistent. They had exact times, places and accurate descriptions of the events they testified to. The witnesses for the defence seemed to be confusing and contradictory. Even on the simplest matters they gave different accounts and the details were definitely lacking. It was like they were making it up as they went along. Some of their accounts of events were almost unbelievable, or so lacking in detail they could hardly be relied upon. He cursed himself for not preparing the witnesses better so they would at least come off as somewhat knowledgeable and consistent with each other. He sighed and asked for a recess, which was granted. He had to come up with something. He thought long and hard about what he was going to say in summation.

At this point in the trial it was all up to him. Everything that would determine his client's fate was now on his shoulders. He would try to give his client as much of a chance to live as possible, but it would be difficult. He looked over at Bennie who was sitting impassively in the prisoner's box. He looked like he was at someone else's trial. Maybe that would work in his favour. It might give the jury the idea that his client was unaware of the gravity of his crime and, if not insane, not completely responsible for his actions either. Or, it could work against him. Maybe the jury would think he was such a coldblooded killer that he didn't care about what he had done or what was going on around him. Either way, Mr. Squires knew that this trial would be talked about for years, probably debated in Law Schools across the country and he would not come out looking very good. He would be criticized for years to come until some other trial came along that took the spotlight off of him.

He had to do something and it had to be dramatic. He went into an office that was provided for him and began to write. He wanted to make sure he brought up every available point that would help his client. When he was finished, he went back into the courtroom and motioned to Judge McKeown that he was ready to begin his summation and closing argument.

Bennie was somewhat pensive as he watched his family who were there to help him out. He felt sorry for his parents, sorry that he had to put them through this. He was thankful they were there doing what they could for him. He had trouble meeting his mother's eyes as she sat there in the witness box. He could tell how much she loved him and didn't flinch when she made some obvious mistakes in her testimony. He knew she had lied on his behalf, not something she would normally do as a God fearing woman, but she had done it for him. He was thankful and loved her all the more for it. Maybe she had to believe what she had said under oath, in order to be able to live with herself, or to be able to somewhat justify what her son had done.

His father's testimony brought up some of the same emotions. Bennie was sad that his father had to be here, but glad that he was doing what he could for his son. He had hoped to see his younger brother, Alexander Cameron, and his sister, Cassie Elizabeth, but he understood their reluctance to show up for the trial. They didn't need the cold and angry stares of the spectators, wondering if they were like him, a cold and calculating killer. Well, he would take whatever punishment they gave him like a man. That was his last thought as his lawyer came back into the courtroom and spoke to the jury.

The Summations

Mr. Squires stood and addressed the jury.

Gentlemen of the Jury, I have not had time to go into the defence very carefully, and there are several other witnesses that would have been called to strengthen the defence if the time had not been limited. I am not going to put Bennie on the stand because he could not add anything to the evidence of his defence. Please don't punish or blame him for my decision.

There was a tragedy at Benton Ridge on March 27th of this year; that is for certain. A man and woman were shot dead. No one really knows what happened in that yard. Bennie doesn't know because he has blocked it out. It is no longer in his memory. What we do know is that Trenholm was a scrapper, a man who likes to fight and is good at it. He was an athlete, a strong and powerful man. He may have struck Bennie and the latter stepped back and fired at both, as Mrs. Trenholm was at the door with her husband.

We also know that Bennie and Olive lived together as man and wife in the past, and Mrs. Swim has stated that she gave her wedding ring to Olive, with which to be married. He and Olive had lived as man and wife, slept in the same bed, so he looked upon it as if Olive was his wife, and this man Trenholm was the usurper. He told his mother the night before he left for Benton Ridge that he could not live without Olive. This young man of twenty-two years had inherited insanity from his mother's side, that you have heard testimony in reference to it. When he arrived at Marston's he told them that he was going to get the Sheriff, to look into the matter and have them both arrested, especially the man who had married Olive, Mr. Trenholm, because evidently Bennie Swim considered that Olive was his wife.

His actions at Carr's, showed that he had not intentionally committed the murders because he made no effort to make his escape. It is unlucky that he had the revolver with him, because he may have come to that place to see Olive, the girl that he loved,

100

the girl that he thought was his wife, the girl that the other man had taken from him, and suddenly when he beheld this man and the girl he thought was his wife, it may have unhinged his mind and the deed was done. Evidently she did not want to marry him, as she was too smart for him. If there is a reasonable doubt that the murder was not premeditated, or if you believe the process of insanity was working on his mind, you can bring in a verdict of manslaughter, or even acquit him on the grounds of insanity. I thank you again for your time and patience.

Mr. Hughes was impressed. His adversary had handled himself well, and even with daunting odds he had managed to put up an excellent defence for his client. It would have been even better if he had been able to acquire several more reliable witnesses, but there was not much to choose from. He was surprised that some of the information in the summation was not mentioned by any of the defence witnesses, but it wouldn't be necessary to question that. He was sure that he had enough with his witnesses and their testimony to bring in a guilty verdict. It was now up to him, to make sure the prosecution did as well in summation as Mr. Squires had done. He stood, faced the jury, and began.

Gentleman of the jury, we must accept the responsibility that the law has placed upon us. The prisoner's counsel puts up a splendid defence. The facts of this case are that Olive Trenholm was living with her husband on March 27th. Both of these parties were murdered between 3 o'clock and 4:30 in the afternoon. Who murdered them? Suspicion rested on Bennie Swim. He was arrested and you have heard the evidence. The girl had been living with Bennie, so she left as she has the perfect right to do, and contract a legal marriage*, with Trenholm. Bennie Swim was not agreeable to that. He loved Olive Trenholm so much that he decided that if he could not have her, then no one else would have her.

Bennie heard of the marriage on Saturday. He got a revolver and ten cartridges from Edmund Estabrooks. He came to Woodstock on Monday March 27th. There is no question of that. Sheriff

---

*   Neither attorney knew that since Harvey was still married to Dorina Burgess, his marriage to Olive was not legal, and, though he didn't know it, Bennie could have had Harvey arrested for bigamy.

Foster was on the same train as him. He reached the Marston place and inquired of Gilbert, the way to the Sharp house. He was shown the way and the next thing we hear is that Leslie Bell heard shots fired and that his father Robert Bell, sees Bennie Swim coming from the Sharp house. There is no question of who murdered Olive. The officer came; they make a search and finally arrest him. They find the revolver with five chambers, two were fired into Olive, one went into Harvey Trenholm's brain, one he fired into his own head, and the fifth one is still in the revolver. As to the plea of insanity, it must be based on something substantial; there were no signs of insanity in Bennie on that fatal day. He made plans previously to acquire a revolver, a gun that he could easily hide, and have enough money for the train ride. He left his home, travelled to Woodstock, then got a ride with a team to Lower Woodstock, then walked to Benton Ridge. He evidently shot Trenholm at the doorstep, then entered the house and shot Mrs. Trenholm while she was in the front room. When the deed was done, he tried to escape, by walking towards Oak Mountain and the Maine Border. It's all too well done for a man with any signs of insanity. With all the evidence presented, I believe that you will find the prisoner, Bennie Swim, guilty of the capital crime of murder. Thank you.

Mr. Hughes let the impact of his statement sink in. He looked over the jury and noticed that the face of each juryman was still as riveted on him, as it had been when he was giving his summation. His account left nothing uncertain, and it was powerfully delivered. It was almost as if his words were a physical presence, hovering in the air, still there to be felt and pondered.

The Charge to the Jury, the Verdict and the Sentence

With the summations completed, Chief Justice McKeown began his charge to the jury. The time was 12:30 p.m. on April 27, 1922.

When a person is charged with such a serious offense that his life is at stake we give him counsel. I want to commend both attorneys for their excellent work in this case. I am sure that no person in Mr. Squires' position could have done anything more for his client than Mr. Squires has done. He did not have much time to prepare for such a difficult case but he was very proficient in his work, showing great determination to deliver the best defence that his client could expect. Mr. Squires did not waste the court's time with lengthy cross-examinations, and any weak spots were paid attention to, and he made the most of it that could be made. I would like to express my conviction that no person could have done it better.

The Crown Prosecutor upon his indictment sets out to prove the accusation that he has made. The burden of proof in a criminal case is always upon the Crown. It makes a claim of wrong doing, that some person has committed an offence, and the Crown has got to prove it. If after the Crown has shown all that it can show, if any doubt remains in the minds of the jury, any reasonable doubt, which springs from a lack of convincing testimony, it must be considered.

There are two classes of evidence: there is direct evidence, and what is known as circumstantial evidence. This case is of the latter sort, circumstantial evidence. A person may come to court as a Crown witness to substantiate a charge that is made and he is able to say, "I saw the accused commit the crime. I was present and I saw the assault or whatever crime he is accused of." That is what we call direct evidence. If the jury believes that the man is telling the truth, the jury is justified in convicting. But when most offences are committed, no one sees the act done, and those bringing a person to justice are compelled to rely on all circumstances surrounding the commission of the crime. That is what we call circumstantial evidence. In this case that is what must be relied upon. No one is able to say here that they saw the act done. The Crown places before the jury what evidence it has concerning all the circumstances known to all the witnesses, and it relies upon those witnesses to show what happened. What is needed is also the possibility of the person being able to commit the crime. By that I mean the accused must have had in his possession the implements to commit the crime. In this case you must be able to have a reasonable belief that he did. It is not enough to just have the opportunity to commit the crime, but to eliminate anyone else who could have done it. Was he armed with the necessary tools to commit the crime? The circumstances must convince you that he was, and there is no other reasonable explanation but that the accused did it. Also, that there is no other combination of circumstances that could have produced the killing which took place there. Unless you are satisfied of that, you are not justified in finding the accused guilty.

At this time the judge called a recess. It lasted until 2:30 p.m., at which time the court proceedings resumed. Judge McKeown continued.

The defence counsel argues that it has not been shown that the accused committed the offence, and it is possible that someone else may have done it. I have told you all on that matter that I think it is necessary to say. It is a question of fact, and being a question of fact, is of course peculiarly and wholly within your capacity to find, without any instructions from me. There are other defences, which are largely questions of law, and as to them I expect you to take instructions from me and to follow the directions I give you. The law surrounds the accused person with safeguards when he is charged with an offence of this kind. Mr. Hughes has just concluded within the last half hour detailing the circumstances by which the crown claims conclusively that no other person but Bennie Swim could have done it. I do not want to simply follow in his footsteps and repeat the things which he said to you. It is impossible for a person to sit here as you and I have been sitting here for the last two days and to follow the testimony that has been given, without coming to a conclusion, as to whether Bennie Swim did the deed or not. That is not for me to decide but for you to decide.

Next we go onto motive. It is not necessary to find a motive for a crime. What motive does an individual have to commit a crime? Sometimes none at all, but in this case you must decide if the motive of jealousy is correct and if it is enough to convince you. While motive does not play directly into the guilt or innocence of the accused, it can explain and strengthen your decision. You have heard from Mr. Hughes and his explanation, of how the accused was so in love with Olive that he could not live without her, and decided that no one else should be allowed to. That was the motive of the crime. If you are satisfied with that, then it should help you in your decision.

Next the Defence counsel offers up the probability of insanity. First of all, it is the responsibility of the defence to prove insanity. While we have heard several accounts as evidence of it running in the family of the accused, it is necessary to understand the law when it comes to the defence of insanity. He has to be insane within the meaning of the law so as not to be responsible for his actions. The law never punishes a man for something that he never intended to do or for what is done by a man when he did not know he was doing wrong. For insanity to exist in this case, what must be seen as true is did the accused know that firing a revolver at someone would in fact do them harm or kill them as was done in this situation. If the person was deemed to be insane at the time of the offence, it would be accepted that he would not be capable of understanding the outcome or result of his actions. If you feel that way then the decision is yours to make. Insanity as a defence must be proven beyond a reasonable doubt. Just because someone has some forms of insanity does not make them free from their responsibilities. If you determine the accused to be insane then you must acquit such person from the charge, and to add that he is acquitted of them on the grounds of insanity. Then the law will take care of him in another way. Understand that you must be able to be convinced that the accused did not know that his actions would cause the death of said individuals, Mr. and Mrs. Trenholm. As you have heard from the testimony of the many witnesses, the defendant did several actions in a calculated way, and in a timely sequential manner that brought him to the place where he now sits. There were the preparations to go to the scene of the murder, his going away afterwards and his remarks to the Sheriff. Whatever his family has suffered in the way of insanity or maladies, does not in any way, reflect on the actions of the accused. You must determine if the defendant himself was capable of understanding that his actions would cause the harm and destruction that did occur. If you feel the accused was aware that his actions would cause death, or serious bodily harm, then you cannot acquit him for reasons of insanity. If you feel that the accused did not know what his actions would probably do, then you can acquit him on the grounds of insanity. Simplified, did he know right from wrong?

The next point we must bring to your attention is the distinction between murder and manslaughter. The counsel for the accused, while not admitting that the accused did the act, and you are not to take it on the part of the learned counsel as an admission that the accused did the act, urged that if you should come to the conclusion that he did the act, then there were grounds connected with the whole transaction by reason of which you could find the accused guilty of manslaughter and not murder. The primary distinction between murder and manslaughter is that a person who feels he must defend himself, even if he needs to cause death, is allowed to do so. Murder is when a person does not give a chance to another to remove themselves from the situation. Better explained, a person must be in danger, or seriously believe that he is in danger of loss of life or serious bodily harm, before he can defend himself with deadly force. In this case, a wrongful act against the accused, such as was his belief that a person who he believed to be his wife was stolen from him, is not sufficient to warrant killing. In order for that to be considered manslaughter, it would need to be sufficient to deprive him of his ordinary power of self control, or that he could not hold himself in control and there had been no time for his passion to cool, that the act of killing under such circumstances might be manslaughter. I consider it to be my duty to say to you gentlemen that under the law the time which had elapsed between the discovery on the part of the accused of her [Olive Swim's] *marriage to Harvey Trenholm and the commission of the deed, throws the greatest possible doubt upon the applicability of this section to which I have been referring to this transaction at all.*

The law distinctly lays down that it must be done in the heat of the moment, momentary passion. If a man allows day after day to pass and then goes to the performance of this act in the spirit of revenge, that does not reduce the crime from murder to manslaughter at all. This further, I conceive it is my duty to direct you, that while the law provides that safeguard or safety valve or whatever view you might take of it as regards to the requirements for this to be considered manslaughter, you must be reasonable in applying the term as it occurs here in this case.

Another matter must be mentioned by me; no matter how much comes to us freighted with all the trouble this case has caused to both families, freighted with the death of two people, and freighted with the circumstances of the capital charge being laid at the door of the accused, we have got to meet that circumstance as citizens of a county which desires that law and order be kept within its borders. It is not a question simply between the Crown and the accused. It is a question of the maintenance of law and order, and of a person who considered himself aggrieved by persons, who had a legal right to do what they did, taking the law into his own hands and meting out death in such a summary and awful manner to people without a moment's time for preparation for the change. The matter will be left with you gentlemen with these instructions unless either of the counsel wishes further instructions upon some other point.

Mr. Squires responded, "I was going to ask that your Honour charge the jury as to reasonable doubt on insanity. In the case of the King versus Clark, it was stated that when there is any reasonable doubt as regards insanity, the benefit is given to the prisoner."

Judge McKeown replied.

Yes, I thought I made it clear as I went along. A view did prevail for some time, as in the case referred to by Mr. Squires, that when a person sets up a defence of insanity he had to prove it beyond a reasonable doubt. This case is not relevant to that because the primary defence here was not insanity, as it was in the case mentioned. The defence here is entitled to reasonable doubt and the benefit of that doubt which is raised. The defence also has got to prove it in such a way that you could be reasonably satisfied that it is so. The expression of the law, which those of us use as a standard, is that it must be clearly proved to the satisfaction of the jury that he is insane at the time he committed the offence. That does not express the certainty that the words, beyond a reasonable doubt express. If there is no other point which either of you wish me to refer to, the jury can take this case into consideration. If any difference of opinion should develop between you when you are discussing the evidence, or any doubt as to the effect of what I may have said on any point, you can return into court and have the evidence read to you by the stenographer or ask for further instructions.

The Jury retired at 3:05 p.m..

The jury was glad that the Judge's charge was over. Listening to him drone on was the hardest part of the trial. Many of the jury members had to stifle yawns, but they understood that it was his job to make their decision clear as to the rules of law. Most of the jury had little idea what the Judge was talking about, but they got the general drift. It wouldn't matter anyway. They knew what was expected of them, and it was an easy decision. Forget reasonable doubt; there wasn't any doubt about what had happened at Benton Ridge, and their verdict would show it.

The Jury returns at 4:00 p.m..

Mr. Squires took one look at the faces of the jury members and knew he had not saved his client from the hangman's noose.

Jury Foreman, George Burpee of Centreville, stood and delivered the decision, "We the jury find that the prisoner Bennie Swim is guilty as charged and bring in a verdict of willful murder."

Judge McKeown then spoke, "Sentence will not be pronounced immediately. Let the prisoner be remanded for sentence later."

There were no cheers in the courtroom. It was as if everyone expected the outcome and they had no emotion left. The people attending the trial who had known both Bennie and Olive were sad it had come to this. Bennie would now pay for his crime; there was not much sympathy for him. He was taken back to the jail where he would spend a sleepless night.

On Friday, April 28th at 12:45 p.m., Sheriff Foster and Constable McCarron escorted Bennie Swim from his jail cell to the courthouse. He walked with a quick step to his place in the prisoner's box. He was dressed as usual in his brown suit with a white dotted shirt and white collar. His only sign of nervousness was when he got up and moved from the centre to the corner of the box. Chief Justice McKeown pounded his gavel on the bench to silence the restless crowd of spectators. He cleared his throat and said in a loud voice, "Bennie Swim, stand up."

The prisoner stood.

Judge McKeown continued, "Have you anything to say or any reason to give why sentence should not now be pronounced upon you? Do you wish to say anything?"

Bennie hesitated for about ten seconds and then replied, "No Sir."

The Chief Justice then read out the sentence in a booming voice.

> *After a trial in which everything which could be said and everything which could be done, was done, the jury unanimously has taken upon themselves the responsibility of saying that you are guilty of the crime of murdering Olive Trenholm. I do not wish to add one ounce of weight to the burden of grief and remorse which I am sure you are now bearing by demanding and necessitating your presence in this room for any length of time. This much however, I do say to you, that in the few weeks of life which remain to you, you call in the services of clergymen of your faith and throw yourself unreservedly in their hands in order that you may to some degree prepare for the ordeal which awaits you and for the passage to that higher tribunal before which all of us must ultimately stand. The sentence is that on the fifteenth day of July 1922, between the hours of five o'clock in the morning and five o'clock in the afternoon of that day, you be taken from the County Gaol of this County of Carleton wherein you will be confined in the meantime, to a place of execution, to be prepared according to law, and there between the hours aforesaid on the said fifteenth day of July 1922, you, the said Bennie Swim, be hanged by the neck until you are dead, and may god have mercy on your soul. Let the prisoner be remanded for execution.*

Some people who were present swear they heard Bennie curse Harvey Trenholm as he left the courtroom.

And that was it. Bennie was a condemned man waiting for his hanging to take place. There were no happy faces in the crowd, but John Swim was satisfied. Roy Swim was satisfied. Now, that bastard would get what he deserved. They would both try to attend the hanging. Bennie's parents left the courtroom sad and dejected. Several reporters tried to get them to say something, but they just walked faster. The reporters tried to get a statement from Olive's family, but they, too, just ignored them.

Bennie was brought back to his cell and started raving about the injustice of it all. He was upset. He didn't understand why he was going to hang. He expected to pay for this crime, but somehow he really thought that he would get life in prison, or less. He had been praying to God harder than he had ever prayed in his life and thought he would be spared. Maybe God didn't care.

Mr. Squires came into his cell to talk to him one last time. He apologized for the outcome. He said that he had tried as hard as he could to do everything that would help his case. He said he couldn't think of anything that he could have done differently, and it was unfortunate that the jury had not given a better verdict. He was being honest when he said that an appeal would not do any good, but he would think about it over the coming days. Mr. Squires and Bennie shook hands and Bennie thanked him for all he had done.

As he was leaving, Mr. Squires said, "I'm not recommending this, but they won't hang a man who is insane."

Bennie thought about what his lawyer had said; it made sense. He had also been talking to several fellow prisoners and they had the same words of advice for him.

"Make them believe you're insane," they said. "They never hang a crazy man."

So, Bennie thought, I will do just that—starting now. He stopped shaving and keeping himself clean. He didn't change his clothes. He ate like he was an animal. He began to rattle the cell doors and acted wild, tearing up his cell. Eventually a doctor was called in to sedate him. The jail guards were familiar with such antics from prisoners. They just shook their heads and thought it will be a long six weeks if Bennie is going to act like this everyday.

Bennie Swim Helps Write a Ballad

A guard at the Woodstock Jail decided there was money to be made by writing a poem about Bennie Swim and publishing it. Bennie agreed to collaborate on making the poem if it would put him in a sympathetic light, and, who knows, maybe even reverse his sentence if enough people complained to the proper authorities. The guard agreed to base the poem on Bennie's version of what had brought him to this point in his life.

The poem turned out to be very sympathetic to Bennie and was a hit with a certain segment of the public even though it was riddled with inaccuracies and outright fabrications. It made him out to be a kind of victim of the situation. It was not well received by those who had accurate knowledge of the crime. Several of the jurors read the poem and shook their heads in disgust. The full text of the poem runs like this:

The Murder at Benton Ridge
Committed by Bennie Swim
Composed by E. K. C. Woodstock, N.B.

Come all young men and I'll tell you
    Of a wrong that was did to me
By a man named Harvey Trenholme
    And a girl who was engaged to me.
My parents they call me Benny Swim
    I was born on the mainstream;
It was there I spent my childhood day,
    Where I used to sit and dream.

Today I am lying in a cell
    Up in the Woodstock Jail,
Thinking of the deed I've done
    And no one to go my bail.
My age is twenty-one, boys,
    And that you all know well,
Brought up by honest parents,
    The truth to you I'll tell.

I was walking along the road one day,
　　This story to you I tell,
I met a man they call John Swim,
　　Who'd lead my soul to hell;
We walked along both arm in arm,
　　When John Swim said to me—
Step into my neighbour's house, Benny,
　　And have a talk with me.

You can have my daughter Olive, Benny,
　　To do with what you like,
If you will get you sister
　　To come and be my wife.
His daughter Olive was handsome,
　　With a dark and rolling eye,
I promised for to marry her,
　　And that I'll not deny.

We lived together for fourteen months,
　　Before our wedding, one day
She fell in love with another man
　　And then she ran away.
She ran away to Benton Ridge,
　　At her father's home she did stay,
To live with Harvey Trenholme
　　Until their wedding day.

When this young man Benny Swim
　　Found out what Olive did,
He said, I'll go and see her
　　In her home at Benton Ridge
I love this girl with all my heart.
　　This girl named Olive Swim,
I would lay down my life for her,
　　Was the words of Benny Swim.

In the year 1922,
　　On the 27th day of March,
I left my home and parents,
　　Not thinking of turning back.

The gun was in my pocket
    And my thoughts were far away,
Of the wrong this girl did to me
    And the man who stole her away.

When I met this girl Olive,
    She was fairer than the rose on the tree,
She was a maiden of eighteen summers
    When she promised to marry me.
I went up to her cottage,
    She being a bride of two weeks,
And I said to Harvey Tremholme,
    To Olive I would like to speak.

I asked for the engagement ring
    I had bought for her one day,
And also my mother's wedding ring
    She had borrowed for her game of play.
Olive, dear, listen to me,
    For I haven't long to stay,
Kindly give me back my rings
    And I will be on my way.

Harvey Trenholme he then got mad,
    He rolled up his sleeves and swore —
Benny Swim, do you see that road?
    Take it and come no more.
I pulled my gun and shot him
    The bullet going through his head,
He fell then in front of me
    Across the doorstep, dead.

And when he fell in front of me
    My mind seemed all a blank,
I fired a shot at Tremholme's wife
    And down on her knees she sank;
Arising to her feet again
    She walked through the front room door,
I shot her again through the back,
    Then she fell on the floor.

Down on my knees I went,
    I saw that she was dead,
I ran out to the hen house
    And shot myself through the head;
And when I saw that I did not fall,
    I to myself did say,
It was better to get away from here,
    And I started on my way.

I walked seven long weary miles,
    It was there I went to bed,
And all night long the girl I shot
    Was rambling through my head.
A-twisting and a-turning,
    No rest could I find,
For the gates of hell wide open
    Before my eyes did shine.

Come all you brave young country lads,
    A warning take from me,
Never do murder the girl you love,
    Whoever she may be.
For if you do, you'll surely ruin
    And find yourself like me,
And die a public scandal
    Upon the gallows tree.

When the poem first came out it was printed in several newspapers. It was received with great interest despite the fact it was a mixture of fact and fiction. It gave a sympathetic but false view of a tragic event that would long be remembered by the people in New Brunswick and beyond. The poem was reprinted as a broadsheet by George Rainsford and sold well for 15 cents a copy. Copies were preserved in many homes and were sometimes later brought out for reading at the table or around the stove on cold winter evenings. The story of Bennie Swim entered the folklore of New Brunswick

Bennie was happy with the way the poem told the story, and now that this version of it was written down and published he came more and more to believe it was the truth. He revelled in his image as a tragic figure and hoped that if enough people complained to the government his death sentence would be commuted and he would be given a life sentence instead.

But he wasn't going to put his faith in that alone; he kept up his impressions of someone who was insane. What he didn't realize is that the jailhouse guards were familiar with such antics. They continually warned him that his crazy behaviour would not be tolerated. But Bennie did not stop. He continued to throw fits and act like a wild man, talking to shadows, and arguing with himself.

Finally, Sheriff Foster came to see him. The Sheriff didn't believe Bennie was insane but, as a guardian of the prisoner, it was his responsibility to monitor every aspect of a condemned man's actions. He decided to wait a few more weeks and then, if the crazy behaviour continued, call in a doctor to assess Bennie more closely. The jail guards talked to the Sheriff as well and gave him their experience on the matter. They tried to tell him that Bennie would calm down after awhile. But the Sheriff took his responsibility seriously. He would take charge of the situation and follow the professional protocol.

The Search for a Hangman Begins

Chief Justice McKeown sent the following report to the Secretary of State (Minister of Justice) in Ottawa.

Sir, I beg to make a report, pursuant to the provisions of the Criminal Code and in compliance with instructions from your department, as follows:

1. That on the twenty-seventh day of April 1922, at a regular sitting of the Supreme Court in Circuit in the County of Carleton, in the Province of New Brunswick, one Bennie Swim was found guilty of the murder of Olive Trenholm, and on the following day, namely the twenty-eighth day of April 1922, I sentenced him to be hanged on the fifteenth day of July, 1922, between the hours of five o'clock in the morning and five o'clock in the afternoon of said day.

2. That no plans nor sketches of the locus were put in evidence at the trial except the photographs numbered one to five accompanying this report. The X at the doorstep shown on photograph number 2 indicates where the dead body of Harvey Trenholm was found.

3. No exceptions have been taken to any feature of the trial and no proceedings in appeal, nor application for a reserved case has been made, and no such action is contemplated so far as I have had any information.

4. With reference to the exercise of clemency, should application be made, I regret to report that I cannot say anything in support thereof. The condemned man not only shot and killed Olive Trenholm, but he is also now under indictment for the murder, at the same time and place, of Harvey Trenholm, late husband of the murdered woman, a true bill having been found against him by the grand jury on that charge also.

5. Accompanying this report I beg to submit a stenographic report of the evidence taken at the trial, as well as the photographs before herein referred to.

I have the honour to be Sir, your obedient Servant Chief Justice Harrison A. McKeown.

Now that the trial was over and the guilty verdict demanded that Bennie be hanged by the neck until dead, the Sheriff had a lot of work to do. He had to apply for an act of clemency. It was just a formality but it had to be done. Chief Justice McKeown let him know that he would not be recommending clemency. At the same time, on May 1st, he took out a page of his personal stationary as High Sheriff and wrote to the Minister of Justice as follows.

Dear Sir,

On the 28th day of April last, Chief Justice McKeown, sentenced Bennie Swim to hang on the fifteenth day of July next for the murder of Olive Trenhom on the 27th day of March last. I understand that your department has an Official Hangman. If this is so I want to plan an application for his services on the 15th of July 1922. Kindly let me know what course it is necessary for me to take in order to have his services.

Signed Albion Foster

The Deputy Minister of Justice, Mr. M. Gallagher, promptly sent Sheriff Foster the following cable.

This department has no connection whatsoever with any hangman. All hangings or executions are to be dealt with at the provincial level and it is your, or someone designated by you (Sheriff Foster), responsibility to carry out the death penalty. Suggest you try the Sheriff of Montreal for information about hiring a competent Executioner.

Bennie Swim's "Insanity" Gets Attention

Sheriff Foster kept an eye on Bennie's crazy behaviour. After several weeks, he gave in. He had no experience in the matters of psychology and though he believed Bennie was faking insanity, he could not take the chance it might be real. Bennie would get what he wanted. A doctor would be brought in to examine him.

First, Doctor Griffin was called. He was the jailhouse doctor and more familiar with the whole case than any one else. He talked at length to all of the jail guard's, especially Moses Moore, who spent the most time with Bennie since he had been appointed the deathwatch guard. Moses Moore reported that after his fits Bennie often seemed to be in a state of near collapse. Dr. Griffin gave Bennie a thorough examination. He found that his heart was in bad condition and his temperature was elevated. Bennie's visitation rights were now denied, which didn't bother him. He didn't want to see anyone anyway. He stopped talking to the guards and attendants. He started sleeping on the floor under his cot with his head wrapped in a blanket. This behaviour worried Dr. Griffin so he began to visit Bennie daily. On one occasion Bennie was sitting on the floor in a rigid position but arose when the doctor asked him to do so in order to take his pulse.

Bennie began to refuse his daily meals. On one occasion, he was acting so badly that it took four men to hold him while the doctor quieted him with a sedative injection. At one point, he ate nothing but a banana for nearly a week. He continued like this for several more days and then began to eat a few slices of bread and drink some milk. Though he now became less violent, the doctor was convinced that Bennie needed to be examined by a psychiatrist. The execution would have to be postponed until a diagnosis was completed.

Dr. Griffin talked to the Sheriff, and a special request was sent to Chief Justice McKeown asking for his help in the matter. The request explained that since the trial Bennie Swim was acting insane and asked that someone with experience in such matters be obtained for a diagnosis. Dr. Griffin and the Sheriff wanted to keep it quiet so as not to alarm anyone, and also to have Bennie observed without him knowing about it. The Chief Justice considered the matter and had a meeting with the Attorney General. They decided to have a prominent psychiatrist examine Bennie.

The Attorney General sent for Dr. Stanley King, Head Psychiatrist at the Fairvale Provincial Hospital for the Insane in Saint John, New Brunswick. Dr. King agreed to take care of the matter and sent a letter to the Medical Superintendent of the Provincial Insane Asylum, a psychiatrist named J. V. Anglin. Dr. Anglin had over thirty years of experience dealing with the insane and had been the President of the American Psychiatric Association in 1918. If anyone could determine if Bennie was really insane or just acting, it would be him. He was dispatched to Woodstock in late May for an afternoon session with Bennie. Somehow, Bennie learned in advance he was going to be examined by a physiatrist, and when Dr. Anglin arrived Bennie turned up the act and gave the performance of his life. On June 1st, Dr. Anglin sent this report to Chief Justice McKeown.

I am submitting the following to the Attorney General (J.P. Byrne) of the Province. In compliance with the directions contained in your letter of May 29th, on May 31st, I made an examination of Bennie Swim confined in the Woodstock Jail, to ascertain his mental condition. It is my opinion that his mind is disordered to an extreme degree. There is no question to that except that he may be feigning insanity. In my opinion he is not shamming, strong as the incentive is for one in his predicament to do so, but this opinion could be substantiated only by having the man under observation for a prolonged period. I think he is not putting it on because he does not appear to be overdoing the part, as an imposter not familiar with the behaviour of the insane would be likely to do. Swim is sleeping well by night. He is not on the alert to show off before observers. On the second time I went in to see him, he was curled up on the stone floor of his cell sleeping and was not easily aroused. He could easily have heard me walking along the corridor for some forty feet before I reached the place where he was and been prepared to carry on. Further, there has been at least one lucid interval of several days duration since he first began acting strangely, in which his conduct was quite natural. It is doubtful if a feigner would show lucidity. I doubt, also his ability to play the part. The jail surgeon thought that the fact of his sleeping so much was suggestive of feigning. His mental trouble is not the maniacal type in which insomnia is prominent, but rather of the demented type. I think a man feigning insanity would assume wakefulness as far as possible. A scheming man would not likely sleep well. Moreover, he often sleeps by day as well as through the night. If this man had no motive to do so, I would not think of feigning in the case for a moment.

Before I saw this man, from what I had read and heard, I expected to find a creature in a state of frenzy over his impending fate. I found none of that. He sleeps well, he eats voraciously and there is nothing in his manner to suggest he is a worrier. Just what his thoughts are, none can say as he cannot be induced to speak. He has not the appearance of a melancholy man, but rather that of one whose mind is blank. He has the appearance of a groveling idiot; he suggests the brute rather than the human. He is rarely erect, most of the time he is on his knees crawling about, picking things off the floor and pulling them to shreds. For a long period of time, as I watched him, he worked at a cap as if wringing out a dishcloth. He is seldom still while awake. His breath is short, and with mouth open, he makes one think of a panting dog. He looked at me while I was examining him only once though he is not inattentive to sounds that he hears. For the most part, he seemed unaware of my presence. Sometimes he would growl when spoken to. He took a chew of tobacco and made free use of it, letting the juice drivel disgustingly down his chin, finally swallowing it. A cake that was given to him, he devoured almost without chewing as if he were famished. His hair is unkempt and his whole person untidy. He had on only trousers and a torn undershirt. Formerly, it is said that he was quite natty as to his dress. He showed no violent tendencies, other than to grip one's hand painfully, or clutch at ones clothing which he would have torn if allowed. He made extreme resistance when taken to be washed and resisted with equal vigour when being returned to his cell. It took three men to handle him in the toilet room. He was told that I had come to secure him a new trial and to get him his liberty, but such talk in no way affected him to all appearance. I am told that he has not recognized his mother on any of her visits.

The history given me by the Sheriff, is that Swim maintained self-control, until he was sentenced, and that immediately thereafter, he stormed and swore as if enraged and kept up this agitation for several days, refusing food, then the mutism followed which is to be observed now and persisted excepting during the brief interval above sited. It is not perfect because when he hears dogs bark at night, he will yell, "Get out." Just when the insanity began,

120

I cannot say and the agitation succeeding his being sentenced may have been no part of it. There is no doubt he has inherited mental instability and was a degenerate, and the bullet through his head, probably has had some share in inducing his present condition. Today I believe him to be insane in your legal sense, as well as in the medical. Recovery is a possibility.

I do not think there is a need of examination by other experts; the man is clearly demented. As I have said, there is a bare possibility of deception, but no expert could determine whether Swim is shamming or not, without an opportunity to observe him under all conditions for a length of time as he could be observed if he were, say in Dorchester Penitentiary. In my opinion, the case is a genuine one of mental disorder and his reason is in all probability permanently overthrown. If let, the man may live on indefinitely. My visit to the jail was unexpected; both by the officials thereof and by the inmates, so that no preparation was made for my coming and the condemned man did not know who I was. I had hoped to make other reports than this to you for I fear, eventually, the man will come to my care. I have too many of his kind now. However, I am doing my duty and giving you the facts impartially.

My credentials to those who do not know me are: Continuous experience in insane institutions since 1888, and the Presidency of the American Psychiatric Association, 1918.

Signed: Dr. J.V. Anglin, Medical Superintendent.

After Chief Justice McKeown saw this report, he was convinced that an application for commutation of the death sentence should be sent to the Minister of Justice in Ottawa. However, being a very cautious and thorough man, he requested another evaluation of Bennie and this time sent for Dr. King. While Dr. King had no doubt he could do a proper evaluation of the prisoner, he was in an uncomfortable situation; Dr. J.V. Anglin was technically his boss. But he had been asked by legal authorities to evaluate Bennie Swim so he would do just that. Hopefully, his views would be the same as Dr. Anglin's.

Dr. King spent more time with Bennie at the Woodstock Jail than had Dr. Anglin. Again, Bennie was not fooled. He knew Dr. King was also a psychiatrist and he gave him the same performance as he had given his predecessor. Bennie drooled, he ranted, he shook the bars on his cell, he preached to other prisoners, he crawled on the floor, he growled, and did anything else he could think of to act insane.

Dr. King spent much time talking to Sheriff Foster in order to learn more about the prisoner. The Sheriff told the doctor that it was around May 22nd that he became convinced Bennie's mind had become unhinged. Bennie seemed not to recognize anyone, including family members, and would rave about cattle and sheep in the grain. He began to sleep on the floor of his cell, and stopped paying attention to cleanliness and proper dress. His cell was unkempt, and he ate like a dog.

Dr. King was not totally convinced of Bennie's insanity, but he eventually wrote a report that stated he agreed with the assessment done by Dr. Anglin and put in a request that Bennie be committed to Dorchester Prison for a longer evaluation. He sent his report to Chief Justice McKeown, who in turn sent it to the Attorney General of New Brunswick, Mr. Byrne. Between them they came up with the decision to have the execution delayed and recommend that Bennie be sent to Dorchester Penitentiary for further evaluation.

The Chief Justice then sent a letter to the Minister of Justice in Ottawa requesting that Swim's sentence be commuted to life imprisonment, and if that was not acceptable, a delay for the execution until September 15th of 1922, so that further evaluation of the prisoners mental capabilities could be made. He included both Dr. King's report and that of Dr. Anglin. He also had it signed and noted by the Attorney General, who also gave his recommendations for a delay or commutation of the death sentence. Chief Justice McKeown, acting on his own authority, and believing that Ottawa would accept his recommendation, then informed Sheriff Foster on July 5th that the execution of Bennie Swim, would be delayed until September 15th.

On July 11th, Mr. Gallagher, Deputy Minister of Justice, sent a letter confirming that the Swim execution would be delayed until September 15th of 1922. It also stated that they would send their own doctors to evaluate Swim.

About this time, a registered package arrived in the Office of the Minister of Justice, Sir Lomar Gouin. It included a 38 five-shot revolver, several cartridges, and an accompanying note that stated.

This is the gun that was used in the killing of Harvey Trenholm and Olive Trenholm, by condemned prisoner Bennie Swim. The spent cartridges are still in the cylinders as when the gun was found, but the live cartridge that was also in the cylinder at the time, has been removed. Signed: K.C. Jones, Solicitor of Woodstock.

Bennie Plans an Escape

Before Sheriff Foster received an Official Notice of Acceptance that the date of the hanging would be delayed until September 15th, Bennie was very uncertain about his fate. He had done all he could to ensure that he would be found too insane to be executed, but he wasn't taking any chances. In June, The Daily Gleaner, a Fredericton newspaper, ran an article about Bennie stating he would not be hanged because he was insane. The story used Dr. Anglin's report as proof and included several names from the Provincial Authorities, such as the Attorney General Mr. Byrne and Chief Justice McKeown. The newspaper story reported that a letter would be sent to the Minister of Justice in Ottawa that would confirm his status as insane and therefore not able to be hanged. Instead, the report said his sentence would be commuted to life imprisonment and he would stay in the Provincial Insane Asylum until he was well enough to be sent to Dorchester Penitentiary for the remainder of his sentence.

Bennie's spirits soared for several days after he learned of this report, and he was back to his old self. He had done it, he thought; he had fooled not just one but two prominent doctors into believing he was insane. Then came the bad news. According to the Sheriff, the article was premature and not altogether accurate. Ottawa had not approved the recommendation and nothing had officially changed. Damn those reporters, he thought, messing with his life like that.

As the days wore on and he still had heard nothing from any of the authorities about what was going to happen to him, he was convinced that nothing had changed and he would still be hanged on the 15th of July. Since it was late June, he was now getting desperate, and his thoughts turned to escaping. All he would need to do was to somehow make it to the Mainstream. Once there, he could hide out in the woods for years, with lots of support from family and friends. He wouldn't be the first to do that. Everyone out there knew of someone's relative that had escaped justice by hiding out deep in the forest. By the time the law came looking for him, he would have plenty of warning and could evade them for as long as it took. But he had to get out of this damn jail first. He dreamed of escaping, but dreams aren't worth much. Bennie needed a plan and good luck.

Good luck came with the workmen who were hired to do general maintenance and any other repairs that the jail needed. The plumbers, especially, had the right tools and tools were what Bennie needed. He had also become familiar with the schedule of the guards, and he knew which ones were likely to take a snooze during the night shift. That was useful knowledge, but first, he still had to be able to get out of his cell.

He studied the bars on the door and figured that was not the way to go. It would take too long to saw through them, even if he had the tools. It would be near impossible to be able to do it without someone finding out. The bars on the window were also a problem. The bolts that held them on were too far away to reach. Even if he were able to remove the bolts or saw through the bars and get out, he would still only be in the courtyard, and then he would need to scale the fence. Anyone from the street would be able to see him, even if he did it late at night and that would look way too suspicious. The best way out was right through the front door.

Bennie began to study the cell door. He noticed that bolts held the cell door to the wall. If he could loosen them to the point where all that would be needed to force the door open was a strong push, he could open it anytime he wanted. There was still the locked cage at the end of the corridor. If he could loosen the bolts to that as well, he could also force it open. If he did it at the right time, all that would be left to do would be to overpower the guard at the end of the corridor, and he would be free. Once outside, he could have some prearranged help to pick him up and then he could make it to the Mainstream.

He thought this plan could work and was worth trying. So, now that he had a plan, it was urgent to put it in motion. Time was running out. It was getting too close to his execution date. He knew that the closer that date came, the more security would be increased, and his chances of pulling off a successful escape would be next to impossible. Things had to happen fast. First he needed to measure the size of the bolt heads. He put some paper up against them, and carefully traced their edges with a pencil. He wanted to be exact because he didn't want any more wrenches than necessary. When he had the opportunity, he looked carefully at the bolts on the door at the end of the corridor. As he had hoped, they were the same size.

Bennie sent a message to one of his uncles and arranged for a visit. When his uncle came to the jail, Bennie explained the situation in a hushed voice. He told his uncle what he needed, and when the guard wasn't looking, he slipped him the piece of paper with the bolt measurements on it. His uncle quietly nodded. He told Bennie not to worry; he would do what he could and would let him know on his next visit.

Later that day, Bennie's uncle stood across the street from the jail and waited. In late afternoon he saw the group of workmen leave the jail and head to a hotel for a few drinks. He sidled up to the bar and studied the men intently before choosing which one he would approach. Most of the workmen were happy with one or two drinks and soon the group thinned out as they each left for home. Bennie's uncle wasn't interested in them; they seemed too responsible. He wanted the one that stayed the longest and drank the most.

When he was left in the company of the last workman, he approached him and said, "Hello friend, can I buy you a drink?"

"Well of course," said the workman. "It would be rude to say no to such a kind offer."

After Bennie's uncle bought the man several more drinks, the two of them had become fast friends. The workman was glad to have met such a generous man, and when the conversation turned to his work in the prison, he was glad to talk in detail about it. He talked about the difficulties of the job and how skilled he was at his trade. Bennie's uncle lapped it up, feigning great interest. He kept the drinks flowing and the workman talking. When the workman was quite drunk but still somewhat coherent, Bennie's uncle offered to take him home in his wagon. The workman was grateful, as he didn't want to walk the long distance to his home in a drunken condition.

Bennie's uncle now got to the reason he was being so friendly. "I'll bet you sometimes forget and leave tools at the workplace, right?"

"It happens sometimes," said the workman. "Why do you ask?"

"Well," said Bennie's Uncle, making sure the workman could see him counting out several large bills before he continued, "How hard would it be for you to leave a wrench and a metal pipe at the worksite tomorrow?"

The workman was suspicious, but when he looked down at the bills and saw it was more than enough to ensure many nights like tonight, he warmed up to the proposition.

"It wouldn't be a problem, but I would only consider doing what you ask because you're such a good friend" he said, pocketing the bills.

Bennie's uncle clapped him on the back and promised to see him very soon so that they could enjoy another night in each other's company. He then gave the workman the measurement of the bolt heads for the wrench and the size of the metal pipe he wanted left behind. He explained where to leave them. When they reached the workman's home, they parted company with the promise to meet again.

The next day, Bennie's uncle paid the prisoner a morning visit and let him know what had been arranged. The workman did as he had promised;

he left the right size wrench and a metal pipe in the pre-arranged place. Bennie spied the tools in the late afternoon on the way back to his cell and, while the guard was distracted, quickly picked them up and hid them in his clothes. Bennie was ecstatic. This will work, he told himself over and over. When he got back to his cell, he hid the tools under his mattress. Step one complete, he thought; his uncle had really come through.

When the lights went out that night, Bennie stayed awake. He waited and waited until finally, a few hours before daylight, he heard the guard snoring at the end of the corridor. Now was the time. He got the wrench out and went to work on the cell door bolts. He was doing all right until one of the bolts squeaked loudly as it turned on its threads. Bennie nearly jumped out of his skin. He looked anxiously down the corridor. The guard gave a grunt, jerked his eyes open for a split second, and then continued snoring.

Bennie looked around his cell for something that might quiet the squeaking bolt. He saw his bar of soap and figured that might work. He scratched shavings off the bar and rubbed them all around the threads of the bolt. He turned the bolt back in so the soap would coat the threads of the hole. It worked well. Using this method, he was able to loosen the remaining bolts with hardly a sound. Step two complete, he thought. Next, he had to get to the bolts on the door at the end of the corridor. This would take more planning; he may even need to have help from another inmate. He considered which of his fellow prisoners could be trusted. He settled on a man called Chase, who had previously been in Dorchester Penitentiary for an extended period of time.

Chase was up for it. He liked antagonizing the guards whenever he had a chance, so he would gladly make a distraction when they were coming back from the exercise yard. As they entered the corridor, Chase set in to making a ruckus. When he refused to obey the guard's order to settle down, the other guard on duty came to help out. They manhandled the prisoner down to the floor, and with his hands cuffed behind his back, led him away to a segregation cell in another part of the jail. Chase continued to rant and tear. The guards, knowing they were responsible for the safety of their prisoner, stayed with him to calm him down and make sure he didn't hurt himself.

Bennie pulled out the wrench from where it was tucked in his belt under his shirt and quickly went to work on the bolts of the cage door. Luckily, they turned easily and he had them all lose in short order. He returned the wrench to where the workman had left it and went back to his cell. Now, all that had to be done was to tell his uncle that all was ready and decide when to make his escape. It had to be soon because the guards might notice the loosened bolts and all would be lost.

On his uncle's next visit they decided on the night of the June 27th for the escape. His uncle would wait close to the jail for Bennie to appear. He would have two fast horses saddled and ready to go. They would make a run for it. There was a lot of forest area near Woodstock where they could quickly disappear. They knew the trails and the old logging roads that would take them to the Mainstream.

Bennie was almost beside himself with anticipation. He tried hard not to show it and kept up his routine of insanity. On the Morning of the 27th, Bennie was given a bonus when the guard failed to properly close his cell door. Bennie then jammed a small piece of wood in the lock mechanism, so it wouldn't latch even when shut all the way. It was like God was helping him out. Now all he had to do was wait for night to come when only one guard would be on duty.

* * * * *

Two of Bennie's fellow prisoners, William Scott and Robert Irvine, did not like jail one bit. They were farm boys who had done a very stupid thing. Generally good and law-abiding citizens, they had gone on a drinking spree. When their money ran out they decided to replenish it by robbing a shop. What they didn't know was that the shopkeeper never left any money in the till overnight. When they didn't find any money, they took what they felt would sell quickly. They took dozens of cartons of cigarettes. Someone saw them, and they were arrested before they had a chance to do anything with the cigarettes.

When they sobered up, they found themselves in front of a judge being sentenced to two years in the Woodstock Jail. Time went very slowly for the boys. They hated being in jail. They were used to life on the farm, and they wanted to get back there. They were not even half way through their sentence when something happened that they could take advantage of and shorten their sentences considerably. The night Bennie was loosening the bolts of his door, Robert Irvine heard the loud squeak coming from the direction of Bennie's cell. He didn't think much about it at the time, but the next day he told his friend, William Scott. They figured Bennie was up to something and decided to watch him closely.

They soon noticed an iron pipe barely visible under the end of Bennie's mattress. They figured he was going to try to escape. They also knew what happened to inmates who squealed on other prisoners. They had been in jail long enough to know what would happen if they were caught doing that. Was it worth the risk? It would be if warning the Sheriff got them out of jail. They asked to speak to Sheriff Foster. When asked what about, they wouldn't say. They told the guard they would only speak to the Sheriff and no one else. They insisted it was really important,. Finally, the guard agreed and the Sheriff was summoned. To make sure that none of the other inmates knew that Scott and Irvine were talking to the Sheriff, they were both taken to a room in another part of the jail.

Sheriff Foster looked at them and could see by the expression on their faces that something important was going on. Irvine began with his story that he had first heard a loud screeching noise coming from Swim's cell late one night. He went on to say that he then saw Swim working on the bolts to his cell door and later on the cage door at the end of the corridor. Scott picked up the rest of the story. He said they wouldn't have said anything except he also knew that Bennie had an iron pipe under his mattress and probably intended to attack the guard on night watch in order to escape.

The Sheriff was incredulous. If this was true, these inmates could very well have saved a guard's life and prevented the escape of one of Carleton County's most dangerous men. He also knew what their fate would be if any of the other prisoners found out what they had told him. Since they were in jail for a minor crime, he was sure he could to get them released immediately with a call to Chief Justice McKeown. First he had to determine if they were telling the truth. He summoned a guard and told him to remove Bennie from his cell to another part of the jail and stand guard over him until further notice. Leaving the two young men in the room, Sheriff Foster went to Bennie's cell, and sure enough, the bolts had all been loosened. He pushed against the cell door from the inside and realized that with a modest amount of strength the door could easily be opened. He then noticed the piece of wood jammed in the lock mechanism. When he turned up the mattress on Bennie's bed there was the iron pipe, right where Scott had said it was.

Sheriff Foster, now thoroughly alarmed, walked to the end of the corridor where he saw the bolts on the cage door had also been loosened. He immediately called for a workman to repair the doors of the cage and Bennie's cell. Next he called Chief Justice McKeown and explained the situation. He asked for immediate release of Irvine and Scott, explaining how they had helped thwart an escape as well as possibly saving the life of a guard. He explained that when word got out that they had talked to the Sheriff about Bennie's escape plan, they would be in grave danger from the other prisoners. Chief Justice McKeown agreed to call the Attorney General and get back to him.

Within the hour, the Sheriff had permission to release William Scott and Robert Irvine. With that taken care of, he went back to the room and told the two inmates they would be released immediately. They breathed a sigh of relief and went back to their cells to collect their belongings. Word quickly spread through the jail that an escape attempt had been thwarted because someone had warned the Sheriff. When the other prisoners saw Irvine and Scott being released, they knew it had to be them. As the two young men were walking down the corridor with their belongings, inmate Chase got their attention with a slashing motion of his finger across his throat. They knew what that meant. If they ever returned to the Woodstock Jail, Chase would be waiting for them. (Robert Irvine and William Scott were never in trouble with the law again. They went back to their farms and became model citizens for the rest of their lives.)

After the release of Irvine and Scott, Sheriff Foster ordered that Bennie be brought to his office. Bennie knew immediately what it was about and was worried he might now be punished severely for his attempt to escape. He knew county jails practiced corporal punishment and he was afraid he might be flogged. Surprisingly, the Sheriff did not have this in mind. He wanted to know how Bennie had gotten the wrench to loosen the bolts and the iron bar. Bennie refused to tell him, and that was that. Sheriff Foster decided not to punish him. He understood why Bennie had tried to escape. In less than three weeks, Bennie would be executed; that was punishment enough.

Bennie went back to his cell and stayed there. He lay on his cot the rest of the day and night and refused all meals. He was very depressed; all that planning and work and being so close to actually escaping, and now, nothing; just waiting to die. It occurred to him he could tell his uncle how the escape plan had been foiled and who had ratted on him, but he knew what his uncle would likely do. While it was a pleasant thought that Irvine and Scott would be made to suffer the consequences of their actions, the last thing he wanted was for his uncle to end up here with a charge of aggravated assault, or worse. No, he would just lie on his cot and take what was coming to him like a man.

*   *   *   *   *

Near the end of June, Chase came to Bennie with some advice. Bennie thanked him for what he had done in distracting the guards.

"Listen Bennie," Chase said in low voice. "All is not lost; there are still ways to get out of jail if you want to. It just takes being really creative. I want you to know that if Irvine and Scott ever show up where I'm at, I'll take care of them for you, OK? Now, don't stop with the insane act. It could still work. I know you're running out of time, so here's something else to think about. When I was in Dorchester Pen, a guy escaped by faking the symptoms of appendicitis. He was taken to the hospital in town for an operation, and that's where he made his escape. Even with a guard, that's the easiest place to escape from. The guy was eventually caught, and he told me what the symptoms were. It's easy to fake and a sure way to get you to the hospital. If you're interested I can tell you."

Bennie was interested. For the first time since his escape was thwarted, he had hope again. Chase was right about the appendicitis trick. Bennie followed his instruction about the symptoms. On June 30th, Bennie complained of severe pain in his right side below his chest. He had also swallowed soap shavings that induced vomiting and produced a fever. He complained of severe diarrhoea and of being exhausted. Doctor Griffin was called to examine Bennie. When asked what exactly was going on, Bennie related all the symptoms for appendicitis. Dr. Griffin didn't hesitate with the diagnosis and with what needed to be done.

"This man needs an operation and fast," he told the Sheriff. "Without an operation, he'll die."

Sheriff Foster was conflicted; he thought this might be another trick. But he would be in serious trouble if it wasn't and Bennie died from not having the operation. You don't refuse the orders of the jailhouse doctor without serious repercussions.

Sheriff Foster replied to the doctor in a loud voice so Bennie could hear him, "If he needs an operation, fine, but it's going to be done here in his cell."

The doctor was stunned; an operation in a jail cell? There was no way he was going to do that. The lack of sterilization would probably kill the patient. He told the Sheriff he could only do the operation safely in the hospital, and if it was to be done that's how it had to be. Dr. Griffin got up and motioned for the Sheriff to follow him to another area of the jail. He wanted to tell the Sheriff in private why he could not do the operation in the jail, but the Sheriff first quickly explained the reason he had wanted Bennie to hear him say the operation had to be performed in the cell; he might be faking in order to get to the hospital and try another escape. The doctor understood but was convinced Bennie was really sick and not faking. He again told the Sheriff he was sure that Bennie was suffering from appendicitis and needed an operation.

When Dr. Griffin and the Sheriff went back to check on the patient, Bennie had made a miraculous recovery, even asking for something to eat.

Dr. Griffin was angry with himself for being fooled by Bennie's appendicitis act, but it was very convincing and doctors are trained not to take chances. Bennie did not come up with any more plans to escape. Sheriff Foster increased security around Bennie at all times; he was not taking any chances.

Bennie settled into the realization that he would soon die. He took Judge McKeown's advice and began to renew his religious faith. He became a model prisoner. He spent as much time as possible with the clergymen Perley Quigg and Hedley Bragdon. He attended all the religious services that were offered in the jail. His mood was better and for the most part a quiet acceptance of his fate seemed to come over him. This didn't, however, mean he slept better. He was still having nightmares about the impending hanging. He had heard about hangings and often would dream about the rope tightening around his neck and the trap door opening. He woke up screaming and covered in sweat. The other inmates were disturbed by Bennie's ordeal, but the jail guards figured it was a good deterrent for any of the prisoners who might one day consider murdering someone.

On July 5th, the Federal Deputy Minister of Justice, Mr. Gallagher, sent a letter to New Brunswick Attorney General, Mr. Byrne, informing him that the request for a delay of the execution of Bennie Swim was granted and the new date for the execution was September 15th, 1922. Mr. Gallagher also wrote that they would be sending their own psychiatrist to examine the prisoner. The Attorney General sent a cable, asking for confirmation of the new date. He received a reply from Ottawa on July 9th confirming the execution delay and the new date for the execution.

Ottawa Sends a Psychiatrist
to Examine Bennie

It is not known what Dr. Anglin and Dr. King thought when they learned that their examination of Bennie Swim was not sufficient to convince the Minister of Justice in Ottawa that Bennie was insane. They almost certainly would have been put out since it was basically telling them their professional judgments were not acceptable. If Ottawa wanted to send their own doctors to Woodstock, so be it. They would certainly confirm the diagnosis of Bennie Swim's insanity.

In early August, a man showed up at the Woodstock Jail. He made his credentials known only to the Sheriff. He was given free reign of the jail and made the most of it. The guards were annoyed by his mysterious presence, but he ignored them. When they confronted the Sheriff, they were told only to allow the man to do whatever he wanted. The man was Dr. Phelan, a prominent psychiatrist from Kingston Ontario. He was very familiar with the behaviour of inmates trying to get out of jail by acting insane. He had seen a lot of such faking in the penitentiary at Kingston and knew what to watch for. His report would say it all. After spending several days in Woodstock, Dr. Phelan sent his report on August 7th to the Minister of Justice in Ottawa, Sir Lomar Gouin.

Sir:

In accordance with instructions, I made an examination of Bennie Swim, now a prisoner in Woodstock Gaol, under sentence of death. In view of the nature of the crime, and the many persons apparently interested in establishing some mental defect in the prisoner, I gave him more than ordinary professional attention in the matter of examination.

The prisoner is well developed physically; never sick in his life, has a fair education as far as reading and writing are concerned, has neither hallucinations, delusions or illusions, and responds intelligently to all my questions put to him. He was negative to all tests for insanity. He sleeps and eats well, but so far as sleep is concerned he has nothing else to do, and therefore, as he says, finds it an easy method to pass away the time, which he finds very slow going. He therefore wishes to get out so that he may go back on the farm to engage in ploughing. A very sensible remark.

Moses Moore, the guard over him since incarcerated, has known him for many years, and says there never was anything noticed in his conduct or actions--he acted like other men always, but his method of existence at home was not far removed from that of the ordinary animal, and living in open concubinage with the girl he murdered, and known to all the country around and the contiguous villages, the tragedy may be considered the result of a depraved rather than a diseased mind.

Since his sentence, he now and then affects antics which he imagines conform to some variety or phase of insanity. Though in prison some time before, he never attempted these manifestations till after his sentence. On being asked why he does these things, he replied that he was told to act silly as the only means of escape. A convict called Chase, who comes from Dorchester Penitentiary, and consequently up to all the tricks of prison life, coached him, and I understand that he had other advice to act the silly part. On my examination, I discovered that the silly acts which he performed were at will and for effect; all feigned, and consequently devoid of every shade of insanity. If a free man, there would be no more simulation.

His deathwatch, Mr. Moore, has given special attention to the prisoner's mental condition since, and though he fooled him, as he did also one of his spiritual advisors, Reverend L.J. Alley, his medical advisor, Dr. Griffin, High Sheriff Foster, and Deputy Sheriff Mooers, there appears to be an unanimity of opinion amongst them now, that he is a faker. This is in agreement with my findings, though they do not know it.

The prisoner has a motive; there is no history of mental affliction in the family, or in himself previous to the commission of the crime; he overacts his part and frequently does not know what to do, to act; he acts when he thinks that he is watched; he forgets sometimes, and speaks quite rationally and then he is ashamed of himself; his skin gets hot and perspires, whereas the skin of a lunatic is always dry and harsh, as the acts are performed without an effort.

In my five interviews with him, he talked and laughed and was very sensible; in my sixth visit to him he began to suspect and at once affected a few movements which were feigned. The prisoner's recent attempt to escape, which was cleverly conceived and almost successfully executed, proved him to be very clever, and far from being insane—indeed the conception showed much intelligence. High Sheriff Foster believes him to be more a knave than a fool.

The prisoner also feigned appendicitis recently, and so cleverly did he stage all the symptoms that the doctor diagnosed gangrenous appendicitis—a fatal disease without an operation. It was proposed to take him to the Hospital in the town, but the Sheriff said, if an operation is to be performed, it will be done in his cell. The prisoner was up and walking around in an hour, perfectly well, asking for something to eat, as he had been on a low diet for three days prior to the doctor's examination. This episode does not indicate a diseased mind.

Again, he is calling attention to the bullet wound in his brain inflicted by himself, as causing him trouble, but I gave the matter a looking into, and I found that the wound is only a scalp wound of no significance whatever—the brain was never touched. The wound has long ago healed.

He also has feigned all along that he could not write, but the day of my examination of him he wrote a very intelligent letter to his mother and asked her to come and see him. He was quite anxious that no one would see his writing, as he was supposed to have written, "Good bye Olive Swim and Sleep" on a piece of paper after the tragedy, but always said that he could not write. The writing in the letter to his mother is the same as that on the piece of paper.

The tragedy was premeditated, carefully planned and with a motive; the revolver being thrown away to avoid detection, thus unlike a lunatic.

I do not find, therefore, that the prisoner Bennie Swim is labouring under a disease of the mind to such an extent as to be incapable of appreciating the fact that he has been convicted for the crime of murder, and sentenced to death. Therefore, if out in the world, and detained for examination as to his mental condition, he manifests no definite symptoms which could form the basis for the regular Certificate required for admission to an Asylum for the insane.

I have the honour to be, Your Obedient Servant:
Signed Dr. D Phelan

When the Deputy Minister of Justice in Ottawa, Mr. Gallagher, read this report, he didn't know what to think. He now had the reports of three prominent psychiatrists, two from New Brunswick and the latest from Dr. Phelan of Kingston. Someone had clearly gotten this very wrong. How could two reports say that Bennie Swim was a complete lunatic and another one say he was intelligent and completely sane? Did the prisoner stop acting for the benefit of Dr. Phelan, or was there some ulterior motive that the doctors in New Brunswick had for saying that Bennie was a lunatic. Maybe they needed patients, maybe they were opposed to the death penalty, and this was a way of preventing another execution. Maybe they were just easily fooled. Whatever the reason, he now had to send another psychiatrist to Woodstock to examine Bennie Swim and it had to be someone with impeccable credentials. He settled on Dr. Devlin from Saint Jean de Dieu Hospital in Montreal, one of the most prominent psychiatrists in the country. Dr. Devlin couldn't go immediately but he could do the examination in the third week of August.

Bennie's lawyer, Mr. Squires, had been doing what he could for his client. When he heard about Bennie's efforts to show he was insane and the attempt to escape, he felt that his client should be told where he stood with the impending execution. Mr. Squires attempts to find out fell on deaf ears, so, taking the bull by the horns, he wrote a letter to the Minister of Justice in Ottawa on August 21 1922.

Dear Sir:

In Reference Bennie Swim

I am writing to know what steps are intended to be taken with reference to the above matter. I may say that I was named by Chief Justice McKeown to act as Attorney for Bennie Swim in his trial here. Since sentence was pronounced upon him he has been acting in an insane manner, so that when Doctor Anglin of the Provincial Asylum visited him, it was his opinion that Swim was insane. He was to have been executed on July 15th. He was reprieved until September 15th. After his violent attacks, he seems to have had a semi-lucid interval. In fact, he was in this latter condition at the time of the reprieve. Lately he seems to have reverted to his more violent condition. I wish you would be good enough let me know at the earliest possible date what the status of his case is.

Respectfully, Frederick Charles Squires, Attorney

The office of the Minister of Justice replied quickly and tersely. "You'll know when we know."

Dr. F. Devlin came to Woodstock and spent several days doing interviews, both in the jail and outside of it. For this case he felt it was necessary to talk to several members of Bennie's immediate family before he talked to Bennie. He was also given free reign of the jail and all the guards were told to provide him with any information he requested. Except for the Sheriff, no one knew exactly who he was, by what authority he was acting, or why he was there. He also did something that none of the other doctors considered. He suspected that Bennie might have a mental defect due to syphilis, so he had Bennie tested for the disease. When he felt he had enough information, he made his report to the Minister of Justice in Ottawa.

Sir: In accordance with your instructions, I have the honour to report that I have examined the condemned prisoner, Bennie Swim, now confined in the jail at Woodstock, New Brunswick. My study of the case consisted in making an examination, observation and interrogatory of Bennie Swim, and of making an interrogatory of the Officers of Justice in contact with him since his crime. Those include: the High Sheriff of Carleton County, Mr. A.R. Foster; his Deputy, Mr. H.B. Mooers; the jail physician, Dr. T.W. Griffin; and Mr. Moses Moore, the Deathwatch. I also made an interrogatory and observation of his father, William Swim, his mother, sister, brother and cousin at their places of residence about twenty miles from Woodstock.

On my first examination on Saturday morning, the 19th of August, instance of Bennie Swim. I invited him to be as frank with me as I would be with him, and I told him, my name, my profession, and the object of my mission — to inquire into his mental condition. At first he made a few untrue statements, which were that he had been arrested for a debt of $4. And he had been in jail for thirty days. This was the only time he made any attempt at feigning whilst I was in contact with him. I again asked him to *be frank with me and proceeded to question him as to the details of the crime for which he had been condemned. He, in answer to my questions, gave me a coherent and connected story, in which all the facts he narrated about his movements on the day of the tragedy, from the time he left home until he was lodged in jail, were true. The distortion he made of the facts as told in court was in regard to the death of his victims.*

At this point of interrogatory his answers led me to believe that the woman, Olive Swim, was shot in the house by Trenholm, his other victim. He also said that Trenholm shot him (the prisoner) and that Trenholm was subsequently shot by the accidental discharge of the revolver in one of the scuffles between himself and Trenholm. The nature of the replies made in reference to the actual cause of the death of his victims was of a character to entirely free him (the condemned man), from any blame.

His statements regarding the crucial moments of the crime, that of the deaths of his victims, were, in the light of the evidence submitted to the court, absolutely false, but they were not those of an insane mind, they were simply, in my opinion the utterances of a condemned man prompted by a motive of self-preservation, or shame, or by both.

Immediately after this my first examination of the prisoner, the Sheriff, Mr. Foster, informed me that Bennie Swim, had spoken of the murders prior to his trial, but had not alluded to them subsequently until the moment of this interrogatory. Doctor Griffin, the Jail Physician, also informed me that the version given me of the crime, corresponded to the one given him by Bennie Swim prior to his trial, and at a time when there was no question whatsoever of the sanity of the accused.

I saw Bennie Swim twice again on Saturday and twice on Sunday, and again on Monday. He was at all these further interviews clear and collected and never showed the slightest sign of insanity. He freely admitted that he had been feigning. He said that he was told to do so by the other prisoners and that they told him what to do. It is my impression that this statement may be partly true, but not wholly so. To the question, "When you grew tired going around on the floor, what did they tell you?" His answer, "They told me to do something else." Question: "Did you ever tell them you were tired of acting?" Answer; "Yes Sir." Question: "Why did you tell them you were tired of playing the fool?" Answer: "Because I was tired, I told them I was going to quit and they told me I was a damn fool, and to keep on. At last I got tired of it and I came out here, (meaning the corridors outside the cell) and got a shave, a wash, and a cleanup. They (meaning the other prisoners) told me to start again." Question: "What did you do?" Answer: "Preach, pray and swear, rattle the bed, and crawl on the floor. They told me to do it all the time. I swore a little, but not on that account." (Here the prisoner referred to being deceived by the other prisoners.) Question: "You rattled the bed a little?" Answer: "Very little; I told them I was making a damn fool of myself."

In speaking of the escape planned from jail, Bennie Swim places all the blame on the other prisoners, and stated they were in on the plot as well as himself; that he at the last moment had rapped on the bars of another cell in order to inform the officer on watch. I questioned him about his boyhood, life and habits, to all of which he gave clear answers. I was informed by the officers of the jail that prior to his condemnation, whilst in prison, he was clean and even particular about his appearance, and this, I was subsequently informed at his home, was characteristic of him. He was quite clean and smart looking during the last two days I observed him.

Recently he has been writing letters home in which he gives expression to a very natural feeling of a healthy mind, the feeling of lonesomeness. I enclose a letter written by him to his cousin. It contains some mistakes in spelling which I attribute to his lack of education. But the letter is most sensible and expresses a very natural wish to hear news of home.

Bennie Swim's letter to his cousin Hattie Idella Swim, Daughter of his uncle, Edward Swim, written on August 17th. Re-written as is with no corrections.

well my dear cousin hattie I thought I wood right and find out how yous all are well hattie I am ofel lomson and I wont you to right to me and tell me how yous all are I wood like to see you so I cood talk to you and tell you some lies out of your cop well I ges chances are slime well hattie right and tell me how yous all are and when you are goning to get marrid and I ges I will close for this time so good by from Bennie I will send yous all the best of wishes Signed: Bennie Swim

My interrogatory and observations of the family of the condemned man, revealed a state of moral callousness but not of insanity in their mental makeup. The parents were either so indifferent that they never tried to see the marriage certificate of their son, and the woman, Olive Swim, his cousin, or, they knew that no such certificate existed. In any case, they allowed this couple to live under their roof as man and wife.

In order to check up the possibility of syphillis existing in Bennie Swim, Dr. Griffin, at my request, took a sample of the prisoner's blood, which was sent to Dr. M.L. Abramson, the Government Pathologist at Saint John New Brunswick, who sent me a report to the effect that his blood is free from any contamination by that disease. Dr. Griffin's report of his physical condition, and my own observation in that regard, likewise failed to reveal any serious physical illness.

I have failed to detect any delusions, hallucinations, or any form of mental aberration in the mind of the accused. He has admitted to me that he feigned insanity subsequent to his trial. He can think intelligently, speak coherently, and acts sensibly when he so desires, as he has demonstrated to me during my study of his mental condition. I am therefore of the opinion that he is not insane, but that he is of sound mind and fully understands the nature and quality of his acts.

I have the honour to be, your obedient servant, signed: Dr. F. Devlin. Report dated August 23 1922.

So, that was it. With two psychiatrists declaring him insane and two declaring him sane, the Minister of Justice in Ottawa would trust the doctors his office had contracted to examine Bennie Swim. As far as the Government of Canada was concerned, Bennie was now officially declared sane. He could be legally hanged.

Sheriff Foster was still waiting to be informed by the Minister of Justice about their decision on Bennie's case. He wrote a letter of inquiry about the same time as Dr. Devlin's report arrived in Ottawa.

To Deputy Minister of Justice, Ottawa Ont.

Dear Sir   Re: Bennie Swim

This man is confined in the county Gaol at Woodstock, N.B under sentence of death, to be carried out on the 15th of September. I understand that your department is investigating the question of his mental condition.

Will you please advise me at the earliest possible moment of the decision arrived at, so that I may make all arrangements for the execution, if necessary. The time is growing short and I naturally would like to hear as early as possible.

Will you also give me any necessary instructions and send me any papers which it may be necessary for me to have. I can, of course, prepare those for which the forms are given in the Code. Is a death warrant sent me? I can find no provision for it in the Code, and presume that the sentence of the court is my authority.

Yours truly, Albion Foster August 23, 1922.

The Deputy Minister of Justice, Mr. Gallagher, was quick with his reply. He sent a cable in which he stated that the law must take its course, the sentence of the court is to be upheld, and the execution is to be performed under local authority.

Sheriff Foster Widens the Search for a Hangman

Sheriff Foster now had to secure a competent hangman to perform the execution. It seemed like a simple matter. He would apply for the services of the most famous and experienced hangman in Canada, Arthur Ellis, or Arthur English as he was also called. Arthur Ellis had been the official hangman since 1913 when he replaced John Radcliffe who died from cirrhosis of the liver in 1911. But he hit a snag when he found out that Arthur Ellis had recently been charged with assaulting his wife and was temporarily removed from duty as Canada's official hangman. The Sheriff had sent Mr. Ellis fifty dollars as a retainer as was the custom for a hanging, before he learned that the hangman was no longer on the job. Mr. Ellis had been ordered by the court to give his wife a certain amount of money every week, but he was not happy with that arrangement and fled the Montreal area. Ellis, however, did return the fifty dollars to Sheriff Foster.

When the Sheriff received the money, he realized he had to find another hangman. With the removal of Ellis, the Minister of Justice in Ottawa decided they would no longer have an Official Hangman for the country and all executions would be the responsibility of local authorities and be done on an ad hoc basis. The Sheriff was informed that hangmen were now being contracted out of the Bordeaux prison in Montreal, so it was there he applied.

He was referred to a man called Scott. When he attempted to retain this person as the hangman, he received a letter back from Mr. Scott saying he would not be able to perform the execution because he was relocating to British Colombia. Mr. Scott then referred the Sheriff to a man called Holmes in Montreal. The prison officials in Montreal also recommended Mr. Holmes as a competent executioner. Mr. Holmes agreed to the request and the Sheriff was satisfied that all the arrangements were now in place. Sheriff Foster sent Mr. Holmes a retainer of fifty dollars.

Capital punishment had been practiced in Canada since the 1700s when those condemned would be hanged in a variety of ways. At first, the logistics were not well attended to, and all it took was a rope with a slipknot coiled thirteen times. But even that was often ignored as it worked just as well with five coils. The noose was placed around the prisoner's neck and they would be hauled up and left to dangle until dead. Often they would stay suspended for hours or days after they died as a reminder to the public of what would happen to those who committed violent crimes. Hangings were commonly done from the yardarm of a ship, if one was available, but just as often outside the local jail. In the early days the only documentation of the event would be a notice recorded in a journal, or perhaps a newspaper account.

Later on, another method was used. A heavy weight would be attached to the other end of the rope and dropped from the scaffold. The condemned man or woman would be jerked upwards hopefully snapping the neck. This was thought to be a more humane technique. The problem with this method, however, was that it looked absolutely appalling when the condemned person swung around like a fish caught on a line. It was soon discarded and the hangmen moved on to the method of using the drop through a trap door.

Hanging a person is not very difficult. Proper hangings start with weighing the prisoner to determine the length of rope needed from the condemned person's neck to the drop point. The formula was to take the person's weight in pounds, less 14 pounds for the head, and divide the remaining amount into 1020. If a person weighed 200 pounds, less 14 for the head, the hangman would divide 1020 by the 186 and get a rope length of 5 1/2 feet. The rope would be tied to the cross bar on the scaffold and the noose placed around the prisoners neck so the lower part of the knot of the noose was on the left side of the neck, just below the left ear. The trap door would be held with a greased slide that when pulled by means of a lever would instantly release the trap door. The prisoner would drop immediately and the neck would snap, killing him instantly. That is, if all went well. If the calculation were wrong and the drop too long, the person could be decapitated. If the rope were too short the neck would not break and the condemned would strangle slowly causing pain until he died.

There is no consistent time it takes for a person to die by hanging, but once the person dropped, a doctor takes the pulse every five minutes until the prisoner is officially declared dead. The original idea of hanging as a form of execution was said to be because a hanged man was not allowed to enter the kingdom of heaven, since Judas Iscariot hanged himself over the remorse he felt for having betrayed Jesus. However, it became the custom to have a clergyman present at each hanging to give the condemned person a last chance at repentance and redemption, or comfort if he or she had already repented. The records kept for hangings in Canada are seriously inaccurate and sometimes simply non-existent. For this reason, it is impossible to know exactly how many people have been hanged in Canada, but a reasonable estimate would be far more than the seven hundred recorded since Confederation in 1867, after which more accurate records were kept.

Jails were the most common place for executions. A scaffold would be built each time in the jail-yard and removed as soon as the hanging was over. Hangings were public events until January of 1869. From then until 1935, they were by invitation only. While not openly public after that, they were still easy to view because jail-yards were often in close proximity to a street. Attempts were sometimes made to restrict the view, but it was often difficult to effectively do so. Even with a fence surrounding the scaffold, the hanging was rarely completely obstructed from public view. Some people would even climb trees and telephone poles to watch a hanging take place.

For the hangmen, it was a profitable job as long as there were enough hangings to keep him busy. When an experienced hangman could not be found, a fellow convict would sometimes perform the hanging in exchange for a reduced sentence. In 1882, Canada opted for an official hangman who would be paid on a yearly basis. The first official hangman was John Radcliffe who had gained his experience in the British Navy. From the accounts written about him he was an unhappy and arrogant man who spent most of his time before and after each hanging drinking heavily and boasting about his job.

The law at the time stated that the clothes of the executed man were to be offered to the hangman as a bonus. Radcliff was known to sell this clothing to augment his income. He even tried to pass off sections of rope as the rope that was used in the hanging. This was a scam because the rope was never given to the hangman; the jail officials usually destroyed it. That didn't stop the enterprising Radcliffe. He was caught buying rope in a hardware store, and if he hadn't been recognized and stopped, it was expected he would have tried to sell it.

John Radcliffe was not one to use an alias as most other hangmen did at the time. He boasted to all who would listen about his job and was regarded as a pariah. This stigma didn't stop many others from wanting to be a hangman, but most of them will never be known by their real names because they used aliases. Arthur Ellis, also a heavy drinker, took over from Radcliffe as official hangman in 1913. He was the first hangman to go on strike when the government of Canada decided, with Radcliffe gone, it would now pay a hangman on a per hanging basis. Ellis refused to perform any more hangings and the government went back to giving him a retainer of $700 dollars a year. He carried on until his assault charge when he was banned from the job until the government realized his skills were needed and he was reinstated.

So this was the situation Sheriff Foster had to deal with. He really didn't like hangings in general, but, as Sheriff, it was his duty to make sure that a prisoner, once condemned to die in his county, would be hanged properly. He was confident that Mr. Holmes, with his recommendations, would do it right. One final detail remained to be completed. He still had not received permission from the Minister of Justice, Lomar Gouin, for the execution. With the delay in the execution date and the additional examinations of Bennie, the situation was confusing. While Deputy Minister Gallagher had given his permission, Sheriff Foster believed he still had to have the permission of the Minister.

Sheriff Foster had something else to decide. While it was legal and acceptable to have the hanging attended by certain invited individuals, he did not want the hanging made into a public spectacle. He was a pious and God-fearing man and had no respect for those who would find enjoyment in watching a hanging, even if a feeling of revenge by certain family members of the victims could be justified. It would be bad enough if everything went well, but he had heard of many hangings that did not go well. Decapitation or slow strangulation was always a hazard. Many things could go wrong and he was not interested in having Bennie's hanging become a source of entertainment. He planned to do everything in his power to keep the hanging as private as possible.

This would be no easy task. First of all, there would be the newspaper reporters to deal with. They were not going to let such a great paper-selling story as the hanging of Bennie Swim pass by unnoticed and unreported. No sir! They had been following this case since it was first discovered, and they had been making sure their readers knew everything about it that had been found out. The hanging would be the grand finale and the newspaper reporters were primed to make the most of it.

The date of the hanging was still September 15th, and the Press had made sure everyone who lived within a thousand miles of Woodstock was fully informed on the case. Sheriff Foster decided to invite only public officials and official representatives of the Press. This would satisfy his responsibility to the public and the interests of the newspapers. He would send out notices to these parties that the hanging would take place at 5 a.m. on the morning of September 15th. He figured this early morning hour, long before the public would be out and about on the streets of Woodstock, would prevent the hanging from becoming a spectacle. The Press accepted this arrangement. A 5 a.m. hanging would enable them to get a full report of all the grim and gruesome details out to their papers early in the day. The story might even make it into afternoon editions, which would be satisfying their readers as soon as possible.

In addition, the Sheriff decided to make sure the scaffold was built well inside the prison fence. He also had planking installed to cover and extend the height of the fence so the view of the jail yard would be completely obstructed. With all this taken care of, he was satisfied he had made all the arrangements to ensure the execution would be as shielded from view as much possible. What he had not fully calculated was word of mouth in the community. That was something he had no control over. For now, he was satisfied he had done everything he could to make sure the hanging would go as properly and discretely as possible.

Mary Kierstead Boyd Goes to Jail

On September 1st of 1922, Sheriff Foster got a telephone call; a woman had just murdered her two children. He couldn't believe his ears. Not again, he thought; another double murder in his county. What was going on? Although he now had experience in such matters, he was not happy to learn that a whole terrible ordeal of this sort would have to be dealt with again. Bennie Swim wasn't yet hanged and now he might have to go through the same thing all over again. But a woman! This was something different. Very few women had been hanged in Canada, These rare cases were usually for killing a lover or an abusive husband and often with alcohol as a catalyst. This woman, he had been told, had killed her children. There would be no sympathy from a jury, that's for sure.

The Sheriff dreaded the thought of how another hanging would affect his nerves. Bennie Swim would be the third hanging he had to participate in. The first was George Gee in 1904 and then Thomas Cammack in 1905. He was only the Deputy Sheriff for those two hangings but it had been very hard on him. Those were long ago and by now he had many more years of experience. The effect on him of those hangings diminished with the passage time, but he would never forget them. Now he had to face the prospect of two hangings close together. Well, he was the Sheriff and he had to do his job.

Once again he contacted his deputy and the other necessary individuals and set out for the Boyd place. When he arrived, Mr. Allan Boyd, the husband and father, led him into the bedroom where two of his four children lay murdered. A young girl and boy lay on the bed, blood all over the sheets from what looked like severe head wounds. Mary Boyd was crying softly in the corner and staring at the bodies of her young children. The Sheriff ordered her outside, placed her in handcuffs and had Deputy Mooers keep her under guard. He then went about the difficult task of helping the coroner and the doctor get the bodies ready for transport. The undertaker arrived shortly and the bodies of the two children, Charlie and Myrtle, were loaded up and taken for autopsy. Sheriff Foster took Mary Boyd to the Woodstock Jail.

As they traveled back to Woodstock, Mary Boyd talked incessantly about a plot to kill her children. Apparently, in a state of hallucination, she believed the Prince of Wales had ordered her to kill the two children. She complied. Like Bennie, she was ready to tell Sheriff Foster everything. He told her over and over not to say anything because it would not be in her best interest when it was time for her trial.

By the time they arrived at the jail, the Sheriff was convinced that this time there would be no hanging. Mary Boyd was clearly insane. Bennie would soon learn what insanity really was and it did not help him one bit. He talked to Mary several times, but he was disgusted with her. When he learned what she had done, he was heard to exclaim, "What is this world coming to." When she asked him how long he was going to be here, he replied "Until September 15th." "Oh," she said. "Then you won't be here much longer."

Mrs. Boyd was one of the few people in Carleton County that had not heard of Bennie Swim and his crimes. She didn't care anyway. She vacillated between not understanding why she was in jail, and not caring about anything. She took to wondering where she was, and began treating the whole situation as a vacation on which she could do as she pleased and not have to worry about all the chores she was used to doing as a housewife and mother. Bennie resented her presence.

If time passed slowly for Bennie before her arrival, it was now almost glacial, because she got on his nerves so badly. She became loud and devout; often praying for all to hear and making the jail seem like a revival meeting. She became a fire and brimstone preacher trying to drive her flock to redemption. Bennie tried to cope as best he could. He would bury his head in a pillow when it became unbearable, or spend as much time away from her as possible. He now understood why his attempt at faking insanity had failed to convince two of the psychiatrists. He was now seeing the real thing first hand.

Bennie Thinks about Life and Death

With so little time remaining, Bennie occupied himself writing letters to family and friends. Some of his family wanted nothing to do with him, but others were sympathetic. He wrote another letter to his cousin, Hattie Idella Swim, congratulating her on her recent engagement to Wilmot B. Shaw. The marriage would take place on April 11th, 1923 almost eight months from now, but since there was almost no chance he would still be alive at the time, he figured he would again send his best wishes now and hope that she had a wonderful wedding and a long life blessed with many children.

He didn't mention his present situation in the letter but he knew that she knew of his circumstances. He didn't care whether she wrote back or not. Hattie Idella was one of the few members of his family he had liked while he was growing up because she was such a sweet person. She was the daughter of his Uncle Edward. They would often see each other at family functions and at church. Hattie was about the same age as Olive, but not quite as pretty. As Bennie sat there in his cell he couldn't help wondering if maybe he had loved the wrong cousin. Well, that was a lifetime ago. He would never know.

All he could do to keep his mind off the hanging was to daydream. He remembered the days of summer, lazing in the sun on the Mainstream, his fishing pole in hand watching the trout nibble on his line while he sucked back on a jar of homebrewed beer, several fish already caught, lying in the grass beside him. They would make a good supper. He could imagine his mother happily cooking them up, frying them in butter in the large cast iron skillet that hung on the wall beside the stove. She would add lots of garlic and wild onions and would serve them up to the family gathered around the kitchen table, making sure Bennie got the biggest piece.

He thought constantly of Olive. He thought about the first time he had seen her; her gingham dress, her lovely wide-open smile and large almond shaped eyes. She was so beautiful, and the way she looked at him made him just about melt. His face would get flushed and he would look down. He remembered how she would smile mischievously when that happened. That was the way he always thought of her, never as he had last seen her, lying on the floor, blood oozing from the bullet holes after she had fallen. No, that wasn't Olive. His mind wouldn't go there, even on his darkest days.

He often wondered about heaven and hell, if they existed, and, if they did, where he would end up? The Reverend Bragdon promised him that God would be merciful and would forgive his sins, even the sin of murder if he fervently believed and confessed his sins. He also would have to pray for forgiveness, so Bennie tried hard to believe and pray. He asked to be baptized, and it was granted to him. Reverend Bragdon was very pleased; another soul saved because of his good efforts. God will now look with special favour on me, thought the Reverend. He was especially eager to baptize Bennie.

On the 11th day of September he came to Bennie's cell and performed the ceremony. He couldn't take Bennie to a river like he usually did for baptisms, so he used a bowl of water instead. Once the baptism was completed, Bennie felt better about his chances of going to heaven. He attended all the spiritual meetings held in the jail and spent a great deal of his day struggling through the difficult passages of the Bible. He wished he had stayed in school longer and learned to read better. He thought that with all he was doing to prove to God he was, after all, worthy of salvation, there might be a good chance he would see Olive again. That was what he wanted. It didn't occur to him that Olive might be happy in heaven with her husband Harvey.

Then, there was always the alternative — Hell, the eternal lake of fire. Walking among the damned is where he might also end up. Maybe he wasn't praying hard enough and that's why he would go to hell. If he did go there, he figured he would meet many other murderers like him, or worse. The idea of spending eternity burning alive would scare him so bad that he would pick up the Bible again and read until his eyes hurt.

Soon, he would hang and all because of Olive. Why couldn't she have married him or at least stayed with him. She loved him once, why did she have to leave him. Hadn't he tried to give her everything she wanted? A place of their own and little gifts when he could afford it. He had part-time work. True, it never paid much but wouldn't love be enough to keep them happy regardless of how much money they had. He was able to give her as much as his father had given his mother. She seemed happy enough. What was it that Olive expected of him? He would never know. And all because of that damn Harvey Trenholm. Well, he wouldn't feel guilty about killing him, no sir, he deserved it, war hero or not, he should have known better than to mess around with another man's beloved.

He wondered if Harvey had known about him before the marriage. Well, he certainly learned what Bennie Swim was made of, that's for sure. It was his bad luck that the first time they met Bennie would be the last person he saw on this earth. Bennie remembered the look on his face when he whipped out the revolver and pointed it at Harvey's head. First, there was a look of stunned amazement. It was clear that what he saw when he looked down the barrel of the gun did not register with him. Bennie wished he had prolonged that split second because he would have liked to see fear in Harvey's eyes, but he didn't. He acted with blind hatred and just pulled the trigger.

Maybe if he had seen fear, he might have spared Harvey's life. No, he thought to himself, that's not true, he went there to kill them both and he did it. The plans were made; he wasn't going to change his mind no matter what. He was on a mission and he accomplished it. Well most of it. He had intended to kill himself as well, but he couldn't even do that right. It wasn't for lack of trying though. It was strange that he failed, probably for two reasons: the angle that he pointed the gun at his head, and the reduced amount of powder in the bullet. It's awkward to point a revolver straight at your head and pull the trigger. In his state of shock, he got the angle wrong. The low powered bullet was pure chance. Well, at least he had honestly tried. He could have fired a second time, but something kept him from doing it. Maybe it was divine intervention and he was meant to hang.

Some people may think him a coward for killing two people like that, but he felt now, that unless they have been put in the same position, they have no right to call him a coward. He now knew it takes more courage to kill someone than it does to not kill them.

Most people don't know when they are going to die. Even if they are very ill and know that it's coming, it isn't the same. They can feel it coming slowly and are usually in pain. They have a better chance to accept it and sometimes even want it to happen. A person like himself that has been sentenced to hang at a certain time, on a certain date, really knows when they are going to die. It's a strange feeling when you are in relatively good health and know that in one moment you are alive and then the next moment you are going to be dead. That's the real punishment.

It wasn't the bars of his cell, or the forced confinement that made life in jail intolerable. These conditions were soon adapted to and it became a way of life. Hardship is relative. Whenever something is taken away, the abrupt change is inconvenient for a while, but soon, if the routine is then stable, it becomes acceptable. You just begin to enjoy smaller pleasures. It's the little things that make you just as happy as the bigger things you had appreciated before. While most people imagine that life in jail must be hell, it isn't. Certain things become very appreciated, like meal times, yard time, a letter or a new book or magazine, newspapers, a good nights sleep, stories about past exploits as described by other prisoners. The situation becomes your life, and after several months you begin to feel you belong. That's not to say you wouldn't enjoy a day away to go hunting or fishing, or to spend time drinking with friends in a bar, but, since that's no longer possible, the days just pass with what options you do have.

That's what Bennie learned from the other prisoners. It explained why so many of them come back again and again for stupid reasons that could easily be avoided. Given enough time spent in prison, and depending on your life otherwise, it can become more comfortable than being on the outside. Ex-convicts begin to see a return to jail as a positive thing, especially when you become one of the lowest members of society when you're released. They are constantly reminded of that and made to work at degrading jobs just to survive and are expected to be thankful for it to boot; no, its often better to be an equal in prison than a loser on the outside.

What made jail intolerable for Bennie was knowing when he was going to die and that each day brought him closer to his execution. He was still praying fervently for a miracle that would keep him alive for many years to come and that gave him a sense of hope; that became his life. He did wonder what the rope would feel like against his skin when it was pulled tight around his neck, whether it hurt to be hanged or not, and if he would have the courage to face death bravely, or if he would break down into a whimpering mess, begging for mercy. It almost came to a point sometimes when he just wanted to get it over and done with.

The Day Arrives but the Hangman Doesn't

Construction of the scaffold did not start until Sheriff Foster received official word from the Deputy Secretary of State in Ottawa that his Excellency, the Governor General, would not intervene to prevent the carrying out of the death sentence the County Court had brought down in the Bennie Swim case.

On the morning of September 12th, Bennie was looking out the window of his cell. A large pile of lumber had just been set down in the yard. Carpenters soon came and began to work. He could see them measuring, sawing and hammering and figured they must be building the scaffold. He was right. Shortly after they had started working, they stopped and put a framework covered with large pieces of cloth around the construction site to prevent anyone, including Bennie, from seeing what was going on. Of course this didn't fool anyone and soon the word spread inside the jail and all around town that the scaffold was being built.

Sheriff Foster didn't want Bennie to see the scaffold being built. He felt that if Bennie watched the construction it might severely affect his mind and emotions. But he needn't have bothered. Bennie was now feeling more and more numb. He was becoming increasingly fatigued from lack of sleep. He had a growing sense of unreality. The carpenters could have been building anything for all he cared.

Sheriff Foster and Deputy Mooers were increasingly anxious as the day of the hanging approached. They had done all they could to make sure it would go smoothly and the prisoner would suffer as little as possible. All the arrangements had been made. A reprieve had not come, so the hanging would take place as scheduled. Twenty witnesses and the official newspaper reporters had been invited and informed of the date and time. All of them sent word they would be there well in time for the execution.

Deputy Sheriff Mooers was in a sombre mood. He had been watching his good friend and colleague, Albion Foster. He was keenly aware of the amount of work that went into putting a condemned man to death and the toll it was taking on Sheriff Foster. He appreciated that he was able to work under the supervision of someone as qualified as Sheriff Foster and grateful he was in charge of this case. Mooers would certainly use him as the example should he become High Sheriff himself one day.

By the late afternoon of the 13th of September the scaffold was completed. The workmen informed the Sheriff and, along with Deputy Mooers, he went to inspect the scaffold. They found no fault with the construction, not that they knew what to look for, but it was up to them to make an official inspection. It would be up to the experienced hangman to make sure the scaffold was constructed properly and indicate alterations if needed.

Sheriff Foster called the hangman, J. W. Holmes, and discussed the upcoming execution going over all the arrangements that had been made. Mr. Holmes ended the call by telling the Sheriff he would start the journey from Montreal that night and would arrive in Woodstock the next morning.

When Mr. Holmes sat down for his evening meal, he thought about all of the hangings he had performed and wondered if he would ever do one without feeling somewhat remorseful, even though it was his job. Well, at least when he did them, they were done right; that thought made him feel somewhat better. With his supper finished, he went out and started his car. While it was warming up, he collected his suitcase from the house and stowed it in the trunk of the car.

Soon after starting out, he made a stop at a hardware store to buy the rope needed for the hanging. He had learned from past experience not to attempt to buy the rope in the town where the execution was to be held. On his first hanging he had walked into a local general store to buy rope and the proprietor wouldn't sell it to him. The storeowner knew Holmes was a stranger and figured why he wanted to buy rope. The proprietor was a relative of the man to be hanged. He literally chased Holmes out of the store. He had to go to another town to buy the rope he needed. This experience taught him an important lesson.

After buying the rope and throwing it into the trunk of his car, he headed towards the highway out of Montreal. He figured that since he had at least an eight-hour drive ahead of him, a drink was in order. Before he even left the city limits he stopped at a roadside tavern and had a glass of whiskey; that was relaxing. Mr. Holmes got back in his car and pulled onto the highway. He didn't notice the car barrelling down the road in the same lane and pulled right out in front of it. The driver didn't have time to slow down or even swerve. His vehicle rammed straight into the back of Holmes' car.

Mr. Holmes was stunned and hurt. He got out of the car and checked himself over. He could stand and walk, but he was definitely injured. He had a severe pain in his side. He looked at his car. The rear end was completely smashed in. He knew he wouldn't be driving anywhere after this. Other motorists stopped and offered assistance. Mr. Holmes was helped into a car and taken to a hospital. After being examined by a doctor, Holmes was advised he needed to remain in the hospital for at least a few weeks and possibly longer while he recovered from his injuries. He asked to use the phone at the nurse's station to call Sheriff Foster.

In the late evening of September 13th the telephone rang in the house of Sheriff Foster. He did not like that because no good news ever comes so late at night. He walked to the phone and picked it up. Mr. Holmes, the executioner, was on the other end of the line.

"Hello Sheriff, I have some really bad news. I have been involved in a car accident and have been injured quite badly. I'm in the hospital right now, and won't be able to travel for at least a few weeks, maybe more. I'm sorry but I definitely won't be able to perform the execution."

Sheriff Foster slumped in a chair. His first thought was to berate the hangman, but realized that wouldn't do any good, it probably wasn't his fault that he was in an accident, and even if it was, it didn't change anything. Instead, he controlled himself, gathered his thoughts, and asked Mr. Holmes if he knew of any other hangmen that could replace him on such short notice. The answer was no, and after several further apologies to the Sheriff, he said goodbye and hung up.

What a problem! Sheriff Foster sat staring at the telephone and wondered what to do next. This had never happened to him or any other Sheriff that he was aware of. He decided that once again the execution had to be postponed; he just didn't quite know how to do it. He decided to call the Honorable K. C. Jones.

Mr. Jones heard the telephone ringing and cursed. No one calling this late at night was going to make him happy. It was the Sheriff. After he told him about the accident and non-arrival of the hangman, Mr. Jones said, "Well Sheriff, you know about the law and the duties pertaining to your job as county Sheriff."

"What do you mean?" Sheriff Foster replied.

Mr. Jones continued. "It's your job to make sure the man gets hanged, and if you can't get a proper hangman to do it then you will have to do the hanging yourself; it's all there in the manual duties of what a county Sheriff has to ensure happens in the absence of a professional executioner. You swore an oath to uphold the law, perform all duties as stated in the Sheriff's Regulations Manual, and any other responsibilities that you may be called upon to do. It's very specific Sheriff, it's your job to perform hangings if need be, I can't make it any clearer than that."

Sheriff Foster knew about his duties but this was one he had no intention of performing. He spoke as plainly and respectfully as he could to Mr. Jones. "Now look, Sir, I don't care if it costs me this job, I don't care if you fine me ten years pay, I don't even care if I go to jail, but there is no way that I am going to be the executioner of Bennie Swim. I don't know how to hang a man, and I wouldn't be able to do it properly, so for that reason you must go down to Saint John tomorrow and ask Chief Justice McKeown to postpone this hanging."

The Honorable K.C. Jones heaved a sigh. He knew that he had an extremely good man in Sheriff Foster, and he sure didn't want to lose him over this. It wasn't easy to replace a County Sheriff, so in reply he said, "All right, here's what I'll do. I'll go to Saint John tomorrow morning by train and wait until the Chief Justice gives me an audience. I'll explain the whole situation to him, but I want your word, Sheriff Foster, that if I fail to convince him to postpone this execution, that you will do it yourself; is that clear?"

Sheriff Foster agreed; it was the best he could hope for. After all, you can't avoid hanging a legally condemned man just because the executioner had a car accident. He knew what his duties were but this was one he did not want to perform.

The Sheriff was sweating profusely when he replaced the receiver in its cradle. He knew that sleep would not be his tonight. He was right; all night long he thought about what happened with the Cammack hanging in 1905. He was Deputy Sheriff back then, and William Hayward was the High Sheriff. John Radcliffe had hanged George Gee properly the year before, even though the hangman reeked of alcohol. Radcliffe knew what he was doing, and it all went well. Sheriff Hayward figured he could do the job when the Cammack execution came up the next year; it looked easy enough. So, instead of hiring an experienced hangman, the Sheriff decided to do it himself. Well, he didn't make the knot as tight as it should have been and the noose was not adjusted properly. Poor Thomas Cammack was strangled for nearly nineteen minutes before he was officially declared dead. Sheriff Foster was not going to take a chance on making a mistake like that. Now, he was worried about the bargain he had made with Mr. Jones.

The next morning, the Sheriff went down to the jail and explained the situation to Bennie. He also talked to his Deputy. They decided together what to do. First, they would learn how to perform a hanging, just in case. They knew there were probably manuals that would explain the procedure. They searched the prison office and located a manual on hanging under some other books in one of the desk drawers. They read through the manual and

155

learned everything they could by just reading and studying the drawings. Sheriff Foster was still very uncomfortable with the subject in general. He really did not want to do the hanging and it showed. Deputy Mooers was not feeling good about it either. They were both in a high state of nervousness as they read and re-read the instructions. The Sheriff called in the head Jailor, Moses Moore, to ask for his advice. They had all seen hangings before, but none of them had performed one, and they didn't want to do it now.

The telephone rang and the Sheriff jumped. It was too early to be from Mr. Jones, but it still might be important. It was a reporter who had found out about the hangman not being able to make it. He asked the Sheriff what it meant for Bennie Swim.

The Sheriff's reply was firm, "The law must be carried out, if we don't get a reprieve."

That was all he had to say, and it was enough for the reporter to understand that Bennie was likely to be hanged as expected on the 15th of September.

In the meantime, Mr. Jones had arrived in Saint John at noon and went directly to the office of the Chief Justice, Mr. McKeown. He was given an appointment for 2:30 p.m.. With almost two hours to wait, he went to a local restaurant and had lunch. At 2:30 sharp he was ushered in to see the Chief Justice. Mr. Jones explained the situation and they discussed it at length. Mr. McKeown was not happy with the position that Mr. Jones had put him in. The Chief Justice pointed out that the execution had already been postponed once, and he was not about to do it again.

"Look" he said, "It's the job of the county Sheriff to do the hanging if no one else is there to do it. That's why we have that rule in place. So, I ask you Mr. Jones, why should I grant another reprieve."

Mr. Jones cleared his throat and chose his words with care, "Well sir, I agree the execution should be carried out as scheduled, but the problem is that Sheriff Foster is in a state of nervous collapse about doing the hanging himself. He has never done one before and if he does, there may be serious problems in the performance of it. As you know, even with a professional hangman, there have still been accidents, and someone without experience is at even greater risk of making a mistake. If the hanging goes wrong we could have some very bad publicity. I told the Sheriff I would do what I could to have the execution postponed. I feel I have given you very good reasons for the request."

Mr. Jones waited apprehensively and finally Chief Justice McKeown spoke. "Fine," he said. "I will grant a postponement until the 6th of October, but that's it. Regardless of what happens, Swim must be hanged on that date; is that clear Mr. Jones?"

"Yes Sir, it's clear and thank you sir."

Mr. Jones left before the Chief Justice had a chance to make sure he had the authority to issue the delay. But he did, in fact, have the authority. When he looked, it was right there in the criminal code

> *A competent Judge has the authority to order a reprieve of a prisoner condemned to be hanged if sufficient reason is shown as to why the death sentence may not be successfully carried out."*

Mr. Jones returned to Woodstock greatly relieved, but he first telephoned Sheriff Foster to give him the good news. The Sheriff was immensely relieved and thanked Mr. Jones for his great efforts.

The Sheriff now wanted the scaffold completely hidden. He had an even higher wall constructed all around the scaffold. When he went out onto the street, he noticed the top crossbar could still be seen. He would have preferred that even that part was not visible, but he wasn't going to order the workmen to make the fence any higher. It would have to do. Word of the reprieve spread quickly through the jail, and for a few seconds, Bennie thought he might not be hanged at all. That hope quickly faded, however, when Sheriff Foster came into his cell and explained that his execution had been delayed until October 6th.

Bennie now had an extra twenty-one days to live. He didn't know whether to be happy about it or upset. In one way it was good news, he had more time to reflect about his life and all that had happened in his twenty-two years. In another way it was bad because the strain that had reached the boiling point would continue for the remaining days. There was nothing he could do about it. He contemplated suicide several times, but the preachers had told him that it was a sure way of going to hell, and he didn't want that. He had managed to accept his fate, and he would do what he could to ensure that everyone saw Bennie Swim walk to the gallows a brave man, on his own two feet and meet his maker unwaveringly. This was easy enough to say, but doing it was something different. He imagined all sorts of embarrassing scenarios such as fainting before he got up the steps, or begging for mercy. It would be very hard on his parents no matter what happened, but to die a coward was his greatest fear.

For now, it was business as usual for him and he would try to just get through the remaining days. Hope was never far from his thoughts. What if by some miracle he would escape the hangman's noose. Wouldn't that be wonderful? But just as soon as he would daydream about living to one day become free, the hope would fade and he would fall into a great depression again.

Sheriff Foster told Deputy Mooers to call all of the witnesses that were scheduled to attend the execution and give them the new date. Most of them were relieved that they were not needed for almost three weeks, but now they all knew that on October 6th the hanging was definitely going to happen. They would go about their business for the next few weeks, but the looming execution was never out of their minds for long.

*   *   *   *   *

Not everyone was content to allow Bennie's execution to take place. There were national organizations that tried to prevent it through repeated letter campaigns, aimed at the Department of Justice in Ottawa. Did they care who Bennie Swim was? No, they didn't even know about him until he was sentenced to death. He then became a cause in the campaign of those who wanted to end capital punishment in Canada. Hundreds of letters addressed to the Minister of Justice, Sir Lomar Gouin, arrived daily but never got any further than a junior secretary's desk. They would be quickly scanned, the senders name and address read, and if they weren't recognized, would be filed in the wastepaper bin. Some letters required more attention. One such letter came from the Canadian Prisoners Welfare Association. This letter made it to the highest level and even received a reply. Several lower ranking officials, including Deputy Minister Gallagher, read it before it got to the Minister.

To Whom It May Concern

We are requesting a commutation of sentence to life imprisonment, for the prisoner Bennie Swim, who is to be executed in Woodstock, New Brunswick on the 6th of October of this year. The reasons for this request as are follows:

The High Sheriff of Carleton County, who is in charge of the execution, has tried to engage the services of several hangmen without luck. He tried to get, Mr. Ellis, then Mr. Scott, and then Mr. Holmes. The Sheriff himself refuses to do the hanging so that is not an option. The execution date has been delayed three times so far and when these kinds of blunders happen in other countries, the sentence of death is commuted to life imprisonment, as is their custom.

Sincerely Yours,

Mr. Bickerdike, President of the Prisoners Welfare Association

The Minister of Justice took this one seriously and wrote the following reply:

> *Clemency Refused; interference with the sentence of court not warranted.*

Another letter that got their attention was from the Anti-Capital Punishment League. It also recorded its reasons for the commutation of the death sentence, to life imprisonment. They were somewhat more forceful in language.

> *To the Minister of Justice, Sir Lomar Gouin:*
>
> *We demand that the sentence of death for the Prisoner Bennie Swim, of Carleton County, in New Brunswick, be commuted to life imprisonment. The Sheriff of that county himself refuses to do the hanging, and has been unable to secure the services of a hangman to date. With three postponements, already, it is cruel to continue this.*

The Minister of Justice sent this reply:

> *We are unable to interfere with the sentence of the court.*

Sheriff Foster also tried one more time to halt the hanging. In mid September, he sent a final appeal to the Minister of Justice in Ottawa, but it also was denied. Deputy Minister Gallagher sent the following reply:

> *Law will take its course. Execution will be under direction of local authorities, subject to judicial order. Minister of Justice cannot interfere.*

And that was the end of any serious effort to halt the hanging of Bennie Swim.

Sheriff Foster Goes to Montreal in Search of Another Hangman

Sheriff Foster now had the unenviable task of finding another hangman by the 6th of October. He had been severely warned about the consequences of his failure to do so. If he failed, he was officially bound to do the hanging himself, and he was not going to do that even if it cost him his job. His state of mind did not improve with the reprieve because so many things had gone wrong that he was not sure of anything right now. As he sat on the train heading to Montreal, he knew that he wasn't going to go back to Woodstock without the assurance he had secured the services of an experienced hangman. The best place to do that was at the Bordeaux Prison in Montreal.

Thanks to the press, word of the failure of the hangman to appear had spread throughout the province, and Sheriff Foster had now gotten many offers from men willing to do the hanging. At first, he took them seriously in the hope that at least one would be an experienced executioner. It soon became apparent that all they wanted was the money and perhaps the status of saying they had hanged a man. None of them had ever done a hanging before. He even wondered if John Swim or his son Roy might have been one of the volunteers. Their interest would be understandable because of the terrible grief Bennie had caused them. The desire for revenge made sense.

There was also the possibility that some of them were friends of Harvey Trenholm. Sheriff Foster had never been in the military himself, but he knew how strong the bonds between soldiers were. He had heard them speak of the brotherhood that develops between men who fight together in war. None of them had given him names he recognized, but that didn't mean anything. Even the official hangmen rarely gave their real names. He shook his head at the thought. What kind of person would eagerly volunteer to hang someone?

Of course there were professional hangmen who did it as a living, but he had yet to meet one or even hear of one that could stay sober before or after an execution. They must have to overcome and cover up serious doubts about their profession. But the law is the law, and someone had to do the job. Alcohol helped get the job done. What mattered was that they do it correctly and prevent as much pain as possible. All the hangmen he had spoken to were convinced that hanging, when done right and the neck is cleanly broken, was a civilized way of execution; it was fast and painless.

What other choices were there? The French still used the guillotine. They seemed to think it was far superior to hanging. Maybe it was, but to have the head lopped off like that seemed so gruesome. Electrocution was beginning to be used in some places as a form of execution, but it was certainly not painless. He had heard that sometimes things went wrong and the condemned man's head caught on fire with flame and smoke coming out from under the mask. Most civilized countries hanged people, so there must be some merit to it. Soldiers could be shot, and if the firing squad did what they were supposed to do, that method could be fast and relatively painless. It wasn't his concern how capital punishment was carried out; he just didn't want to be the one to do it. But he was the Sheriff; he would follow the law as it pertained to his county, which meant he had to find another hangman.

Sheriff Foster arrived in Montreal late in the evening and retired to a hotel near the train station. He had telephoned the Warden of Bordeaux Prison earlier that day and set up an appointment. Under normal circumstances, he would have made all the arrangements by telephone but not in this case. He wanted to make sure that nothing went wrong this time. He wanted to meet the hangman personally and make sure he would be able to come on the required date. He wanted to look him in the eye and shake his hand to ensure a personal contract of sorts. He had brought the money needed, and even extra, just in case. He was exhausted from the full day of travel and fell asleep almost immediately. It was one of the few times in the recent weeks that he slept through the night.

When he woke up, the sun was just creeping over the horizon. He got dressed and went down to the restaurant for a large breakfast of eggs and ham. When finished, he paid his bill and proceeded to the prison. When he arrived at the outer gates of Bordeaux Prison, he was impressed. Located at 800 Gouin Boulevard in West Montreal, it had taken three years to build and was completed in 1912. It had six wings in a star shaped design. The prison was constructed to house up to 1200 inmates. It was the most modern penitentiary in Canada. Each cell had a flush toilet and electricity. The public was outraged when they learned that prisoners had such modern conveniences. Some local people were furious that the inmates were living in better conditions than many Montreal residents were at the time.

The Warden was waiting for Sheriff Foster and immediately took him on a tour of the prison. Compared to the Woodstock Jail, it was amazing. While he appreciated the tour, he was there for one reason only, and that was to secure the services of a competent hangman. They at last returned to the Warden's office. Sheriff Foster explained what it was he needed. The

Warden listened patiently and then gave his visitor his advice and what further information he could offer.

"Sheriff Foster," he said. "I was quite surprised to learn of your predicament. I checked with the Department of Justice in Ottawa and it appears that your situation is a first in the whole of the Dominion of Canada. What I mean is that it has never happened before that a hangman engaged has not been able to show up and perform an execution. Now, we have a problem here, sir. Let me explain. We do all of our hangings from a second story balcony so the prisoners are able to see it and, hopefully, be deterred from ever considering murder. What happens when a person is hanged is not very nice. Normally, we use only the Official Executioners, but as you know, Mr. Ellis was taken to court for beating his wife, and the only reason he is not in jail, is because he pleaded an engagement in Vancouver; whether that is true or not, doesn't change things. He is no longer able to provide his services here, and the only other official hangman we have is Mr. Holmes, and his accident is the reason for you coming here today. So I regret to tell you, sir, that I can't help you. There's no one I can recommend in good conscience."

Sheriff Foster was sickened with the news.

"Are you telling me there is no one here qualified to do a hanging," he asked.

"I didn't say that," replied the warden. "We have some guards here that have assisted in hangings and are somewhat qualified but not to the level that Holmes or Ellis are. Now, if you want, I can speak to them and they can decide if they want to take on the responsibility of performing the hanging of your condemned prisoner. To make matters easier for you, I can say, and you can report, that they come highly recommended. What I suggest is that you take two of them and pay them the usual salary. That way you can be sure the hanging goes successfully. Would that be agreeable to you?"

Sheriff Foster didn't have much choice, so he agreed. The only other option was to perform the hanging himself and that was not going to happen if there was an alternative. The warden then summoned two of his guards into his office. The Sheriff took stock of each man. One was a large boisterous type with a ruddy nose, probably from too much drink. The other was smaller with a lean and wiry body. He seemed to be a much more serious type. Both men looked hardened from many years as prison guards, so a hanging shouldn't adversely affect them. Sheriff Foster explained about the execution and gave them the date of October 6th. He asked each in turn if he felt qualified to perform a hanging and each replied that he did. The larger man said he had experience because he had done lots of hangings of coloured folks down south.

The Sheriff doubted that but let it pass. He insisted that they come three days prior to the hanging to ensure there was plenty of time in case something went wrong. Finally, he asked each man his name. There was an awkward silence as the two guards looked at the warden.

"You know how this works, sir," said the Warden. "Real names are rarely given in such matters." Then pointing first to the larger man and then the smaller, he said, "This is Mr. Mark Allan Doyle and Mr. Frank Gordon Gill."

The two men exchanged nods with the Sheriff, who then said. "Here's fifty dollars for each of you as a retainer. You'll get the rest of your salary when the hanging is completed."

They agreed. The Sheriff continued, "All right then, I'll see both of you in Woodstock no later than the evening of the 3rd of October. Agreed?" The men nodded.

"And thank you Warden for your help in this matter," the Sheriff concluded. The Warden shrugged and they shook hands.

Sheriff Foster left the prison and headed directly for the train station. When he arrived he purchased his ticket and learned he would have to wait until almost noon before a train departed for New Brunswick. He would have lots of time on the way home to think about what had transpired. He appreciated the Warden's help but was somewhat apprehensive about the two men he had hired to do the hanging. They seemed all right but he had his doubts about the larger one. Why had the Warden said there was no one he could "recommend in good conscience" and then called up these two?

Doyle bothered him for some reason but Gill seemed to be a better fellow. He saw Doyle as a braggart, loud and forceful and probably a terror to the prisoners on his watch. Sheriff Foster had good men working for him in the Woodstock Jail and would never tolerate a guard abusing a prisoner. Maybe things were rougher in a large penitentiary like the Bordeaux prison. He didn't like the choice of Doyle but there was nothing he could do about it.

As the train headed northeast along the St. Lawrence River before turning south to New Brunswick, the Sheriff found himself dozing off. It was a scenic journey with spectacular views, but not for the Sheriff. When he wasn't sleeping, he found himself thinking about changing jobs. Maybe he had taken his occupation as far as he should go with it; it was too great a strain, the mental and emotional stress was getting to him. He was now 50; he shouldn't be doing this much longer.

*   *   *   *   *

Prison guards Doyle and Gill, as they came to accept their temporary names, finished their shift and headed straight for the local tavern. Doyle took a glass of whiskey with a beer. Gill just had a beer.

"Isn't this great," said Doyle. "Over two months pay just for hanging a man? I wish we could do it more often.'

Gill looked Doyle in the eye and said, "Yeah, but we never actually hanged a man before. What if we mess it up?"

Doyle laughed, tossed back the last of the whiskey, and said, "Look, it's not difficult, I've been standing beside the hangman lots of times, and so have you. We know exactly what goes on. We've been there from start to finish so we know what has to be done. I even prepared the rope and tied it around that last guy's neck. What was his name? Who cares, it's not important. How hard can it be? We just need to remember to do exactly like we've seen the hangman do it. Besides we've got plenty of time before we leave for Woodstock so if you want to check in with Holmes and get a recap on what we have to do, go ahead, but I'm not going to bother. I know it will be a snap."

Doyle raised his beer and laughed at his pun.

Gill wasn't so convinced. He thought a visit to Mr. Holmes to learn everything he could about doing a hanging was a good idea and would do this as soon as he had the chance. The visit with Mr. Holmes went well. Gill took notes and listened carefully to everything the professional executioner told him. Holmes covered the need to weigh the prisoner, the formula for the correct length of free rope, fall distance, and all the other details to get correct to make sure the condemned man's neck would be cleanly broken. Gill asked questions about anything he didn't fully understand and didn't leave until he was completely satisfied that he could do this hanging successfully. Now, all he had to do was accept the fact that he was going to kill a man. Yes, with the government's permission, but he was still wondering how it would affect him mentally in the days and years afterwards.

Doyle didn't have any problem with the upcoming hanging. He was a prodigious drinker and knew that whatever problems he might have could easily be remedied by the right amount of whiskey. He didn't particularly care how the hanging went. No matter what, hanged men all eventually die; if the hanging was painful, so what. Since they were all murderers, he had no sympathy. He figured they hadn't had any sympathy for their victims so why should there be any sympathy for them. If the law wanted them dead, so be it. Someone had to do it; with such good pay, Doyle was happy to do it.

Sheriff Foster arrived in Woodstock late in the evening. He thought about going to the office, but he was exhausted and there was nothing that couldn't wait until the next morning. He went directly home and fell asleep almost immediately once he hit the bed. It had been a tiring trip and a stressful day. The next thing he knew the sun was shinning into his room. After coffee and breakfast he headed down to his office at the Woodstock Jail. Deputy Sheriff Mooers was waiting to hear the result of his trip to Montreal.

Sheriff Foster gave Mooers a full account and ended by saying, "We now have two professional hangmen that come highly recommended by the Warden of Bordeaux Prison."

He didn't like lying to his Deputy, but he sure as hell wasn't going to tell him the truth — that these "professional" hangmen were actually amateurs with minimal experience. God help him, if that information began to circulate. He would have a seriously hard time defending his choices if anything went wrong. No, it was best if he were the only one who knew the truth. Come hell or high water, he would stick to his story. Now, all they had to do was wait. October 6th wasn't far away.

Bennie and the Sheriff
Wait for the Hanging

Bennie was worse off because of the delay. Now that he had another twenty-one days to suffer, he was having a hard time of it. The reprieve made it hard to believe he was really going to die after all. Wasn't it cruel and unusual punishment that he had his execution date changed so many times? As the 15th of September came closer and closer, he finally accepted that he would die on that date.

Yes, the first time it was his choice; the delay happened because of his insanity act. That was really something! He actually thought he could convince the authorities he was really insane. And he came close to succeeding, at least with two of the doctors. The family stories about his fits certainly helped, as well. Damn the other two doctors. He hadn't realized that the one guy lurking around the jail was a psychiatrist. If he had, he would certainly have done a better job of acting insane. Now that Mrs. Boyd was in a cell close to his, he learned what it was he should have done to convince Doctors Phelan and Devlin that he was insane. Well, that was done and over with. He sure as hell wasn't going to get another chance at that.

As the days slowly passed, Bennie thought how ironic it was that he could now feel his mind becoming seriously unhinged. Who could be normal when he was waiting to be hanged? He tried to be brave, but how much can a person take. What does it mean to be brave? For him, it now meant to act as normal as possible and to be able to enjoy the remaining time he had left. But even that was hard to hold on to. Every little thing bothered him. A fly buzzing around his head was enough to make him cry out in frustration. His cell always seemed too hot or too cold. Headaches came frequently, and even with medication there was little pain relief. Eating was a joke. He had no appetite at all. The food all tasted metallic. It wasn't the fault of the cooks. No one else had a problem with the food. In fact, they thought it was pretty good. The stress was making it hard to hold down even the smallest meal. In the last few days he barely ate anything.

At the rate things were going, he would die from starvation if there were another delay of the execution date. He could feel the sombre looks of the Deathwatch, Mr. Moses Moore, the man there to make sure he didn't take his own life, and to make his remaining time go by with as little stress as possible. But his presence was a constant reminder that the day was coming soon. Once again he thought of somehow ending his own life but he didn't want to give them the satisfaction of a breakdown such as that; besides, if he had any chance of entering heaven that was definitely not the way to do it. His spiritual advisers had expressly told him that life was a gift from God and only God had the power to decide when it started and when it ended. No, he would just take the hours and minutes as they came, and try to stay on this earth as long as possible.

He could not fault the care he received. He was thankful for all of it, but it still didn't make the days easier. His time was diminishing. If he could just hold on for the few remaining days, that would be acceptable. Distraction was the key, but even that was hard. He would try to read, but gave up after he had read the same paragraph several times and still have no clue what it was about.

Pacing back and forth in his cell was now his main occupation. It helped, but in his weakened condition he tired easily, and it was not a good feeling of being tired, like after a long day in the fields on the farm; it was a nervous tired, like his mind was still reeling. When he got a chance to go out in the yard, heavily guarded and in chains, he still couldn't relax because of that damn scaffold. It stood there mocking him, and even though they had tried to cover it up, it was so obvious. Everyone knew what was under all that cloth, especially him.

*   *   *   *   *

Sheriff Foster managed to get through the days before the execution in a much easier way than Bennie. With the new double murder case pending, he had a lot of extra work, and he welcomed this distraction. This one was an easy case compared to Bennie Swim's. Mrs. Boyd would not hang. She might not even make it to trial. The Doctor was certain that her mental state was such that she had no idea that bludgeoning her children was wrong. Even with the stories she told of her reasoning, it would never make her anything other than truly insane. She would certainly be sent away for treatment in Saint John, and would probably die in the insane asylum.

She was a perfect prisoner, always keeping her cell neat and tidy, often reading her Bible and thanking all those she came in contact with for the good things they brought her. The Sheriff hoped her calm demeanour would help Bennie but it didn't. It couldn't be helped. He did what he could for his prisoners. Now all he had to do was wait for the hangmen Gill and Doyle to arrive. It would be just a few more days, and Bennie's hanging would be a part of Carleton County's history.

That's what he wanted, to get back to the normal problems of being High Sheriff of a county. He liked his job, but sometimes the strain was almost too much. He realized from all his past experience that he was a resilient man. Whatever the job required, he was always able to get through it. Sometimes it took longer to recover and sometimes it took more out of him, but he always seemed to end up feeling stronger inside.

He remembered that a philosopher had once said "whatever does not kill you makes you stronger." This is the way he felt. The Bennie Swim case proved the point. He was probably the only County Sheriff that had hired two hangmen for an execution. County Council had not liked the double expense, but he didn't care. He did what he had to do and to hell with their penny pinching.

Hangmen Doyle and Gill
Arrive in Woodstock

On the evening of October 3rd, Sheriff Foster was waiting at the Woodstock Train Station for Doyle and Gill to arrive. As the train from Montreal pulled in, Sheriff Foster said a silent prayer. "Please make everything go smoothly, Lord; have both hangmen arrive without problems."

As he waited for the passengers to disembark, he thought about the consequences if these men didn't arrive. He didn't have to worry. He soon spotted Doyle as he came lumbering through the crowd of weary travelers. Then he saw Gill, laden down with both of their suitcases. He greeted them and noticed the strong odour of alcohol wafting from Doyle's breath. He had expected this but hoped the hangmen would be sober at least for the first couple of days. Gill was sober; he was glad of that.

It was late and dark, so he wanted to deliver them to the rooms where they would spend the next few days. Sheriff Foster had prepared a place for each of them to stay in the Woodstock Jail. It seemed logical to him because it would be free lodging for them, close to the hanging sight and out of the way of the general public.

He had heard many stories about what could happen to an executioner found bragging about why he was in town. Even though most people accepted that someone had to do the job, many folks felt it was a disreputable profession and were not always discreet about what they said about it. The Sheriff wanted the hangmen to stay at the jail so he could keep an eye on them, especially Doyle. He wanted to monitor the amount the hangmen drank. He knew it was a common habit of executioners, but he intended to make sure their drinking did not prevent them from doing their job properly.

As they pulled up to the jail, Doyle was the first to speak. "This doesn't look like a hotel to me Sheriff."

Sheriff Foster sighed, and then said, "Well it's not. I thought it was best if you stayed in the jail until you were ready to board the train back to Montreal."

"That's not what I expected," Doyle replied. "I'm used to much better accommodations, and I will not be treated in this manner. I suggest, Sheriff that you find me a room in the best hotel in town or I'll be back on the train to Montreal tomorrow morning, and you can forget about me performing this execution. And you can forget about getting back the retainer you gave me."

Gill didn't know what to say; he didn't care where they stayed. It was only for a couple of days so what did it matter. He tried to placate his partner. Doyle knew the Sheriff wanted him to stay at the jail so he could watch his drinking; that didn't sit well with him, no sir. He wouldn't be watched and treated condescendingly like that. If he chose to drink it was his business and no small town Sheriff was going to control him. He wouldn't stand for it. Sheriff Foster looked at each man in turn.

Gill broke the silence. "What if I stay in the jail and Doyle here can stay in a hotel. Would that be all right Sheriff?"

Sheriff Foster didn't want to call Doyle's bluff, but it angered him all the same. He agreed, and after settling Gill in the room that had been prepared for them, he went with Doyle to find a place in one of the town hotels. They went to the Carlyle Rooming House where the proprietor agreed to accommodate Doyle for the few days he would be in Woodstock. With both of the hangmen settled in, the Sheriff breathed a sigh of relief and left for home.

Early the next morning, Sheriff Foster showed up at the hotel and knocked on Doyle's door. There was no response. He didn't hear any movement. He pounded on the door. Finally, he heard some cursing and a bleary eyed Doyle opened the door. He told him to get dressed and come to the jail to inspect the scaffold. The Sheriff left Doyle mumbling about the ungodly hour. He wanted Doyle and Gill to inspect the scaffold to make sure that it was correctly built. Gill had already taken a close look at it, but in deference to Doyle when he got to the jail, he checked it over again with him. Doyle made a brief inspection and declared the scaffold was satisfactory.

With that done, the Sheriff again went over the list of those who would be the witnesses to the hanging. Counting himself and the two hangmen, there would be a total of twenty-three people. It was a lot, but it would insure that if anything went wrong, there would be an accurate accounting of what happened.

He read over the list of names: Albion Foster, Sheriff; Mark Allan Doyle, Hangman; Frank Gordon Gill, Hangman; Hedley V. Mooers, Deputy Sheriff; Dr. Thomas W. Griffin, Jailhouse Physician; Dr. L. D. McKintosh, Physician; Dr. N. P. Grant, Physician; Moses Moore, Deathwatch Guard; Reverend H. Bragdon, Clergyman; Reverend Perley Quigg, Clergyman; Hardy Crane, Bridge Superintendent; Harry Bell, Alderman of Woodstock; Gladstone D. Perry, Warden of Carleton County; Charles W. Clark, County Counselor; Avon Nevers, Liquor Inspector; S.W. Lynott, Editor of the Carleton Sentinal; Manzer Clark, Produce Merchant; George Thornton,

Merchant; Edward Caldwell, Salesman; Fred Seely, Salesman; Burrill Hatfield, Farmer; Henry DeWitt, Undertaker; Owen Kelly, Chief of Police for the Town of Woodstock.

It was an impressive list. He was happy with it. He had tried to get as many titled people as possible but there weren't that many who were willing to see a hanging up close. He made sure that all of them were good men of sound character and strong constitution. When he made the list, he contemplated asking family members of the victims, Harvey and Olive, but that might be asking for trouble. Seeing the person that murdered their loved ones, even about to die, could anger them to the point where they might make a spectacle at the execution. No, he thought, it was best if just unrelated and unbiased members of the community were there. What might be a problem was that number of people in such close proximity. Twenty-three didn't seem like too many when he made up the list, but as he would soon find out, this was a lot of people, and they took up a lot of space. About half of them had to be present in an official role, but he could have left a few out. Well, he wouldn't change the list now.

The Last Days of Bennie Swim

Bennie was not enjoying his last days on earth. It didn't matter that everyone was so nice to him, or that he got to see his parents more often than usual. He was feeling ill and weak and his throat hurt. Once again, Doctor Griffin was called in. He diagnosed tonsillitis, gave him pain killing medication and left. It didn't make much sense to do anything else since the execution was the next day.

Bennie felt like he was not far from collapse. He had pain in his head, but figured that was just stress and there was nothing that he could do about that. Maybe the painkillers for his throat would take care of the pain in his head as well.

He felt pathetic. He tried to remember back when he was more of a man, back when he could feel joy, hunger, and being normal. That's what he wanted most; just to feel like his old normal self again for his remaining time. But no way could that happen. He felt like an eighty-year old man, weak, miserable, absent minded and dispirited. When he went out in the yard, he was able to see the now uncovered scaffold—grim, foreboding, mocking. He stared at every board every nailhead, the cross beam, all of it. The only thing missing was the rope. He imagined walking up the steep flight of stairs, hoping he would be able to do it without assistance.

Please God, he thought to himself, don't let me break down. I want to be brave, but it's so damn hard. I should have kept my body in better shape, instead of lying on my cot day after day just waiting. And now the time is almost here. Last night I hardly slept at all, I heard every hour strike on that damn clock. I have to be brave, even cheerful for when my parents come. God, what must they be going through? Why did I put them through this? Why didn't I just take their advice and find myself another girl. Love, that's why. Such a strong feeling! And jealousy. What did it get me?—a date with the hangman and shame for my family and friends. If only I could change it all, if only I could go back in time.

Sheriff Foster did whatever he could to make Bennie's last day go as easily as possible. He asked Mrs. Boyd, who was now waiting for her own trial for killing her two children, if she would play some of her gramophone records so that Bennie could enjoy soothing music until his spiritual advisor came.

He thought that he was doing Bennie a favour, but when he mentioned it, Bennie was adamantly opposed.

"Oh no, don't let her play that thing anymore," he burst out in a loud and petulant manor. "I'm sick of it; the damned thing sounds like a washing machine to me."

Fine, thought the Sheriff, just trying to help. He could see that Bennie was not in a good frame of mind. Well, who would be, considering what he was going through?

Bennie was taken to a meeting with the hangmen. He couldn't figure out why there were two of them. He was treated with respect by Gill, but the other one was an entirely different matter. Bennie felt Doyle was arrogant, and indifferent. He didn't really care, since it wouldn't make any difference what this hangman thought of him; but still, considering the way everyone else was now treating him so considerately, it was annoying to be shown no respect by hangman Doyle.

They didn't have much to say to each other. The only thing required of Bennie was to be weighed. Doyle watched as Gill weighed Bennie three times to be sure they had his weight correct. The weight of the condemned man determines the exact length of rope — the drop length — to be tied to the cross bar. Gill had seen the decapitation that could happen when the rope length was too long and he sure didn't want that. Or worse, if the rope wasn't long enough the prisoner would be slowly strangled, writhing in agony for many long minutes. No, they had to make sure they avoided any error on weight and on the drop length of the rope.

Bennie called in his spiritual advisor. He wanted to clear some things up. Since it would be his last chance, he wanted to leave his parents and everyone else he was close to with a better version of the murder. He thought about what would sound the best. Hopefully, it would give his parents some comfort.

When Pastor Bragdon came into his cell, they shook hands and Bennie started right in, "Reverend, I want to make a full confession of the crime and some other things."

"Fine," said the Reverend. "Let me get my notepad and we can begin."

So Bennie began, "First I want to say I was never insane, that was a complete act I thought up after talking with one of the prisoners here. He led me to believe that if I was convincing enough, they would never hang me, so in my desperation I tried it. Problem was, I didn't really know what an insane person would act like, so I just did some things that I thought would make me look insane. As you know, Dr. Anglin was fooled, and so was

Dr. King, but those other two psychiatrists' were not fooled. So, it was useless for me to even try it, although it did delay my execution by a few months.

"As for the actual events that happened when I went to the Sharp farm, well, here goes. When I walked up to the house I knocked on the door and Harvey Trenholm opened it. He began to sauce me; then Trenholm jumped on me. Olive came to the door, I guess because she heard the ruckus. The revolver was in my raincoat pocket, and it fell out. Trenholm picked up the revolver and I took it from him. He then went into the house. Olive had an old trunk up home. Trenholm had a piece of paper with her address for sending the trunk to her. He wanted to see the revolver, said he was going to fix me. I said no. He then stepped towards me and got me by the shirt collar and started to back me into the woodshed. That's when I shot him in the left temple. Olive came to the door again and said, 'Bennie, I've ruined you, and we all deserve it.' I shot her as she turned from me, then I shot her again in the left breast. Then I thought I was doomed so I put the revolver in the back of my ear, pulled off a shot and fell along side of her. I just laid there a minute or two and then got up and went to the sheep pen and sat down at the door. And you know the rest."

Reverend Bragdon covered up a sigh. He knew this latest version was definitely not truthful, but he wasn't going to say so. What did it matter now if Bennie wanted to believe it all happened this way? So be it. There was no use challenging him. The Reverend knew most of what had happened by speaking to others and being in the courtroom for much of the testimony.

"OK Bennie," Pastor Bragdon offered. "If that's what you say happened then sign it here and I'll witness it for you. Now, do you want this revealed to others today or do you want it to stay a secret until after the execution?"

"Oh," Bennie replied, "I hadn't thought about that. I think it's best if you wait until I'm dead and gone before you let it out to the press."

"That's a good idea," said the Reverend, not so much because it was a good idea but because if it came out earlier, it would be ripped apart by the newspaper reporters, and if Bennie chose to speak with them again he would be challenged and totally discredited.

Reverend Bragdon spoke softly. "Your family will be visiting you this afternoon; that should be a comfort to you Bennie."

Bennie hesitated and then said, "Yes it will. But to tell you the truth, I think it will be really hard on my mum, and I hate to see her so upset. My dad is also hurting, but he shows it less. I know what I did was wrong, very wrong, but what I'm sorry for the most is the way I hurt my parents."

Reverend Bragdon thought about what Olive's parents would feel if they heard this latest statement from Bennie, but he said nothing about it. Instead he told Bennie that if he is truly repentant, he could still have a chance of going to heaven.

"I am, Reverend, I really am," Bennie whispered.

*   *   *   *   *

Mr. and Mrs. William Swim arrived at the jail in the early afternoon of October 5th. They didn't want to be there but felt it was the only thing they could do for their son, considering the circumstances. They would not be there the next morning for the hanging; that wasn't expected of them. There is only so much parents can stand. Most parents will never have a son or daughter executed, but for those that have, it must be one of the most depressing and heart wrenching experiences anyone could go through.

As they greeted Bennie, they saw how sad and distraught he was. He seemed to have aged several years from the strain and he looked ill. This was all understandable considering what he must be feeling, but it was still very hard to see him this way. Eva hugged her son, and William did the same.

"How ya holding up, Bennie?" his father asked.

It was a redundant question, but just one of those things men say when they don't know what else to say.

Bennie wasn't about to tell them the truth, so he just said, "I'm fine," even though he was sick and scared.

They all looked at each other helplessly before his mother spoke. "Listen son, there's not much left to say here but I want you to know that no matter what happened, you're still my son and I love you. I wish you hadn't gone and done what you did, but now it's between you and God, and we know He is merciful, so there's a good chance you'll be forgiven by Him. I want you to think about that from now until tomorrow, OK?"

She wanted to say until "your last breath," but she couldn't bring herself to say it.

William sat quietly as his wife spoke. He couldn't think of anything better to say, so he remained silent.

Bennie, not wanting to upset his parents any more than they already were, broke the silence. "So how are Cassie and Alexander, I would've liked to see them one last time."

His father spoke up. "Listen Bennie, I know they would've liked to come and see you too, but what they really want right now is to remember you the way you were, the way we all were, happy and carefree, in the better times.

I think it's best for them not to visit you. Please don't hold that against them. They are still young, and with everything that's happened, it's been really hard on them."

Bennie nodded. "Sure," he said. "I understand."

The rest of the visit included Reverend Bragdon saying several prayers and reading Bible passages he felt might comfort Bennie and his parents. All too soon the time came for his parents to leave.

Sheriff Foster came to the cell and quietly said, "Ten more minutes folks."

Bennie then asked his parents about plans for his burial. William looked at his wife for a second, trying to decide whether they should tell Bennie the truth or not. The truth was that when he approached the church elders about his son's burial they were sympathetic, but also adamant that murderers could not be buried in the church cemetery. "That's consecrated ground," he was told. They said they spoke for the whole congregation. The members of the church would be appalled to think their dear departed ones could be side by side with a convicted murderer. Eventually, they came up with a compromise. Bennie could have his own plot outside the fence that surrounded the cemetery.

William didn't want his son to know that, so he said, "Well son, as it stands, we have a nice place for you up in the Coldstream Hillside Cemetery. That's where most our family are buried and when it comes time for us, we'll be there too, right close to you."

Bennie thought about it. He remembered the place well, and it suited him. He would be overlooking the Becaguimec River. This was much to his liking. But what Bennie really longed for was to be beside Olive. After all that had happened, he still considered her his wife

William continued, "Bennie, who do you want as your pallbearers? I know it doesn't mean much to you right now, and maybe we shouldn't be talking about it, but we'll do what we can for your last wishes."

Bennie hesitated and then spoke up, "I want you, Alexander, Uncle Jesse, Uncle Edward, and Charles Hamilton. The rest, you can choose."

"OK, we'll work it out," his father replied. "Well, I guess this is it. Listen Bennie, don't worry about being brave, OK? Just accept what happens, and if you want to cry, scream or whatever, it's OK. No one, especially us, is going to think any less of you."

Eva looked deep into her son's eyes and couldn't hold back the tears. Her sobs were heard throughout the jail, and it tore at Bennie's heart something awful. He also started to cry. Mother and son held each other tightly. No further words were spoken. Finally, William had to gently pull his wife away from his son. Eva continued to sob as he led her away from the cell, down the corridor and out onto the street.

Bennie lay on his cot for the rest of the afternoon and evening, just staring at the ceiling. He didn't know what to feel, what to think, what to do. He listened to the clock across the street, as it rang out the hours. He kept his eyes closed for the remainder of the night, but he didn't sleep.

Bennie thought he would have been better off if the execution had happened back in September when it was supposed to. With the reprieve, he actually had some hope that it may not happen at all. But now he was completely wrung out, totally exhausted, and it was so damn hard to keep himself sane for what little time he had left.

*   *   *   *   *

Sheriff Foster was now keeping right on top of things. He wanted Doyle to spend the night at the jail. He wanted him close by so he could keep an eye on him. He told his deputy to go over to the Carlyle House and bring Doyle back to the jail.

"If he protests, too bad for him," the Sheriff said in voice Deputy Mooers had not often heard before. "You are under orders to drag him here if you have to, but he stays here tonight, and that's for sure."

Deputy Sheriff Mooers felt the urgency in the words spoken to him. He knew Sheriff Foster was really feeling the strain. Mooers did as he was told, and, as expected, Doyle was not happy about it, but he packed up all of his belongings and came along to the jail without protest. He had figured this would happen, and it was probably a good thing since he wanted to leave Woodstock as soon as the hanging was done. He made sure he had a bottle of whiskey in his valise so he could fortify himself in advance for the grim task he would be performing tomorrow morning. He could feel the eyes of the Sheriff on him after he got to the jail, but he didn't care. He did things his way, and to hell with anyone else who felt the need to judge him.

Gill didn't drink anything all night except tea. He wanted to be clean and sober when the time came for the execution. He had nothing against fortifying himself with liquor on occasion, but in this case, not until the hanging was over. There would be enough time for getting drunk afterwards if he so chose.

Sheriff Foster sat and waited for the night to pass. Though it was still several hours before the execution was to take place, a small group of people began to gather outside the jail. They wouldn't be able to see much, but they would know what was happening by the noise that the hanging would create. The Sheriff wondered about these people. What could entice them to be at the scene of a hanging? Thrill seekers or bored people, perhaps. He also wondered if John and Roy Swim would be there. That would make sense, at least from a revenge point of view. The Sheriff thought of his son, Glen. He loved his son, and wondered what he would do if anything happened to him. Glen was only eight now, but he could understand the hate and anger that John Swim and his family would be feeling towards Bennie for murdering their precious, Olive. Well, if they could see Bennie as he was right now, some of that need for revenge might dissipate. Whatever Bennie used to be, he was now just a jumble of nerves, a pathetic little figure waiting to die.

Some of the witnesses also began to arrive. They came early enough so they would be fully informed as to their role in the matter at hand. Most looked weary. It was likely that none of them had been able to sleep much, knowing what they were about to witness. Gill and Doyle went out to the scaffold to examine it one last time. Both could see nothing that would impede a proper hanging. They fastened the rope to the cross beam and the other end, the noose, lay draped beside the railing, waiting to be put around Bennie's neck when the time came. Both hangmen went inside and waited for the appointed hour. Doyle was taking sips from his bottle. He would be properly fortified for the execution.

Bennie lay on his cot for the whole night with eyes closed. He tried to distract himself with visions of life from his past, but that didn't work anymore. He was conscious of every sound the prison made: the footsteps overhead made by people walking around, the water running from a faucet ,and the quiet steady breathing of his deathwatch guard as he came to the cell to check on him every few minutes. Bennie wanted Moses Moore to think he was sleeping, so he kept his eyes closed and tried not to move.

It worked. It was actually written in the local papers that he had to be awakened when it was time for his execution. That wasn't true, but Bennie would have liked the rumour that he had slept soundly the night before he was hanged. Bennie thought, in some desperate way, that maybe if he kept his eyes closed it would never happen. He was wrong of course, but desperation clutches at false hopes. The night passed slowly; there was a ringing in his head, his stomach was in knots and his heart was racing. At 4:15 a.m., the prison came alive. He heard noises, lots of noises, coming from everywhere.

Twice to the Gallows:
A Botched Hanging and a Legal Scandal

Sheriff Foster kept his eye on the clock. When it struck 4:15 a.m., he said to all present, "It's time."

No one had to ask what he meant.

It was October 6th, 1922. Sheriff Foster, the two hangmen, and Deputy Sheriff Mooers waited outside the cell. Reverend Bragdon, Reverand Quigg, and Dr. Griffin entered Bennie's cell. A jail guard had already been there with a small tray of food. Bennie roused from his cot, sat up and got dressed in his grey trousers, blue coat and low cut tan shoes. He tried to eat something but all he could manage were a few sips of tea and a couple slices of grapefruit. When he was done eating, the service commenced.

First, there was the singing of the hymn, "I Heard the Saviour Say," and then the reading of Psalm 51.

Reverend Bragdon told Bennie to pray during the reading and then began, "Have mercy upon us, O God, according to thy loving kindness: according unto the multitude of thy tender mercies blot out my transgressions. Wash me thoroughly from mine iniquity, and cleanse me from my sin. For I acknowledge my transgressions: and my sin is ever before. Against thee, and thee only, have I sinned, and done this evil in thy sight: that thou mightest be justified when thou speakest, and be clear when thou judgest."

He went on reading until the passage was finished. Bennie kept his head bowed the whole time. He was now racked with sobs and slumping sideways on his cot. Doctor Griffin and Reverend Bragdon reached out to physically support him. Reverend Quigg began another hymn. He asked those assembled to join in, but only a low murmuring came from the others in the cell.

When the service was over, Bennie asked to speak to one of the newspaper reporters. The reporter from the Globe stepped up and Bennie addressed him directly with a surprising show of determination.

"First of all," Bennie said. "I want to thank Sheriff Foster for all he has done for me and my family. The kindness he has shown has been well received. I also want to thank Dr. Griffin for all his help in keeping me feeling as healthy as possible. The officials here at the Woodstock Jail have always treated me fair, and I appreciate what they have done for me. I sincerely believe that I am going to find a new and good life in the hereafter, so for that I want to thank you, Reverend Bragdon, and you Reverend Quigg, for teaching me that God is going to forgive me. So I now say goodbye to both of you men of God, and again I thank you."

At 5am sharp, the Sheriff spoke in a voice that could be heard throughout the jail, "The hour is at hand, gentlemen."

He tried to make his voice sound authoritative, but he could feel the unsteadiness in it. He motioned to the executioners and Doyle now took charge. He marched into Bennie's cell. Bennie looked him in the eyes, shook his hand and said, "So you're the guy; I don't bear you any ill will, and I will do my best to walk steadily up the steps to the scaffold."

Doyle was taken aback. He had not expected this, but for the sake of propriety, he shook Bennie's hand again and nodded. Doyle was reeking of liquor, but no one seemed to care at the moment.

Bennie continued, "I wish that my arms not be manacled, but left free." The Sheriff looked at Doyle, but Doyle said no to Bennie's request. His arms were then secured with handcuffs and his legs with restraints.

"Sheriff, these handcuffs are hurting me," Bennie said.

Sheriff Foster loosened them and asked Bennie, "Is that better?"

Bennie nodded, "Yes, but I am feeling cold."

Doyle couldn't believe his ears. The man was going to be dead within minutes and here he was complaining about being cold. Someone went to get Bennie a sweater. The handcuffs were removed so Bennie could put on the sweater and then refastened. The whole group then proceeded to the jail yard and the scaffold.

Bennie was weak and stumbling so hangman Doyle supported him on one side and hangman Gill on the other. He walked unsteadily but well supported up the scaffold steps to the platform. The platform could only accommodate three people so hangman Gill returned to ground level ready to enter the enclosure at the base of the scaffold. Reverend Bragdon joined Bennie and hangman Doyle on the platform. Bennie stood on the trapdoor. Hangman Doyle placed a black cap over Bennie's head.

Bennie spoke up in a strong voice, "Please God, have mercy on my soul!" Reverend Bragdon led Bennie in the Lord's Prayer. Bennie said the words silently while Reverend Bragdon spoke them aloud. As they were praying, hangman Doyle placed the noose around Bennie's neck and tightened it. Gill was looking up at the procedure, and was suddenly alarmed to see that Doyle had placed the noose on the wrong side of Bennie's neck. It was supposed to be placed so the rope ran behind the left ear, but instead Doyle had placed so it ran up along the right ear. He was about to say something, but then thought maybe from where he was, he was just it seeing wrong.

Out in the jail yard, Reverend Quigg led the witnesses and officials in the hymn "What A Friend We Have In Jesus." Not many people were actually singing, but it was a momentary distraction from the spectacle before them. The crowd that had gathered outside the screened off fence near the steps of the jail could tell the end was near.

Bennie was praying. Hangman Doyle was getting impatient. He wanted this to be over with so he could get back to his bottle. Reverend Bragdon droned on with the Lord's Prayer. When he got to the part "…for thine is the kingdom…," Doyle pulled the lever, which tripped the trapdoor. Bennie dropped like a stone. His body slammed against the lower side of the scaffold with a loud thud. Everyone went silent; even the crowd outside stopped talking. They all knew what that thump meant.

Reverend Quigg started up another hymn, "Sin Has Left A Crimson Stain." He was the only one singing and didn't bother trying to get the others to join in. Instead, they were all watching Doyle, who was now walking rapidly down the steps and talking loudly to those near scaffold.

"Get out of the way! Get back! Don't open that door! I'll be the first to check on him."

Once he opened the door and entered the enclosure, hangman Gill and doctors Grant and Griffin joined him.

Doyle took one look at Bennie's body swinging slowly back and forth and said in a loud, bragging voice, "Clean and pretty, clean and pretty, that's how I like to see a job done."

The crowd outside became angry when they heard the hangman's bragging. Many of them were Bennie's relatives and friends, and they didn't like the flippant attitude of the hangman.

Bennie was dangling about a foot off the ground. Dr. Grant took out his stethoscope and listened for Bennie's heart. At the same time, Dr. Griffin was taking Bennie's pulse. The doctors concurred there was definitely a heartbeat, but they figured it would stop any second and Bennie could be declared dead. The body stayed suspended for several minutes.

Finally, in annoyance, Doyle yelled out, "He's dead as a doornail! Cut him down!"

Gill, who had returned to the platform of the scaffold, assumed that was the final verdict and began to cut the rope. Dr. Grant was just about to pass the stethoscope to Dr. Griffin when they realized the rope was being cut. Doyle stepped out and Deputy Sheriff Mooers came in to hold up the body to ensure Bennie didn't just hit the ground like a sack of potatoes. With the rope cut and the noose removed, Mooers and Gill carried Bennie's body back into the jail and laid it out on his bed.

The people outside the jail had the feeling something was wrong, even though they hadn't seen the hanging. The crowd became loud and boisterous, and then began to shout curses at hangman Doyle.

Sheriff Foster motioned to Deputy Mooers and said in an anxious voice, "Get Doyle upstairs; make sure he's safe and put a guard outside his door."

The Sheriff then spoke to the doctors. "What's going on, do we bring in the Jury?"

The doctors looked at each other. Dr. Grant was the first to speak, "No, he's still alive."

"What," exclaimed the Sheriff. "But he's going to die any second, right? How could this happen?"

"Well," Dr. Griffin replied hesitantly, "I've just examined him and there's a dislocation between the third and fourth vertebrae, but his neck is not broken. Bennie's not going to die from this injury."

Dr. Grant, who was still listening to Bennie's heart through the stethoscope, spoke up. "He's getting stronger; I can revive him if you want."

"No, no! Oh good God, no," the Sheriff exploded, almost screaming.

No one had ever seen Sheriff Foster in such a state. Two other physicians, Dr. Mapleback and Dr. McIntosh who were also present, took turns listening to Bennie's heart.

"It's true. He's definitely getting stronger," Dr. McIntosh said. "If we just leave him here, he's going to regain consciousness any minute now."

Sheriff Foster was beside himself. With great effort he pulled himself together. Then, looking at Bennie, who was visibly breathing, the Sheriff leaned forward with his hands flat on a table for support, faced his attending officials, and said in a loud but quavering voice, "The law states that he'll be hanged by the neck until he's dead, and that's what's going to happen. We have to do the hanging again."

Deputy Mooers went to get Doyle but, having availed himself of his pocket flask, the hangman was now drunker than ever. He could hardly stand up. Hangman Gill would have to do it. Gill was brought in and informed of the situation. He shook his head and knew that what he had seen was right after all. The misplaced rope must have been the cause of the failed hanging.

Gill was stone cold sober and acted immediately. There was enough rope left from what they brought with them for a second hanging. He cut the right length. He climbed up, tied the second rope to the crossbeam and quickly tied the noose on the other end.

Once again Bennie ascended the scaffold, but this time carried carefully up the steps like a sack of grain by Deputy Sheriff Mooers and Reverend Bragdon. Gill was on the scaffold waiting for them. He steeled himself when Bennie's body arrived. Mooers and the clergyman had to hoist Bennie up so Gill could place the noose properly around his neck with the rope running up just behind his left ear. This was not easily done since Bennie's head flopped forward and had to be held in place just so. His feet rested on the trapdoor but they had to hold him up until Gill pulled the lever that snapped the door open. No one on the scaffold said a word, but the commotion of the second hanging could be heard on the street, and the thud of Bennie's body hitting the side of the scaffold a second time was unmistakable. The crowd outside went quiet and then exploded with plenty to say and none of it good.

This time, Bennie's neck was broken. To be sure he was dead, his body was left suspended for nineteen minutes. Once again, all the doctors checked for a pulse and when none was detected, Dr. Griffin declared Bennie Swim dead. The body was brought back into the jail, and again laid out on a bed. This time the Jury of Witnesses was called in and they all observed that Bennie Swim was officially dead.

Dr. Griffin prepared "A Certificate of Execution of Judgment of Death."

> *I, Dr. Thomas Griffin, Medical Officer of the Common Gaol, of Carleton County, Province of New Brunswick, Hereby certify that I, this day examined the body of Bennie Swim on whom Judgment of Death, was this day executed in the said prison, and that on such examination, I found that the said Bennie Swim was dead. Dated this sixth day of October, in the year one thousand, nine hundred and twenty two.*

Coroner Wallace Hay wrote the "Official Notice of Death."

> *An Inquisition taken for our Sovereign Lord the King at the Town of Woodstock in the Parish of Woodstock in the County of Carleton on Friday the sixth day of October, A.D. 1922, before W. Wallace Hay, one of the Coroners of our Lord the King for the said County of Carleton, upon the oath of Hazen Scott, Manzer Clark, George Thornton, Hardy Crane, Fred Seeley, Edward Caldwell, Gladstone Perry, Robert Bell, Harry Bell, Avon Nevers, Burrell Hatfield, and Anson Marginow, being*

good and lawful men of the said County, duly sworn to inquire for our Lord the King, as to the death of Bennie Swim, and those of the said jurors whose names are here unto subscribed, on their oaths do say:

That the said Bennie Swim came to his death by hanging in the Common Gaol, in the County of Carleton, on the sixth day of October, A.D. 1922, in pursuance of sentence of death upon him passed on the 28th day of April, A.D. 1922, by his Honour, Chief Justice McKeown, for the murder of one Olive Trenholm.

And so do further say that the said Bennie Swim came to his death by execution of judgment of death and by due process of law.

IN WITNESS WHEREOF the said Coroner has subscribed his hand and affixed his seal, and the said Jurors have subscribed their hands the sixth day of October, A.D. 1922.

Coroner Wallace Hay and each of the twelve jurors signed this document. Coroner Hay then conducted a quick inquiry by asking the Jurors for any further comments; there were none.

Bennie's body was wrapped in the blankets of the bed where it had been placed. Jesse Foster, Bennie's uncle, had agreed to collect the body and convey it to the Undertaking Rooms of Henry DeWitt. The undertaker prepared Bennie's body for burial and placed it in a coffin. Jesse Foster picked up Bennie's body and took it to the Baptist Church in Rockland for the funeral. On the long ride back to Rockland, Jesse must surely have remembered when he had "persuaded" William Swim to get married to Eva so their first child, Bennie, would not be illegitimate.

* * * * *

Sheriff Foster had more work to do. First, he had to place a notice on the jailhouse door.

We, the undersigned, hereby declare that Judgment of Death was this day, October 6th 1922, at 5 a.m. executed on Bennie Swim in the Common Gaol of the County of Carleton in our presence and sight.

Signed: Albion R. Foster, High Sheriff of the County of Carleton, and Hedley Mooers, Deputy Sheriff, and Gaoler, of the County of Carleton.

184

He didn't mention that it actually took an hour from the time of the first hanging until Bennie was officially dead after the second hanging, but the fewer people who knew that the better. It wouldn't be long, however, before word of what had happened became known and spread like wildfire. It was just inevitable.

Next, he had to deal with Doyle. Sheriff Foster was so angry he didn't trust himself to confront Doyle alone, so he brought Deputy Sheriff Mooers with him. Doyle, for his part, was happily nursing his whiskey in his secure room, unaware that he had botched the hanging.

When Albion Foster walked in, Doyle looked up and said, "Well, Sheriff, I guess I'll be leaving soon."

Sheriff Foster blew up!

"You stupid son of a bitch! What the hell happened? We had to hang the man again because of your incompetence. Do you know what that means? I now have to ask the Attorney General to conduct an investigation into this hanging. You can expect to be called back here in the near future. And if that isn't enough, there are people in this town ready right now to beat the hell out of you for the way your incompetence hurt Bennie and for the disrespectful and arrogant way you treated him. And, frankly, I should let 'em."

Sheriff Foster stormed out of the room before Doyle could gather his wits.

He told the Deputy Mooers, "You bring that drunken idiot and Gill out to Teeds Mills in the afternoon, just before the train comes through that stop. There's no way I'm going to let them show up at the Woodstock Station, or worse, be walking around town before their train leaves for Montreal. I don't want any more problems because of Doyle."

This was a wise decision. Teeds Mills was about six miles out of town just off the Hodgdon Road. It was an isolated siding, which is just what the Sheriff wanted.

With the two hangmen taken care of, Sheriff Foster went back and discussed the situation with the remaining officials who had witnessed the execution. An Inquiry was going to happen, and soon. He informed the witnesses to remember all they had seen and done before and after the hanging and write it all down, just as it had happened. The Sheriff then put pen to paper and wrote a long letter to the Attorney General of New Brunswick explaining what had happened with the execution and the need for an Inquiry.

He was answered soon enough. On October 11th the Honorable J. E. Hetherington, Provincial Secretary-Treasurer replied saying that he would be personally in charge of the Inquiry, and it would start in Woodstock on the second day of November. Sheriff Foster was fully satisfied with this reply.

*   *   *   *   *

Meanwhile, once on board the train for Montreal, the man who called himself "Doyle" now wanted nothing more to do with the name, or any of the events that had happened in Woodstock. Still smarting from the dressing down he had gotten from Sheriff Foster, he discussed the events with his co-worker, previously known as "Gill."

"Listen," he said. "There is no way we are coming back here. Right? I mean, we did what we came here to do, and if things didn't work out as well as we'd hoped, well then it's not our fault."

His co-worker looked him in the eye and said, "Yes it is our fault. It's your fault for putting the rope on the wrong side of his neck. It's your fault for not waiting until he was declared dead before you ordered the rope cut. Most of all, it's your fault for getting so drunk you didn't realize what you were doing wrong. It's my fault for not stopping you when I saw the mistake. It's my fault for letting you do the hanging while totally drunk, and for not making sure you did it right. But most of all, it's my fault for agreeing to do this in the first place. Oh, but your right about one thing; unless we end up being dragged back there in chains, there's no way in hell we are ever going back to Woodstock.

When "Doyle" and "Gill" arrived in Montreal, they both went directly to their homes hoping to put the whole ugly scene behind them and have a good night's sleep with no nightmares. But whether they liked it or not, they were now real hangmen with a botched hanging to their credit. The next morning, when they presented themselves to the Warden of Bordeaux Prison, he asked them how the hanging went. Both men hesitated, looked at each other, and then both said, "Fine," at the same time. The Warden knew from the look on their faces they were lying, but it was not his concern so let it go and thought no more about it.

The Funeral of Bennie Swim

Jesse Foster came back to Henry DeWitt's Undertaking Rooms later in the day of October 6th to collect Bennie's body. The undertaker had done a fine job with the coffin. Jesse loaded Bennie onto his wagon and started up the road toward Rockland. He was headed for the Baptist Church where Bennie's funeral would be held the next day

It was a grim and depressingly long journey for Jesse and a time for reflection on all that had happened. He remembered his nephew as a child running around the countryside chasing butterflies or heading down to the river to go fishing for trout. Bennie was always whistling back then. He seemed happy when he was alone, entertaining himself, but he was often moody and quiet when in the company of others. He should have been destined to have a long and happy life. How sad the way it turned out. It was all because of Olive. Not that it was her fault in any way, but she just affected Bennie in a way he couldn't get over and that was the early death of them both.

Maybe she really had loved him at some point when they were together, or maybe she just wanted to be with someone until someone better came along. He understood his nephew's belief that he and Olive were married. Lots of couples on the Mainstream lived without benefit of a legal marriage, and to them they were married and referred to themselves as such. But Olive wasn't that type of girl. She wanted something more. She twice left Bennie, trying to get away from him, and when that Trenholm fellow came along, she saw what she was looking for. Well, it came to a bad end for all of them. Poor Harvey Trenholm; he believed he had found himself a beautiful young wife and probably had no clue that Bennie even existed. So now, all that remained was to bury Bennie.

Jesse knew about the two hangings. He was there outside of the jailhouse early in the morning, and he knew what had happened. He had heard the loud voice of one of the hangmen, being very arrogant and disrespectful to his nephew. It made him angry, but there wasn't much he could do about it. It's a good thing that he had not later crossed paths with hangman Doyle; there would have been a terrible row, and Jesse himself may have ended up in prison. He pondered about whether he should tell Bennie's parents about what had happened. No, they had enough to handle with their grief right now. Eventually, they would probably find out, but why make a bad day worse for them now?

When Jesse arrived at the Rockland Baptist Church, the pastor and a couple of local men helped carry Bennie's coffin inside. He then went out to the home of William and Eva, Bennie's parents, on the Mainstream where the wake was in progress.

When he arrived, he found his sister, Eva, and William surrounded by guests. William was drinking heavily. Jesse offered his condolences, but it was a hollow gesture. It wasn't a sudden death or one brought on by disease. It was one that everyone knew when and how it was going to happen. They were all prepared for it as best they could be but still very depressed, especially for the way it happened.

But a death was a death and family stuck together in such situations. There were large trays of food laid out on a table in the kitchen area. Jesse suddenly realized how hungry he was. He hadn't eaten since early morning. He heaped a big mound of mashed potatoes and a slab of roast beef on his plate and drowned it in gravy. The food was good Mainstream fare and the sharing was well appreciated. He stayed for several hours. As he was preparing to leave, he promised Eva and William he would be at the church early for the service and for his role as pallbearer.

The next day, Saturday the 7th of October, folks started gathering at the church in the early afternoon for Bennie's funeral service. It was a perfect day for a funeral and a burial. The rain came down hard and cold. The sky was gloomy. Reverends Quigg and Bragdon had each prepared a reading and a sermon they hoped would be well received by the congregation. They were both astounded by the number of people who were showing up for Bennie Swim's funeral.

Reverend Bragdon remembered Olive's funeral and how only a few people had showed up. It then dawned on him that most of the people were not here because they had cared that much about Bennie while he was living. Many of them probably didn't even know Bennie or anything about him other than the way he had been treated when he died. But they were a part of the community, and wanted to show their feeling for the way Bennie had unnecessarily suffered. Many folks felt that hanging, as a method of carrying out capital punishment, was a relic of the dark ages and should be abolished.

While no one felt sympathy for what Bennie had done that caused him to be hanged, they wanted to show sympathy for the family and their solidarity against hanging itself. As Reverend Bragdon looked out at the crowd he figured there must be over three hundred people that had showed up.

This was way more than any other funeral in the area that he could remember. It was going to be a long funeral procession with over one hundred and fifty teams. It was going to stretch from the church all the way to the cemetery. This was going to be a funeral that would be talked about for a long while, that's for sure.

When Reverend Quigg got up to begin the first reading he too realized he had never seen anything like this before; and to think, way out here in Rockland, close up by the Mainstream. After a Bible reading Reverend Quigg talked about sin and how none of us are as pure as Jesus was, so it wasn't our place to judge the man we are here to bury.

"Bennie may have done some bad things in his life," Reverend Quigg said. "But there was a lot of good in him too. His life could have turned out differently for sure, but let all of us here always remember Bennie when we knew him at his best. Bennie was one of us, a child of the Mainstream, *and a child of God.*"

He emphasized the last line for the benefit of those who had come out only because of Bennie's notoriety. He wanted to leave them with a message that touched their hearts.

He continued, "Knowing that we have a loving God and a forgiving God, and knowing that Bennie fully repented and prayed to God for forgiveness when we were with him in his jail cell, let us all believe that Bennie is now in a far better place than he was before."

And with that, he led the crowd in a hymn. He was careful to remember what hymns had been sung at the execution; he sure didn't want to sing one that would make some folks think of the hanging they were so angry about. He chose "The Old Rugged Cross." Reverend Quigg started it off in a strong voice and slowly, with more and more feeling, the whole congregation joined in.

> *On a hill far away stood an old rugged Cross*
> *The emblem of suffering and shame;*
> *And I love that old Cross where the dearest and best*
> *For a world of lost sinners was slain.*
>
> *So I'll cherish the old rugged Cross*
> *Till my trophies at last I lay down;*
> *I will cling to the old rugged Cross*
> *And exchange it some day for a crown.*

On and on they all sang right to the last verse.

To the old rugged Cross I will ever be true
Its shame and reproach gladly bear.
Then He'll call me some day to my home far away
Where His glory forever I'll share.

So I'll cherish the old rugged Cross
Till my trophies at last I lay down;
I will cling to the old rugged Cross
And exchange it some day for a crown.

Some of those attending the funeral had never heard the hymn before. It was a new one, written in 1913 by an American, George Bennard, but it was fast becoming a favourite in some churches. The people that didn't know the verses soon caught on to the chorus and amplified the singing each time it came round. The old church just swelled and resonated with the voices of the faithful, singing loudly for all to hear.

When the song was done, Reverend Bragdon began his sermon. He looked down at the family of Bennie seated in the front row. William was looking like he had aged fifty years since the time that Bennie had been arrested. He tried to think what he must have had to go through. Eva, in the same way looked so different, so haggard and drawn, nothing like the happy smiling woman he had known over the years. But what else could be expected with such a family tragedy?

Cassie Elizabeth, Bennie's sister, was seated beside her husband, Frank Ogden. He gave her what support he could, but she looked like this was the last place on earth she wanted to be, not so much because of the sadness of Bennie's funeral, but because all of these strangers were intruding on the family's grief. For her, it was also a matter of shame. She couldn't believe her brother had killed two people and brought so much shame on the family. She hated the stares that she got everywhere she went. Strangers, and even people who used to be friends, all seemed to look at her like she was also capable of murder. Maybe it ran in the family. She had become almost a recluse, hardly leaving the farm except to go to church or other necessary trips to town. There was nothing she could do about it. She would try to keep to herself, if at all possible.

Alexander Cameron was another story. Bennie's brother almost revelled in the notoriety that had developed after Bennie's arrest. If he had any trouble with someone, they thought twice about messing with him now. He figured that was a good thing, even if they talked about him and his family behind his back. He could take that, because one look in their direction and they stopped talking. Most would even look down at the ground, or quietly walk away.

He hadn't seen his brother since the arrest, and it pained him to think of him now in a coffin only a few feet away. He had been close to his brother for a while, especially when they were younger, but they had drifted apart when Cameron found work in Peel and Perth-Andover. He wished now he had made an effort to see his brother when he was in jail. But regrets don't count for much in the end, and it was the end for his brother Bennie.

Reverend Bragdon started his sermon. "We are here to say goodbye to one of our own, someone we all loved at one time, someone from *our community*."

He said these last words in a way that showed some disdain for those that had come merely for the entertainment of being at a notorious murderer's funeral. As for the reporters that were there just so they could write up this part of the story, well, it was their job. He understood that this was something they had to do.

Reverend Bragdon continued. "Bennie was a good man for most of his life, which can be attested to by the countless stories from his friends and relatives. I'm not going to sugar coat it none. We all know what happened and how he died, but I want everyone here to realize that it was the Devil that got into Bennie Swim. The Devil can be powerful, he uses tricks and deceit, and no matter how much we pray, how good we are, sometimes the Devil manages to slide in at our moments of weakness and that's what I believe happened with Bennie. We have a good and merciful God, powerful and strong, and we have to keep praying to protect ourselves, but we can never be sure when the Devil may find a way into our lives, so we have to be continually vigilant in our fight against him, never letting up for a moment, always keeping ourselves true to God and his Son, Jesus Christ.

"I was there when Bennie knew his final moments were approaching. He prayed right up until his last breath. And you know what I saw, I saw the calmness in his eyes, because he knew he was going to meet his Saviour, and he truly believed that God had forgiven him. I saw it in his face, and I want you all to know that. Let us pray."

He then led the congregation in the Lord's Prayer. "Our Father, who art in heaven, hallowed be thy name." When he came to the last line, "For thine is the kingdom, the power and the glory, forever and ever...," his voice had become a little unsteady with emotion and the congregation fell into complete silence. After a long moment, the Reverend recovered and pronounced the concluding, "Amen." Again, a pause, and then after raising his hand and saying, "Let us sing," he led the parishioners in the old favourite that everyone knew, "Shall We Gather at the River."

> Shall we gather at the river,
> Where bright angel feet have trod,
> With its crystal tide forever
> Flowing by the throne of God?
>
> Yes, we'll gather at the river,
> The beautiful, the beautiful river;
> Gather with the saints at the river
> That flows by the throne of God.

When the hymn was finished, Reverend Quigg motioned the pallbearers to rise and move forward. The six men gently lifted the coffin and carried Bennie out to a wagon in front of the church. First the family, and then the congregation rose and followed the pallbearers outside. The Swim family got into the wagon directly behind the one carrying Bennie and the procession started out for the Coldstream Hillside Cemetery.

Most of the other people attending the funeral got into their own wagons and followed. There were so many wagons that they stretched far down McBernie Road. Bennie's coffin was unloaded by the pallbearers and laid on the ground beside the gravesite. Once everyone had arrived at the cemetery and crowded around the gravesite, Reverend Bragdon prepared for this final part of the service. The rain poured down mercilessly. A parishioner stepped up and shielded him with a large black umbrella. He waited until everyone had settled down before beginning his prayer. He raised his voice and repeated the familiar words.

> *I am the resurrection and the life, saith the Lord; he that believeth in Me, though he were dead, yet he liveth; and whosoever liveth and believeth in Me, shall never die. I know that my redeemer liveth, and that He shall stand at the latter day upon the earth; and though this body be destroyed, yet shall I see God; whom I shall see for myself, and mine eyes shall behold, and not as a stranger. We brought nothing into this world, and it is certain we can carry nothing out. The Lord gave, and the Lord hath taken away; blessed be the name of the Lord. Amen."*

Reverend Bragdon then motioned for the pallbearers to lower the coffin into the grave. After this had been completed, Reverend Quigg began his prayer.

Unto Almighty God, we commend the soul of our brother departed, and we commit his body to the ground; earth to earth, ashes to ashes, dust to dust; in sure and certain hope of the resurrection unto eternal life, through our Lord Jesus Christ, at whose coming in glorious majesty to judge the world, the earth and the sea shall give up their dead; and the corruptible bodies of those who sleep in him shall be changed, and made like unto his own glorious body; according to the mighty working whereby he is able to subdue all things unto himself. Merciful God, the Father of our Lord Jesus Christ, who is the Resurrection and the Life; in whom whosoever believeth, shall live, though he die; and whosoever liveth, and believeth in him, shall not die eternally; who also hath taught us, by his holy Apostle Saint Paul, not to be sorry, as men without hope, for those who sleep in him. We humbly beseech thee, O Father, to raise us from the death of sin unto the life of righteousness; that, when we shall depart this life, we may rest in him; and that, at the general Resurrection in the last day, we may be found acceptable in thy sight and receive that blessing, which thy well-beloved Son shall then pronounce to all who love and fear thee, saying; come, ye blessed children of my Father, receive the kingdom prepared for you from the beginning of the world. Grant this, we beseech thee, O Merciful Father, through Jesus Christ, our Mediator and Redeemer. Amen.

After the prayer, both ministers threw dirt on the coffin. Friends of the family then threw flowers onto the coffin, after which the crowd slowly, and with little conversation, walked back to their wagons. Bennie's family waited with the two ministers until everyone had left before throwing their flowers into the grave. They said their silent farewells and left. The gravediggers would soon come to fill in the grave. There was no stone to mark Bennie's grave. The expense was a factor but there was also a worry that the grave may be disturbed, or worse, defiled. It was some time before a simple wooden marker was placed at the head of the grave. "Rest in Peace Bennie Swim. Born October 22nd 1899. Died October 6th 1922."

Within a couple of decades it was rotted away and the actual location of Bennie's grave would almost be forgotten once all those who knew where it was had themselves passed on. Maybe it was for the best.

Sheriff Foster did not attend the funeral. He wanted to but didn't think his presence would be welcome.

The Inquiry into the Execution

There was a bad feeling, even disgust, on the part of some citizens about the way the hanging of Bennie Swim was conducted. One of the letters to the editor of the Carleton Sentinel gave an accurate picture of the sentiment at the time.

The revolting scene enacted at the Swim execution in Woodstock calls for a word of comment. After the Benton Ridge tragedy when two persons were shot to death, Bennie Swim was apprehended by the law officers and lodged in the Woodstock Jail to await trial on the charge of murder. He was tried, and on the evidence submitted, was found guilty by a jury of fellow citizens of the crime of which he was charged. The presiding judge pronounced sentence of death concluding with these words. "You will hang by the neck until you are dead and may God have mercy on your soul." As to the right or wrong of capital punishment, I am offering no opinion here but I believe that Swim, like every other criminal to be hanged, had a right not merely to a "jus ad rem" but to "jus in rem" and to be hanged as perfectly as human ingenuity could devise. The law especially says, he shall be "hanged" not strangled, not tortured. Our human laws forbid the torturing of the dumb brute, and have not a human being, in being put to death, have as much consideration as a dog?

Hanging itself is as crude and revolting a manor for executing a criminal as can be devised, and the law seems to take cognizance of this in as much as it implies that the hanging by neck until dead presupposes that once the criminal is shot through the trap, death immediately follows, and the rope is not cut until the life is extinct. The shooting through the trap, the destruction of life and the hanging by the neck until dead are but one continuous act, and accordingly, preclude the torturing of the criminal by repetition of this act.

I am not a lawyer, but I have grave doubts that the intention of the law is to have the act of hanging repeated indefinitely on the criminal. I shall be told that it's not the first time that a person

194

was hanged more than once. What has that to do with the legality or illegality of the repetition of the act? Abuses are abuses whether committed by ruler, makers of laws, administrators of law, or observers of laws, and traditional abuses are worst of all, and, time with all its mellowing influence, cannot give to abuse the sanction of law. Hanging, so long as it is the law of the land, should be one continuous act, and if it is not, as presently in the law, the people should see that it is.

Assuming that the official statement given to the press is correct, Swim was shot through the trap and before he was dead, was cut down, either officially or unofficially. If officially, I believe he was legally dead, if unofficially, then illegally. I offer no reflection upon the Sheriff, the doctors, or the clergymen who attended when I say that had I been present as Bennie's spiritual advisor, and [as he] was carried up the scaffold steps [a secomd time], it would only have been after superior physical force had overcome my physical resistance, for I believe [with] the official cutting of the rope, Swim was dead in the eyes of the law. If Bennie Swim was not the first man to be hanged more than once, then let him, in the name of our boasted civilization, be the last. The press has given us a statement from certain officials present, why have we not heard from the law officials of the crown.

Thank you, Mr. Editor, I am yours truly. Charles J. McLaughlin

*　　*　　*　　*　　*

Sometime prior to October 17th, a meeting of government officials was convened by the Honourable J.P. Byrne, KC, Attorney General of the Province of New Brunswick. As the result of this meeting, it was announced that J. Bacon Dickson of Fredericton was appointed as a commissioner "to conduct the Inquiry into the circumstances surrounding the execution of Bennie Swim, who was hanged last week, in Woodstock, for the murder of Olive Swim Trenholm, and her husband, Harvey Trenholm." [The trial records show that Bennie was charged and convicted only for the murder of Olive.]

The announcement continued.

On account of the feeling which has been aroused throughout the province, and especially in the vicinity of Woodstock, owing to the different nature of the execution, the Attorney General felt that an investigation should be held for the purpose of giving the public the facts in connection with the affair. Mr. Dickson will commence the investigation immediately and the formal inquiry will be held in Woodstock, under the authority of the royal commission to take evidence under oath. All the witnesses to the execution will be brought forward and an endeavour made to fix the blame attaching to the unfortunate affair, on the proper party or parties.

Sheriff Foster was immediately contacted by a reporter and made the following statement over the telephone:

I welcome an investigation, my conscience is clear, and I have nothing to fear. I did everything I could do except to carry out the execution myself, and I wouldn't do that, my friends wouldn't have let me, even if I had been willing. I brought two executioners who were both recommended by competent authorities as capable and experienced as such, and one of them was said to be the official hangman of the Province of Quebec. I have nothing to cover up in the regrettable occurrence. The whole trouble was that the condemned man was cut down too soon, after the trap had been sprung the first time, and the investigation will reveal whose fault that was. I also want to say that I appreciate the absolutely correct and fair report of everything in connection with the case which has appeared in the press.

*   *   *   *   *

The Warden of the Bordeaux prison in Montreal sat staring at two letters from the New Brunswick Attorney General's office. A separate letter asked him to pass them on to the two guards he had sent to Woodstock to conduct the hanging of Bennie Swim. The third letter also asked him to confirm that the hangman known as Doyle was the "Official Hangman of the Province of Quebec."

"Official hangman of Quebec, my ass," he spluttered out loud. "Where the hell did they get that idea?"

Now what was he supposed to do? He remembered the county sheriff arriving in his office back in late September, and how desperate he was to obtain the services of an executioner. The man almost had a fit when he was told there was currently no official hangman, and there was no one else he could recommend in good conscience. When the sheriff pressed him, he suggested two of his experienced guards might do. Well, it's all history now, thought the Warden, and his helping the sheriff of Carleton County had come back to bite him in the ass. The Warden carefully reviewed the whole situation again and then called for the two guards that had gone to Woodstock for the hanging.

"Doyle" and "Gill" meekly entered the Warden's office and sat down. It was rarely good news when the Warden wanted to see them. The Warden passed the letters to the guards. Doyle looked at the part about him being the Official Hangman of Quebec and turned white. He couldn't remember saying that to anyone, but who knows what he may have said in one of his drunken conversations while in Woodstock. When he read the part requiring that he and his partner attend an Inquiry into the hanging they had performed, he felt almost sick. "Gill" read the letters and just sighed. He had nothing to hide, but he knew it would not turn out well for either of them if they returned to Woodstock for the Inquiry.

The Warden looked at both men. He cleared his throat and spoke firmly. "Obviously, something went wrong with the hanging. But what happened is no concern of mine. That's your problem, not mine. Luckily for both of you, they can't make you appear for this inquiry. They don't have the legal jurisdiction to force you to attend. If it becomes a federal matter, that would changes things; but for now, you're safe. So what I'm going to do is inform them that I have passed these letters on to you both. I will also tell them that the train leaves Montreal at 7 p.m.. and they, meaning you two, will arrive the next afternoon on November 3rd. That's all I'm going to do. If you choose to go, fine, but if I were you I would just ignore this summons."

With that he dismissed them. They left his office and took the Warden's advice. They would not be going to Woodstock.

*　*　*　*　*

J. Bacon Dickson sent the following description of the Inquiry in a formal letter to the Honorable J. E. Hetherington, Provincial Secretary-Treasurer in Fredericton.

> *Sir, By Letters Patent under the Great Seal of the Province of New Brunswick, bearing date the eleventh day of October, A. D. 1922, I was appointed a Commissioner under Chapter 12 of the Consolidated Statutes of New Brunswick, 1903, respecting Investigations by Commission, and Department Inquiries, and was authorized and required by the said Commission to investigate*

and inquire into the matter of the execution of Bennie Swim and the conduct of officials taking part therein, which Commission is annexed to this report.

Upon receipt of the Commission, I appointed Thursday, the second day of November, A.D. 1922 at ten o'clock in the forenoon at the County Courthouse in Woodstock, New Brunswick, as the time and place for entering upon the investigation.

I obtained a list of persons present at the execution of Bennie Swim and summoned or requested the following persons to be present and give evidence.

Albion R. Foster, High Sheriff of Carleton County
Hedley V. Mooers, Deputy Sheriff of Carleton County
Dr. Thomas W. Griffin, Physician
Dr. L. D. McIntosh, Physician
Dr. N. P. Grant, Physician
Moses Moore, Deathwatch
Rev. H. Bragdon, Clergyman
Rev. Perley Quigg, Clergyman
Hardy Crane , Bridge Superintendent
Harry Bell, Alderman, Woodstock
Gladstone D. Perry, Warden of Carleton County
Charles W. Clark, County Counselor
Avon Nevers, Liquor Inspector
S. W. Lynott, Editor of the Carleton Sentinel
Manzer Clark, Produce Merchant
George Thornton, Merchant
Edward Caldwell, Salesman
Fred Seeley, Salesman
Burril Hatfield, Farmer
Henry DeWitt, Undertaker
Owen Kelly, Chief of Police of Woodstock

The investigation was held at Woodstock on November second and third, A.D. 1922 and the witnesses above named appeared and gave evidence.

I obtained from Sheriff Albion R. Foster, the names given to him by the two hangmen employed for the purpose of carrying out the death sentence. The names given were, M. A. Doyle, and F. G. Gill. I attempted to communicate with these men by letter with a view to having them attend the investigation and give evidence. After my return from Woodstock I found that my letters to these men had been returned to Fredericton, while I was in Woodstock.

While at Woodstock on the second day of November, I received the following telegram:

Montreal Nov. 2nd-22

J. Dickson   *Woodstock N.B.*

PROTEST INQUIRY LEAVING 7 P.M.   *"Doyle"*

The Canadian Pacific Railway train leaves Montreal for the east at 7 p.m.. If the sender of this telegram had taken that train he would have arrived in Woodstock on November third about 1 p.m.. I kept the investigation open until the afternoon of November third, but the hangman Doyle did not appear and I am fully convinced that he did not arrive in Woodstock on that day. Before leaving Woodstock I stated to the press that I would hear the evidence of either of the hangmen at Fredericton if they would appear before me there. I have had no word from either of them since.

Honorable W. P. Jones, K.C. appeared as counsel for Sheriff Foster and T.C.L. Ketchum, Esquire, appeared as counsel for the Canadian Prisoners Welfare Association.

The Stenographic report of the evidence and proceedings are returned herewith.

When Bennie Swim was sentenced to hang, the Sheriff at once proceeded to secure the services of a hangman. He states that he first endeavoured to secure the services of Arthur Ellis, who has been carrying out the death sentence in different parts of Canada for some years and who has become looked upon as the official hangman of Canada. He was unable to secure the services of Ellis. Ellis recommended a man named Holmes, who has also been the official hangman at many executions in Canada. The Sheriff endeavoured to secure the services of Holmes without success. (The Sheriff did not mention the accident that occurred when Holmes was on his way to Woodstock.) He then appealed to the Sheriff of Montreal and on the recommendations of the Sheriff of Montreal and of the Governor of the Jail at Montreal, he employed a man who gave his name as M.A. Doyle to carry out the execution. To make sure that a capable man would be on hand, he employed a man named F.G. Gill as a substitute. Gill was also well recommended. I am fully satisfied that the Sheriff did all in his power to have a capable man on hand to carry out the execution.

Both hangmen, Doyle and Gill, arrived in Woodstock several days before the day set for Swim's execution. Gill stayed at the jail and Doyle stayed at a hotel in Woodstock. On the evening before the execution, Doyle went to the jail and both hangmen stayed there until after the execution the next morning. All of the witnesses examined by me were agreed as to the main facts regarding the execution. I will outline the facts concerning, which there was no dispute and will later deal with certain matters which require special attention.

At about five o'clock on the morning of October sixth, Sheriff Foster notified the persons who were assembled at the Jail that the time had arrived for carrying out the execution. The hangman Doyle went to Swim's cell and placed the handcuffs on Swim. Swim then walked to the scaffold with Doyle and Gill on either side of him, and Deputy Sheriff Mooers following. Doyle, Gill and Deputy Sheriff Mooers went up to the scaffold with Swim. Doyle placed the black cap on Swim, arranged the noose about his neck, and sprung the trap. After two or three minutes, the door of the pit was opened and Dr. Thomas W. Griffin, the jail physician, Drs. L. D. McIntosh and N. P. Grant, who had been requested by the Sheriff to be present, and a visiting doctor, entered the pit. Doyle, Gill, Deputy Sheriff Mooers and some others also went into the pit. Swim's body was hanging suspended by the rope with the feet about a foot from the ground. Swim was unconscious. The doctors proceeded to examine him. After they had made an examination, Gill cut the rope by which the body was suspended. I will refer to the circumstances under which the rope was cut later. Deputy Sheriff Mooers supported the body in his arms as the rope was cut.

This would be about two or three minutes after the doctors had entered the pit and between five and eight minutes after the trap had been sprung. The body was then carried out to the corridor of the jail and placed on a cot. It was there examined again by the doctors. It was found that Swim's neck had not been broken by the fall and that he was breathing. Dr. McIntosh and Dr. Grant remained with Dr. Griffin for between twenty and thirty minutes after the body had been placed on this cot. During this time the body was examined by the doctors from time to time, and their opinion was that the pulse was beating stronger and the breathing improving. Dr. Griffin remained there and continued to examine the body from time to time and came to the conclusion that Swim would live or that there was a chance of recovery. He notified the Sheriff of his decision and Swim's body was carried to the scaffold again by Deputy Sheriff Mooers and the hangman Gill. The noose was placed about his neck by Gill and the trap sprung. The neck was badly broken by this second fall. After about nineteen minutes, the lifeless body was cut down and delivered to relatives for burial. Between three quarters of an hour and one hour elapsed between the first and second hanging. Swim never regained consciousness from the time the trap was first sprung until his death.

The evidence of the doctors can leave no doubt in one's mind that life was nearly extinct at the time the rope was cut and that Swim would have died from strangulation within a few minutes if allowed to remain hanging. The question at once arises; under whose authority did Gill cut the rope? Dr. McIntosh states that while he was talking with Dr. Grant, he heard someone say "Cut him down." The voice sounded like Doyle's. He turned around and Gill was cutting the rope. Others state that they heard Doyle make other statements such as, "He's dead as a doornail." about this time. Dr. Griffin states that he gave no order to cut the body down, and none of the persons present heard such an order given by Dr. Griffin or by any other person except Doyle. It appears that Doyle was very officious at this time and it was necessary for the Sheriff to request him to go to the jail. I have come to the conclusion that it was on Doyle's order that the rope was cut. One can readily understand how some incident or some remark overheard by him may have led him to the conclusion that the doctors had agreed that Swim was dead. However, he should have obtained definite instructions from Dr. Griffin, the physician in charge, before giving such an order.

Nothing was disclosed at the investigation to throw discredit on any other person taking part in the execution.

Many reports regarding the execution have been circulated, some entirely false and others gross exaggerations of the true facts, and I feel it incumbent upon me to deal with several of these reports.

The report has been widely circulated that Doyle was drunk when he attempted to hang Swim and that it was on account of his drunken condition that the first attempt proved unsuccessful. Eighteen of the witnesses examined by me saw Doyle at the time of the execution or just previous thereto. Of these, only one witness, Dr. N.P. Grant, was at all certain that Doyle was intoxicated. Dr. Grant states that he saw Doyle when he went to Swim's cell and at once came to the conclusion that he was intoxicated. He also saw Doyle on the way to the scaffold and noticed him stagger. Three other witnesses, Reverend H. Bragdon, Deputy Sheriff Mooers, and Manzer Clark suspected that Doyle had been drinking, but were not sure. Reverend Mr. Bragdon, when asked if Doyle showed any signs of intoxication at the time of the execution, said "Well, I can't say. I was impressed that probably he was under the influence of liquor, but I do not know it." Later when questioned on the same subject, he said, "Well in our conversation, I thought he was rather an autocrat and was impressed that perhaps he was drinking. I expected he was drinking; maybe that helped me to think he was. I expected anyone that hangs a man to be drinking." And when the question was asked, "It is taken for granted, I suppose, a man ought to have a little stimulant and you were rather pre-disposed to think that he had been drinking?" his answer was, "I must confess it."

Deputy Sheriff Mooers stated that he saw Doyle stagger once going through the hall and it struck him that there was something wrong with Doyle. Manzer Clark, when asked if Doyle appeared intoxicated at the time of the execution, said "Well, I don't know. I met him going down the stairs. I was at the foot of the stairs. He went down all right but he looked to me like a man that was drinking maybe. I never met him before and I cannot tell you whether he was or not."

All of these witnesses including Dr. Grant, when questioned as to the extent of Doyle's intoxication, stated that he appeared perfectly capable of carrying out the death sentence. The other fourteen witnesses saw no signs of intoxication about Doyle at this time. These witnesses, included Sheriff Foster, who saw and talked to Doyle frequently during the night; Dr. Griffin, who was in Swim's cell when Doyle prepared Swim for the gallows and who saw Doyle at different times during the execution; Dr. McIntosh who talked with Doyle for two or three minutes at about one o'clock in the morning and who saw Doyle at different times during the execution; Reverend Perley Quigg, who was in Swim's cell when Doyle arrived; S.W. Lynott, the Editor of the Carleton Sentinel, who talked with Doyle for about twenty five minutes between one and two o'clock in the morning; Moses Moore, deathwatch; Gladstone Perry, Warden of the County of Carleton; Edward Caldwell; Fred Seeley, Burrill Hatfield; Avon Nevers; Harry Bell; and Charles Clark; all of whom saw Doyle at some time during the execution. From the evidence of these witnesses, I have come to the conclusion that if Doyle had taken any liquor, he did not show signs of it to any marked degree on the morning of the execution. It certainly had not affected him to such an extent as to interfere with his carrying out the execution.

A report has been circulated to the effect that Doyle was brutal in his treatment of Swim. This brutal treatment consisted in his springing the trap before Swim had finished praying, in his handling of Swim, and his remarks to him. It would appear from Swim's last words that his prayer was finished at the time the trap was sprung. It would not be expected that Doyle would notify Swim just when he intended to spring the trap. In reference to Doyle's handling of Swim, Reverend Mr. Bragdon states, "I considered him very gentle, a little rough in speech, but his treatment in the handling of Bennie seemed rather gentle." No witnesses present saw anything out of the way in this respect. In reference to the remarks made by Doyle to Swim, it is impossible for me to come to any conclusion from the remarks as quoted by the witnesses. It would depend upon the attitude of Doyle and the manner in which he uttered the remarks. I have come to the conclusion that Doyle was not as considerate of Swim's feelings as he should have been under the circumstances. The fact that after the trap was sprung, he desired to measure the distance between Swim and the floor and generally so conducted himself so that it was necessary for the Sheriff to request him, to go into the Jail, lends me to the conclusion that he did not look upon the affair in a proper light.

Another report has been circulated to the effect that there was more or less hilarity among those present at the Jail on the night preceding the execution, and that the whole affair was not carried out with fitting solemnity. This report would appear to be altogether false. Again I quote Reverend Mr. Bragdon on this point. When asked the question "Was the affair conducted in a reasonably serious manner without frivolity or commotion?" he answered, "I admired it for the solemnity and order and still quietness." The evidence all of the witnesses gave was to the same effect. My conclusion is that the Sheriff should be commended for the order kept, especially after the first attempt to hang Swim proved unsuccessful.

While not a part of my duty, I feel that having been in close touch with the facts regarding this regrettable affair, it would be well for me to deal briefly with our system of capital punishment.

The sentence of the court is that the prisoner be hanged by the neck until he is dead. The duty of carrying out this sentence is placed on the Sheriff. He receives no instruction from any official source as to how the details of this gruesome task are to be carried out. As our Sheriffs have no knowledge of hanging and as no official information is available, they are obliged to secure the services of a professional hangman and this procedure has become almost universal in Canada. But the Sheriff's difficulties do not end with the decision to employ a professional hangman. There is no official of this description. He must employ some person on the recommendation of others without any responsibility in the matter, and quite naturally, dependable citizens are not making their living by hanging. The wonder is that there are not more affairs of this nature.

Again, our Criminal Code provides that the execution takes place within the walls of the prison. In most of our prisons, no provision is made for the execution of prisoners and this section is interpreted to mean that the execution must take place on the prison premises. Many of our prisons are situated in the residential sections of our cities or towns. There is nothing to obstruct the view of the residents or the public from what takes place there. The Jail at Woodstock is a striking example of this. The yard is small, bordering on the street and there is nothing to obstruct the view of the public from what takes place therein. The Swim hanging would have been hardly more public if the scaffold had been erected on the street.

This state of affairs might well be remedied by providing that executions take place at some central prison under the supervision of a competent and experienced man and where proper equipment has been provided.

I have the Honor to be, Sir

Your Obedient servant, (signed) J. Bacon Dickson

* * * * *

Bennie Swim was hanged by the neck on Friday the 6th of October, 1922. Twice, in fact, the second time until he was dead. Bennie had murdered both Olive and Harvey Trenholm. There was no dispute about the crime. Swim confessed to committing the murders. (Actually he never confessed to simply murdering Harvey, only Olive. He continued to say that Harvey assaulted him and he shot him in self-defence.) What was in dispute, however, was Swim's state of mental health and the circumstances surrounding his execution. Though enabling legislation in the criminal code allow for the relevance of both factors, the Inquiry only dealt with the latter in its investigation.

The story of Bennie Swim's execution is full of drama, pathos and blunders: reports of a drunken, inexperienced hangman; reports of rough and disrespectful handling of the condemned right up to moment of the hanging when Doyle, the hired hangman, was accused of springing the trap door beneath Swim's feet before he was finished praying; reports that on the night prior to the hanging "there was more or less hilarity among those present at the jail;" and, central to the investigation by Commissioner J. Bacon Dickson, a botched hanging, which then had to be repeated.

Though Dickson dismissed some of the reports of wrongdoing, it is clear that Swim had to be hanged twice. The first hanging did not break his neck. When he was cut down, the four doctors present realized that not only was he not dead, but that his pulse was getting stronger. After an interval of approximately an hour, Swim, reportedly unconscious throughout, was taken back to the scaffold in the jail yard, and hanged a second time. There he swung for nineteen minutes until it was clear to all that he had finally expired.

The evidence is fairly clear that the officials involved in the hanging did what they were required to do to the best of their abilities. Those who were in contact with Doyle noticed that he had been drinking, but they did not agree on his state of drunkenness. Their reports range from relatively sober to stumbling drunk. In all probability, Doyle was under the influence when he botched the hanging. It seems likely that Doyle was a man who could drink heavily and remain relatively functional. He was not impaired to the point of being totally incompetent, just mildly incompetent. There's even the possibility that if Doyle had been completely sober, he may have made even more mistakes.

Sheriff Foster, who was there the whole time, kept an eye on Doyle and periodically talked with him. He would not have let Doyle do the hanging if he thought Doyle was seriously intoxicated. If he had had serious misgivings about Doyle, he could have turned to Gill, the back up hangman. The fact that the Sheriff used Doyle for the first hanging means he did not see him as too drunk to perform the execution.

So, that was it. The Inquiry was over and no one was punished, sanctioned, demoted, fired, or even blamed. If Doyle and Gill had shown up and been questioned, the report of the Inquiry might have been different. As it was, the officials were satisfied. They were fine with the report and everyone concerned just went back to their regular lives. Everyone except Bennie, that is; and if the subsequent reports of strange doings at the Woodstock Jail are to be believed, Bennie Swim had a second coming.

Epilogue: Hauntings

Out on Benton Ridge, William sharp was having a bad time in his house during the days that followed the double murder. He wasn't one to believe in ghosts and supernatural goings-on; he was far too good a Christian for that. But many strange things were happening in his house that he couldn't explain. It seemed like no matter how tired he was or how little sleep he had gotten the night before, he often couldn't sleep through the night without being awakened to the sound of a woman screaming. This didn't happen every night, but it happened often enough to make him think about it even when it wasn't happening.

At first, he chalked it up to his neighbour down the road having a marital spat, but when he got up and went out to investigate, the screaming would stop. The screaming happened late at night and usually sounded like it was coming from inside the house. William Sharp considered calling the local minister, but that would make him look foolish and maybe a bit crazy, so he didn't pursue it. The last thing he needed was for his neighbours to think he had lost his mind. Instead, he tolerated it for over a year and a half.

As if the screams weren't bad enough, he could also feel his whole body shiver like he had walked into a cold room. But that wasn't all; there were times when he felt like someone or something was touching him on the shoulder from behind. He thought maybe his imagination was working overtime, but the sensation was so real. He couldn't go into the front room without remembering the sight of Olive's body lying sprawled out on the floor. The image remained vivid in his mind. He hoped that as the days wore on and the months passed, he would be able to forget about it, or at least have it all recede enough so he could tolerate it, but that never happened. Then one night, after he had gone to bed, and before he fell asleep, the screaming began. It was somewhat muted at first, but began to increase in volume and was so real, he got out of bed and headed down the stairs to find the source.

What he saw when he entered the front room was enough to make him almost faint. There was the apparition of a woman lying over the prostrate form of a man. He couldn't believe what he was seeing. He was stone cold sober and wide-awake. It took him several long seconds to steady his vision. What he was seeing was clear as day and then the apparitions disappeared. He was left staring at the empty room. Nothing looked disturbed. Everything was peaceful except his heart, which was beating a mile a minute. This had to stop, he told himself. There was no way he could ever sell the farm if anyone else heard about these crazy happenings. That was one more reason not to tell the minister. But he sure didn't want to live here anymore. Not alone anyways.

William then hired a man to live-in and work on the farm. After a couple weeks, the man just up and left without explanation. One day William met the man in town and over a few drinks, learned why he had left.

"That house is cursed, and that's all I'm gonna say," the man said emphatically.

That was enough for William. He now knew it wasn't just him who was seeing or hearing strange things going on in his house. He recalled some days last winter when no matter how much wood he put into the stove, he couldn't get the house to heat up properly. It was eerie because it wasn't on the coldest days this happened. It could be on mild days with no wind. It was like a constant cold draft wafted throughout the house. He couldn't remember ever having that problem before, and some years had been way colder than the winter of 1923. Something strange was going on, and he didn't know what to do about it. It preyed on his mind

But he sure didn't want to give up either. No sir, whatever was going on with the house, he figured it had to do with his former tenants being shot to death, Harvey on the front steps and Olive in the front room. But ghosts, that was more than he could handle. He kept hoping it would all just end, and he could chalk it all up to his imagination.

After eighteen months had passed and things were no better—in fact, they were getting worse—he decided it was all too much. William Sharp decided to take action before he was driven crazy. He had heard about hauntings before, and in every case it seemed like the only way to stop them was to have a cleansing of the house, a sort of exorcism, performed by a priest or minister. But he couldn't do that because everyone in the area would come to know about it. His friends and neighbours would tease him mercilessly and even ridicule him behind his back. He would be regarded as tetched and his reputation would suffer. He sure didn't want that, so, torching the house seemed to be the only option. He really hated to do it, but it was better than being driven insane or losing his good standing in the community.

Now, it's not a simple matter to get everything you want to save out of a house and set it on fire. People would ask suspicious questions, especially if you had all your belongings just sitting out front. No, he had to make it look like an accident. He could get away with taking some important stuff out of the house, but most of it would be lost. He didn't care. There was nothing in the house that couldn't be replaced. But still, he should take out what was important to him. Also, why replace stuff that was costly? So he made a list of what he would save: certain pieces of furniture, all-important documents like deeds, and photographs could be saved without suspicion.

Over the next few days, William gathered everything he wanted to save and loaded it up in his wagon. Then, he began visiting his friends, who became concerned when he showed up at their door with all sorts of goods and asked if they could store some things for him for a few days or perhaps weeks. He offered no explanation, but his friends knew something was going wrong with William Sharp. They didn't question him because friends did what friends asked them to do.

After he had removed everything from the house he wanted to save and had gotten it distributed, he sat in the half empty house and pondered when would be the best time to burn it down. Early in the morning, he thought, that would be the best time. He didn't want his neighbours rushing to help and maybe managing to save his house, or worse, he didn't want them risking their lives in the attempt. No, he would wait until early one morning when everyone near by would be asleep. So, in the early hours of September 4th, 1923, William Sharp sat at his kitchen table with the kerosene lantern turned low and a bottle of whiskey, which he drank until it was almost empty. Then he walked around the first floor of the house pouring kerosene over the floor and splashing it on the walls. Once this was done, he stepped to the front door and threw the lantern against the wall. The effect was immediate. A great circle of fire engulfed the front room, spread with a flash to the kitchen, and, as the flames grew in intensity, rose rapidly up the stairs to the second floor.

He stood and watched until the heat was too much to bear and then walked calmly out the door and away from the fire's reach. No one was going to save this house even if they showed up. As he stood and watched his house going up in flames, he was sure he heard a woman's scream from deep within the inferno. It became louder and louder, but then, as the house started to implode, the screaming stopped. William was certain he had made the right decision.

*   *   *   *   *

The story of Bennie Swim and the scandal of his hanging had become a footnote in local history, when strange things began happening at the Woodstock Jail—strange, unaccountable and downright intriguing things. Guards began to notice strange occurrences happening inside the jail. As they were all men of reason and logic, the guards at first dismissed the occurrences as just figments of their imaginations, especially since the strange happenings all seemed to be on the graveyard shift — as the shift after midnight was commonly referred to.

It all started simply enough. First, they heard footsteps. Guards began to hear someone walking on the floor above them. That meant someone was walking where they shouldn't be. An inmate on the loose was a problem. The first time this happened a guard rushed upstairs to find out who was there. Nothing. No one was there. After this had happened several times and no source could be found to explain the noises, the guards began to question if they had really heard footsteps at all. But several guards heard the footsteps at different times and were willing to talk about it with each other. Half in jest, they figured maybe the Woodstock Jail had a ghost.

But why now, they wondered? It must be Bennie. No one heard phantom footsteps before the execution of Bennie Swim, and two other men who had been in jail here had been hanged in the jail yard; George Gee in 1904 and Thomas Cammack in 1905. So, to ease their minds, they began to call the footsteps the ghost of Bennie Swim. When he was alive, Bennie was known to be a restless young man so maybe his ghost was the same and needed to walk around at night.

If that had been the only strange happening the jail-keeper and his guards had to deal with, it wouldn't have been a problem. A man can get used to a few phantom footsteps now and then, but other things of a suspicious nature also began to happen. Faucets in the sinks began to turn on for no reason. At night, a guard would hear water running in one of the lavatories. He would go in, find the tap running and securely shut it off. Later that night, the water would be running again and no one had been in the room. This didn't happen every night, but it happened often enough to make the guards increasingly edgy. What in the world was going on?

Bennie's ghost apparently became bored with such small antics and decided to step it up a bit. Slamming doors would scare the bejesus out of the guard. So that's what Bennie did. A couple of guards were sitting in the office early one evening when they heard a loud bang, exactly like the sound of a door slamming shut. They both jumped up and ran to the hallway of the cellblock where the noise had come from. They checked every door and window, but they were all locked. None of them could have made that noise.

Stories of Bennie's ghostly powers grew and included being able to make things disappear. One guard swore that he looked out window at the Cenotaph by the Court House, and all he could see was the base; the statue of the soldier normally perched on top was not there; it was gone. He could see very clearly all around. The base of the statue was visible, but the soldier had disappeared. Not trusting his eyes, he went outside just to make sure, but by then the statue of the soldier had returned, and all was as it should be.

Another strange happening became a regular occurrence; the protective cover for the front of the fireplace was knocked to the floor with a loud bang. At first, the guards thought a downdraft from the fireplace chimney had blown it over. But that had never happened before, and the trouble with that explanation was that it happened on nights when there wasn't any wind as well as on nights when there was. The ghost of Bennie Swim was as good an explanation as any.

Attics, of course, are often places of ghostly activity, and the Woodstock Jail was no exception. One guard told the story of going to the attic for some supplies stored there. He suddenly had the eerie feeling of being entangled in a cobweb but there was no cobweb in sight. The feeling ran down the back of his head and across his shoulders. He rubbed his head and the back of his neck and continued on with his business. Then, as he was about to leave the attic, he heard a distinct voice. It was a strong whispering voice that said, "Come on back."

He stopped and looked around, but couldn't see anyone. As he was just about to turn off the light and leave the attic, he heard the voice again, louder this time, saying, "Come on back." Again, he looked around; no one else was in the attic. He simply had no explanation for the presence of the voice. He waited, finally turned off the light and left the attic.

As the stories of Bennie's ghost accumulated, other details were added. For example, in the winter, all the attic windows of the jail save one would be covered with frost. The window looking out on Maple Street never became completely frosted. There always remained an open circle in the middle of the window. The guards figured Bennie kept this open so he could look outside. It seems reasonable that the attic would be Bennie's favourite place. It's also where he made the most racket.

One guard vividly recalled the time he was up there early one morning to put some items back in storage when there was a loud bang right beside him. He described it like the sound of a heavy metal object that had fallen from a good height. He looked around to see what it could possibly have been, but everything around him was perfectly in place. He could see nothing that would explain it. Nothing had dropped or fallen. He searched in the other rooms of the attic, and again, nothing could be seen that was out of the ordinary. Everything was in its place, where it should be. It was a full moon night, so maybe Bennie was feeling extra mischievous. When the guard went downstairs, another guard working on the second floor asked him what the loud noise was in the attic. Even one of the inmates, having heard the noise, commented on it. Eventually, all these goings-on were just passed off as Bennie being Bennie and were more or less ignored.

But some things are hard to ignore. Unaccountable noises are one thing, and even voices can be uneasily accepted, but other, even stranger things, began to happen. For example, the jail at that time had a dumbwaiter that was used to transport things between the first and second floors. Guards began to report it now seemed to have a mind of its own, or else Bennie was up to more of his tricks. The dumbwaiter would suddenly go up and down for no reason. All the prisoners would be locked in their cells with only one guard on duty, and the dumbwaiter would move from one floor to the other and back again. Strange, indeed!

Still more stories have come to light. Apparently, Bennie not happy with just noises and voices and began to pilfer food from the kitchen. Now, ghosts are not normally known to eat, but perhaps Bennie's ghost was different. At least he got blamed for the missing food. Guards would come down to the kitchen to make themselves a sandwich. If the front door bell rang or if something else occurred that needed their attention elsewhere, they would lock up the kitchen and deal with the matter at hand. When they returned sometimes the loaf of bread they had left out, would be half eaten, or at least half of it would be missing.

Bennie must have liked the kitchen almost as well as the attic because it was in the kitchen that he was often accused of turning on the water taps. Several guards reported they always made sure the taps were off before locking up the kitchen. When they later returned, the taps would be open and running freely. It was the same with the lights. Guards would make sure the kitchen lights were off, but when they later came back, the lights would again be on. This happened when no one else was in the building and the cells were all locked down for the night. One time a guard was checking out the segregation cells in the basement and could hear the water running. He checked the showers and the taps were turned on. This happened when the segregation cells had been unused for some time.

Over the years, some of these strange events happened to new guards who had not been informed about the ghost of Bennie Swim. Had they been forewarned, it could be thought their imaginations had been spurred on by such stories as often happens when ghostly activities are reported. But no, without prompting, sober men entered the Woodstock Jail and had strange experiences.

These accounts are actual experiences as reported by several of the guards who have worked in the Woodstock Jail over the years since Bennie's death. If it is the ghost of Bennie Swim, maybe he wants to make sure he is not forgotten. There's nothing like a good ghost story to keep history on the edge of its seat.

Afterword

Bennie Swim was a complicated person. Reports and rumours that he was stupid, an idiot, a hillbilly, a simpleton, or even worse, are not true. There is plenty of evidence to refute these stereotypes. His early life is not well documented, and what most people know about him dates from March 27, 1922, the date on which he murdered Olive Swim Trenholm and then killed Harvey Trenholm. (I make a distinction between Olive's death as a murder and Harvey's death as a killing because Bennie was convicted and executed only for Olive's murder. He was indicted for the murder of Harvey, but he was not tried for it nor was it proven to be an act of murder. Bennie claimed the killing of Harvey was self-defence. He may have made up that story after the fact to make himself look better. I have told the story of the killing as a simple murder. I may be wrong about this. Bennie persisted in his story to the end. There is no way to know for sure. If he had somehow managed to be found not guilty of murdering Olive, he would have then been tried for the murder of Harvey Trenholm.)

Bennie Swim very cleverly attempted to fake insanity and was quite convincing. Sheriff Foster believed what he was seeing was the real thing and got the ball rolling by informing higher legal authorities. Bennie managed to fool two prominent New Brunswick psychiatrists, Dr. King and Dr. Anglin. Had the Department of Justice in Ottawa accepted their findings, Bennie would not have been executed. He would have been sent to an insane asylum instead.

Bennie planned two escapes, one of which might have succeeded if not for being turned in by two of his fellow inmates. Sheriff Foster foiled the second attempt by insisting that if he needed surgery for appendicitis, it had to be done in the jail. He was not taking a chance on Bennie escaping from the hospital. The attack, which fooled the doctor, had been skilfully faked and Bennie recovered.

Bennie planned his crime systematically and in detail. He managed to get everything in place and implement his plan, except for one thing — he failed at suicide. Some things he did could be called stupid, and some things that happened were just plain unlucky for him. Getting on the train with Sheriff Foster from Hartland to Woodstock was bad luck. Asking directions to the Sharp place, and talking to Enoch Gilbert and Mrs. Marston about the reason he was going there was not a smart thing to do, at least if he planed to get away and escape detection, which he may not have, considering the suicide attempt.

Roy Swim meeting up with Enoch and learning that Bennie was looking for Olive would have been lucky for Olive and Harvey if Roy had caught up with Bennie and stopped him. That would have been lucky or unlucky for Bennie, depending on how you look at it. It might have been unlucky for Roy since Bennie had a gun. As it happened, Roy missed him by only a matter of minutes.

William Sharp being in Benton was lucky for him. Had he been at home, he might have been a victim as well, although if he had answered the door, Bennie might not have started shooting. Even if he had, Olive might have had a better chance to escape. So much depended on luck one way or the other. Bennie's behaviour may look pretty stupid to us, but it was driven by his unbearable loss and passionate jealousy.

After the murders, he wrote a note and left it at the scene. That was like he was begging to be caught. The only thing he didn't do was to sign it, but he might as well have. At this point, leaving such clear evidence probably didn't matter since he planned to put a bullet in his head as well. A curious question about the note comes up; for whom did he write it? The way it's worded, it seems to be written for Olive, or perhaps her lingering spirit.

After he tried and failed to kill himself, self-preservation must have taken over. Despite the wound in his head, he pulled himself together and, with what must have been great effort, started out over snow-drifted fields and through the woods. He managed to make it all the way to Mr. Carr's house, a distance of six miles. Once there, he came up with an explanation for the head wound. While his conversation with Carr was somewhat disjointed, Bennie inquired logically about the nearest doctor and when the train left from Debec. However, his question about how far the Rogers place was from the Sharp farm is baffling. It didn't seem to serve any purpose. Maybe he had a good reason for asking it. When he asked about the train from Debec was he thinking of going back to the Mainstream or heading for the Maine border? When he realized that staying at Carr's was not an option, he walked another mile to Mr. Doherty's and ended up there for the night. At this point he probably knew he would be captured and was so tired he just wanted to sleep.

There is no way to know for sure what Bennie Swim was thinking and feeling at any stage of that fateful day. Maybe he didn't have a definite plan of murder. Maybe he just set out to confront Olive one more time and reacted to the situation as it unfolded. Maybe he was single-mindedly bent on murder or maybe he was volatile and somewhat unhinged. The evidence leans toward the former — well-planned murders carried out by a distraught but logical mind. This is the view around which this story of Bennie Swim has been constructed. One thing for sure, he took a lot of questions with uncertain answers to the grave.

Mr. Frederick Squires represented Bennie at his trial. Would the case have turned out differently if Bennie had had a better lawyer? Chief Justice McKeown, the trial judge, gave his opinion that Mr. Squires did an excellent job in the defence of his client. A memo written by an official in the Department of Justice in Ottawa, however, showed that they were not as impressed with Mr. Squires as the trial judge. The memo described Squires as a fourth rate lawyer who had encouraged his client to act silly to give the impression of insanity. The memo also alluded to Squires coaching the defence witnesses to make up stories to bolster the impression that Bennie came from an unstable family with a long history of mental illness.

A part of Squires' defence was to convince the jurors that Olive, as well as Bennie, regarded their relationship as a common-law marriage. Defence witnesses testified to the fact that Olive clearly regarded herself as Bennie's wife by quoting her to that effect and by her asking for a wedding ring as a sign of the relationship. If they testified in this way on the directions by Mr. Squires, he certainly bent the ethics of his profession, but it also shows he did everything he could to create sympathy for Bennie in the hope of saving him from the gallows.

When the case first went to trial, Bennie was indicted for the murder of both Olive and Harvey. Mr. Squires did manage to hold Bennie's conviction to just the murder of Olive. Harvey's killing was given a reasonable doubt; there was a good possibility of it having been manslaughter, not murder. Overall, Mr. Squires didn't have much to work with. The prosecution called nineteen witnesses who all gave convincing evidence.

Along with Bennie's immediate confession to Sheriff Foster, there was no question of his guilt. The defence called only three witnesses. The main focus of their testimony was to provide evidence to refute the prosecution's contention that Bennie was completely sane and that Olive and Bennie were not married. In the end, this defence didn't really matter. The evidence for pre-meditated murder was overwhelming and the insanity defence was not convincing. Even if Bennie had had the best lawyer money could buy, it is very unlikely the trial wouldn't have ended any differently. Mr. Squires probably did as much as any lawyer could do given the circumstances.

The fact that he never filed an appeal indicates he felt there was nothing more he could do for his client.

Another question about this case is why Bennie didn't die when he shot himself in the head. I have alluded to the probability that the bullet in the chamber of the revolver when Bennie pulled the trigger on himself may have been lacking in powder. It's the best explanation I can come up with. When Bennie obtained the 38-calibre revolver from Edmund Estabrooks on March 22nd, he was not given the proper ammunition for the gun. Edmund didn't have any 38 shorts, which is what the gun was designed for. Bennie was given ten rounds of 38 longs, which is a much more powerful bullet. These bullets were too long for the chambers of the revolver. To be used in this gun, they had to be shortened.

There are three ways Bennie could have shortened the bullets: he could have filed down the lead bullet heads, he could have clipped off the ends of the bullet heads with a pair of pliers, or he could have whittled them down the way you whittle a piece of wood. Lead bullets are soft enough to shave with a sharp knife.

To shorten the bullets with a file, Bennie would have had to put the cartridges in a vise, or rig up some other way of holding them firmly in place while he worked a file around the tips of the bullet and shortened them enough to fit the gun. This would have taken longer than clipping or whittling but it would also have been the best way to shorten the bullets. They would have ended up more uniform with less chance of being damaged.

Clipping the head with pliers might have worked, but the force required could damage the bullets in a way that would compromise effective firing. Clipping might also inadvertently dislodge the bullet head from the casing, in which case the gunpowder in the casing might spill and the whole assembly have to be put back together.

If Bennie shaved down the bullets with a knife, the force of the effort could also have dislodged the lead bullet from its casing and spilled powder on the floor. Whatever he did to the cartridges to make them fit the cylinders of the revolver worked pretty well, at least for the first three bullets fired. They did their job, but the fourth bullet didn't and this fact needs more explanation.

Bennie aimed the gun at the right side of his head and fired. The explosion must have sounded like a cannon going off. The percussion alone from a 38 long must have caused damage to his eardrums. Why didn't a bullet with the power of a 38 long break a hole in his skull and travel right through his brain as it had when he shot Harvey? There are two plausible theories.

First, Bennie almost certainly did not place the end of the barrel flat against his head. Holding the gun in that position would be somewhat awkward and require a certain amount of concentration. He must have instead raised the gun at an angle and fired. Yet, even at an angle, a full power 38 long would likely have broken the skull and caused serious damage. But even if the angle was such that the bullet didn't hit the skull but only penetrated between the skull and the scalp, that doesn't explain why it travelled only a few inches and stopped over Bennie's right eye. A fully charged bullet would have exited the scalp and travelled a long way before coming to a stop.

Here we come to the second theory, which I have added to the story as a plausible explanation of why Bennie Swim failed to commit suicide, or even badly injure himself. If the bullet had a greatly reduced charge of gunpowder, it might have hit his skull with a grazing blow and, with much weakened velocity, deflected along the curve of the skull and come to a stop without exiting.

Something like this must have happened. If Bennie had levelled the gun against his head and fired, the bullet would have killed him. The angle shot theory must be part of a convincing explanation of what happened. The defective bullet theory adds plausibility to the explanation. The only explanation for a bullet to fire at less than full power is that it does not carry a full charge of gunpowder in its casing. My telling of the story includes a description of how a cartridge might have lost its full charge of gunpowder when Bennie modified the heads of the bullets. We will never know all the facts of the case with certainty, but the explanation I have offered is consistent with the evidence. If Bennie Swim had succeeded in killing himself by the sheep pen on William Sharp's farm on that fateful day, the case would have disappeared into the archives of New Brunswick's legal history. His death was delayed by only a few months, but the circumstances of his trial and execution have become legendry in New Brunswick history.

*   *   *   *   *

Bennie was the last person executed at the Woodstock Jail, but he was not the last to die there. Over the years inmates came and went, but a few did not leave in the same condition in which they entered. The Woodstock Jail has seen suicides. The building is still there, right behind Carleton County Court House, but it has not been used as a jail since 1993. It is still the location of the County Sheriff's office and maintains a daytime holding cell for prisoners during their trials in the courthouse next door. No one spends the night there anymore. The building now also houses a regional office of the provincial Department of Health and Inclusive Communities. The Woodstock Jail is a notable example of historic architecture and is on the Town's register of heritage buildings. The New Brunswick Government has closed all county jails and replaced them with large detention centres in Moncton, Saint John, Edmundston and Dalhousie. The federal government operates maximum-security prisons at Renous and Dorchester. If Bennie Swim is still haunting the Woodstock Jail, I hope he's not bothering the nice lady who works in the office on the second floor. If Bennie's ghost only comes out at night, he must find the empty jail a mighty lonesome place to hang out.

*   *   *   *   *

Over the years, as more people died in Coldstream, Rockland, and the Mainstream area, the Coldstream Hillside Cemetery was enlarged. Bennie no longer has his own spot outside the fence. The wooden marker has long since rotted away but with the help of some older local residents, you can find out where his grave is located.

The Mainstream has always been called *the* Mainstream, not just Mainstream. It was a settlement area with a distinct identity along the main course of the Becaguimec River and was still largely forested in Bennie's time. The Mainstream has changed a lot since then. The land William Swim owned is now mostly fields and in the hands of a local farmer who is a descendent of Ida Ross Swim and Edward Swim. William and Eva's house is long gone, but the outline of the rough foundation where it stood can still be seen. The Mainstream is now a mixture of deserted houses interspersed with new homes. When a house is abandoned, no one now attempts to take any of the building materials for reuse. The houses are just left to Mother Nature and eventually they fall in and rot away. The Becaguimec meanders along through the area with forest on one side and wetlands on the other. The Mainstream is an especially beautiful natural area within easy reach of the towns of Hartland and Woodstock.

Benton Ridge has changed a lot as well. One by one, over the years, the farms failed and people moved away. Once a thriving community, the area has mostly been abandoned and left for the forest to take over. There's nothing left of John Swim's farm. The house and barn have long since been torn down and carted away. The forest has reclaimed all of the carefully tended fields and orchards. The only evidence left of the determination and hard work that John and his family put into making the farm a success are the large piles of rocks pulled from the fields to make the land tillable. Scattered amongst the trees are old farm implements, wagon wheels, buckets and tin cans rusting and rotting their way back into the earth.

William Sharp's farm is gone as well. The barns, sheep pens, fields and orchards have all have been lost to Mother Nature. A new modern house painted light blue now stands where the old farmhouse once stood. The new house sits among the very maple trees that Harvey Trenholm was getting ready to tap for making maple syrup on the last day of his life. Harvey was carving sap spiles when Bennie Swim knocked on the door.

The Carr and Doherty farms at Oak Mountain have suffered the same fate as the farms on Benton Ridge. The forest has reclaimed the land and now an occasional hunter enjoys its solitude. A part of Oak Mountain is now a provincially designated protected forest area.

The town of Benton once boasted hotels, sawmills, a train station, a tannery, general stores and several churches. Benton is now diminished to a handful of homes clustered along the Eel River where it is spanned by a covered bridge. Two churches remain, but their congregations are far smaller than they used to be. The train that once stopped in Benton on its way from McAdam to Debec Junction and on to Woodstock and points north is now long forgotten. The tracks have been torn up and the railroad bed is now used by snowmobiles in the winter and all-terrain vehicles during the other seasons. Many of the small roads that once connected farms in the area are now covered with good size trees. Ducks Unlimited has built a low concrete dam and spillway on the Eel River near Benton, which enlarges and conserves an important wetland area. A boat landing at the same site provides upriver access for canoeists and fishermen. Time has moved on, as have many of the descendants of local families. But stories remain, and the story about what happened at Benton Ridge on March 27th in 1922 is still well known.

* * * * *

Although this book is not about capital punishment, it does play a large part in the story. The scandal of Bennie Swim's botched hanging did not change the way executions were carried out in Canada. Bennie was the last person hanged at the Woodstock Jail, but he was not the last person hanged in New Brunswick. That dishonour goes to Joseph Pierre Richard who was hanged in Dalhousie on December 11, 1957. The last person hanged in Canada was Ronald Turpin in Ontario in 1962. From 1963 to 1976, when the death penalty was abolished in Canada, a moratorium on executions was in effect. The Canadian Government routinely commuted death sentences to life imprisonment. On July 14, 1976 a free vote was held in Parliament on a bill to abolish capital punishment; it passed by a vote of one hundred and thirty to one hundred and twenty-four. Several attempts in Parliament to reinstate capital punishment since then have all failed.

*   *   *   *   *

To complete this story, I have compiled the following biographical information on the people who were in someway connected with the Bennie Swim case.

William Swim, Bennie's father, continued to live in his home on the Mainstream. He died there September 2, 1923, less than a year after Bennie was hanged. He was buried close to his son in the Coldstream Hillside Cemetery at Rockland.

Eva May Foster Swim, Bennie's mother, continued to live in her home on the Mainstream for seventeen years after she lost both her husband and son. In 1940 she left the Mainstream to live with her daughter, Cassie Elizabeth, first at Tracy Mills and then in Stickney. She then died on December 24, 1949 at the age of seventy-five. She was also buried in the Coldstream Hillside Cemetery beside her husband and close to her son.

Cassie Elizabeth Swim Ogden, Bennie's sister, continued to live in Tracy Mills with her husband, Frank Ogden. They raised six children, William Thomas, Benjamin Franklin, Eugene James, Mary Gladys, Marrion Faith, and Katherine Elizabeth. Cassie and Frank later moved to Stickney, a town on the east side of the St. John River between Hartland and Woodstock. Frank died in 1980 at the age of eighty-two and Cassie Elizabeth died in 1984 also at the age of eighty-two. Cassie and Frank were buried in the Stickney Cemetery close by the Saint John River.

Alexander Cameron Swim, Bennie's brother, stayed somewhat in the background. There is no record of his birth. In 1970, using his sister Cassie Elizabeth as a witness, he filed for a "Late Registration of Birth." He lived with one of his aunts for a while and then with a niece. He eventually bought a house near Perth Andover. On one occasion he became angry with a neighbour, Wayne Allan Cannon, for trespassing on his land. Alexander took out his 22-calibre rifle and shot Wayne Cannon in the chest. Wayne was not hurt badly, but the shooting would set off a chain of events that ended in Alexander's death.

Alexander Swim was never charged for the shooting but for several years afterwards there was bad blood between Swim and Cannon. On the 27th of July 1989, it was determined by witnesses that Wayne Canon went to Alexander Swim's house and shot him once in the head with a 22-calibre rifle.

He then saturated the house with gasoline and lit it on fire with Alexander still inside. The trial lasted several weeks. Wayne Allen Cannon was acquitted of the murder. Alexander Swim was buried in the cemetery along the river road just outside of Florenceville.

Jesse Foster, Bennie's uncle, who retrieved Bennie's body after the hanging, continued to live on his farm about four miles from William and Eva Swim's place on the Mainstream. In 1938, at the age of fifty-nine, he married Helen Adams who was twenty-one at the time. No children are recorded. Jesse died in 1963. He is buried in the Coldstream Hillside Cemetery beside several of his family members.

John Swim, Olive's father, continued to live on the farm at Benton Ridge, near the site of his daughter's murder, for several years. His date of death is uncertain, but according to neighbours, it was sometime around 1943. He was buried beside Olive in the Benton United Church Cemetery.

Phoebe Ann Wiley Swim, Olive's mother, left her husband, John, and went to live in Houlton, Maine with their youngest daughter, Alice Pearl. Whether she ever returned to New Brunswick is uncertain.

Roy Byron Swim, Olive's brother, continued to live at Benton Ridge on the family farm. Unfortunately, Roy died of pneumonia on February 12, 1930. He was only thirty years old. He was buried in the Canterbury Community Cemetery.

Rita, Roy's wife, continued to live on the Swim farm until close to her death in 1960. According to neighbours, she became somewhat unhinged in her later years. The stories have it that she sometimes dressed in an evening gown and pearls and wandered through the forest between her house and the place where Olive was murdered, acting like she was on her way to a fancy dress ball. She was buried beside her husband in the Canterbury Cemetery. Their son, Ellery, eventually left Benton Ridge and moved to McAdam where he lived until his death in 1993.

Alice Pearl Swim Plourde, Olive's younger sister, left the farm at Benton Ridge with her mother and settled in Houlton, Maine, where she worked in various homes as a housekeeper. She later entered nursing school and obtained her diploma. She was then employed at the hospital in Millinocket, Maine. She met Fred Plourde, a clerk, in Millinocket. They were married in Edmundston, New Brunswick on the 16th of September 1927. Alice Pearl was twenty-one at the time. Her husband, Fred, was thirty. They lived in Millinocket and her husband Fred is buried there. I have been unable to find any record of Alice Pearl Plourde living in Maine after her marriage, or that of any children. If there are children I have missed, I apologize for the inaccuracy. Alice Pearl did return to visit her family in New Brunswick on occasion, and, in 1959, she registered her birth in New Brunswick using the Late Registration of Birth process.

Dorina Rose Burgess, Harvey's second wife, never used the Trenholm name according to the records I have found, nor did she ever apply for a divorce. She moved to Saint John and worked as a housekeeper until her death from tuberculosis on February 8, 1928. Her death certificate shows she continued to claim her status as having been married to Harvey Trenholm. It also indicates she was a widow. If she knew Harvey was dead, she must have learned how he died, in which case she must also have learned that he had married again without getting a divorce from her. She was buried in Fernhill Cemetery near Saint John.

Gladys Gertrude Trenholm, Harvey's daughter with his first wife, Bessie Gertrude Hayward Trenholm, continued to live with her grandparents, James and Jemima Hayward, in West River, Albert County, until she moved to Saint John, New Brunswick in 1929. Gladys married her stepbrother, Egbert Arnott Burgess, in Saint John on the 9th of February 1929. Egbert Burgess was Dorina Burgess' son by her first marriage. Gladys was twenty and Egbert was thirty. Egbert worked for the New Brunswick Power Company. They lived at 162 Queen Street in Saint John. They remained childless throughout their marriage. I could find no records of their deaths.

Mary Kierstead Boyd, who was charged in the double murder of her children, and was in a cell close to Bennie's in the Woodstock Jail, was sentenced to life in the insane asylum in Saint John. She died there in 1928 after having spent just over six years confined to the asylum.

Sheriff Albion Rudolph Foster continued on as High Sheriff of Carleton County until 1926, when he passed the reins to Frank L. Tompkins. When a replacement for Sheriff Tompkins could not be found in 1935, Albion Foster again took over as Sheriff and served in this capacity until his death on February 6, 1945. He was seventy-three years old. Albion Foster was buried in Greenwood Cemetery in Hartland. His son, Major Glen Foster, then took over as High Sheriff of Carleton County and kept the position until 1954.

Hedley V. Mooers remained Deputy Sheriff of Carleton County for several years but he never realized his dream of becoming High Sheriff. His trade throughout his life was as a harness maker. He continued working as a harness maker and a Deputy Sheriff for most of his life. He and his wife Emma raised six children. Deputy Sheriff Mooers died in 1941 at the age of seventy-seven. Emma died in 1939. They were both buried at the Methodist Cemetery in Woodstock.

Hangmen F. G. Gill was never mentioned again in any reports. My attempts to find out who he really was have failed. Hangman M. A. Doyle offered his services for an execution in St John's Newfoundland in December of 1922. The condemned man's name was Wo Fen Game. He had been convicted of killing three men. Doyle offered to do the hanging for $100 plus expenses. He was politely turned down and a fellow convict who was serving a term for bestiality performed the hanging. His compensation was a reduction in sentence

* * * * *

Here ends the extent of my research and my reconstruction of the Bennie Swim story. I have created and presented as complete and accurate an account of this story as my research supported. Where I have used my imagination to create conversations and to describe the context of the action, I have done so with the intention of getting closer to the truth, not distorting it.

Dominique Perrin
Fredericton, New Brunswick

Acknowledgements

Writing this book has been challenging, but the rewards have been well worth it. I have met so many amazing people. My only regret is I did not always get full names when I started my research in 1993. Other names did not get recorded and have disappeared from my memory. I regret that I am not able to acknowledge all the people who assisted me. If you helped me with my research and are not mentioned here, please accept my apologies.

This project got a boost from the encouragement of Kellie Blue McQuade of the Carleton County Historical Society. The first time I met with her in her office at Connell House in Woodstock, I wanted to know what she had on file about Bennie Swim and the murders at Benton Ridge. She handed me a small stack of maybe five pages, which was interesting but very lacking in detail. She suggested that if I was interested enough to research and write up a more complete account, she would be happy to read it.

Several years later, I presented her with my manuscript. She liked it enough to pass it on to Keith Helmuth, Publisher and Managing Editor of Chapel Street Editions. He gave me the encouragement and editing assistance to rewrite the manuscript and make it into a book. I will be forever grateful to him and the team at Chapel Street Editions for their skills and hard work in bringing this book to life. Special thanks go to Karen Arnold, who did the copy-editing.

Others who played an important part in my research are Roger Way of Woodstock and Earl Blackie of Oak Mountain. Mr. Blackie helped me identify the locations of some of the key action. Tommy Porter, of Riceville, was able to recall some of the stories that his older friends and relatives had passed down to him, which he kindly shared with me at his kitchen table.

Descendants of Cassie Elizabeth Swim Ogden provided me with updates on what happened to some of the other relatives of Bennie Swim. Mrs. Swim, of McAdam, related by marriage to Roy Swim, helped me with information detailing what happened to Roy, Olive's brother.

I would also like to thank the staff of Estabrooks Store, in Coldstream, who gave me leads on who to talk to for locating Bennie's final resting place. Mr. Ross of Mainstream helped me find exactly where Bennie was buried and recounted the circumstance related to his burial. The staff of the Provincial Archives of New Brunswick helped me find many of the official documents related to the case. The caretaker of the Benton United Church Cemetery, and the present day pastor of the Meductic Baptist Church were also helpful to my research.

Last but not least, my thanks to all the Seeleys, the Swims, the Fosters, the Sharps, the Marstons, the Franklins, and the Mooers, who shared their stories and knowledge of Bennie Swim and the murders at Benton Ridge.

About the Author

Dominique Perrin grew up in Oakville Ontario attending Maple Grove Public School and Perdue High School. His favourite subject was Literature. During high school, he wrote several short stories but they never made it into publication.

He later spent twenty-six years in the Canadian Armed Forces, most of it in Europe. After retiring from the military, he dedicated his time to becoming a jazz musician.

In the early nineteen nineties, he lived in Woodstock for several years working with the local militia. It was here he heard the story about a twenty-two year old man that had been hanged twice at the Woodstock Jail for the murder of his beloved and her new husband. Intrigued, he wanted to know more. He combed the library for local records of the story. Unable to find a full account, he started talking to people who knew about the case. He heard many different versions of the Bennie Swim story. He determined to find out the truth of what had happened and began his research.

Dominique Perrin regularly plays in the jazz clubs of several European cities His instruments of choice are the alto sax and harmonica. He lives in Fredericton, New Brunswick where he also performs and provides lessons in advanced saxophone.

CPSIA information can be obtained
at www.ICGtesting.com
Printed in the USA
BVHW040352140323
660059BV00002B/7